Rights of the Child

Children's Well-Being: Indicators and Research Series

Volume 11

This new series focuses on the subject of measurements and indicators of children's well being and their usage, within multiple domains and in diverse cultures. More specifically, the series seeks to present measures and data resources, analysis of data, exploration of theoretical issues, and information about the status of children, as well as the implementation of this information in policy and practice. By doing so it aims to explore how child indicators can be used to improve the development and the well being of children.

With an international perspective the series will provide a unique applied perspective, by bringing in a variety of analytical models, varied perspectives, and a variety of social policy regimes.

Children's Well-Being: Indicators and Research will be unique and exclusive in the field of measures and indicators of children's lives and will be a source of high quality, policy impact and rigorous scientific papers.

More information about this series at http://www.springer.com/series/8162

Brian Milne

Rights of the Child

25 Years After the Adoption of the UN Convention

Springer

Brian Milne
Le Brande
Calès, France

ISSN 1879-5196 ISSN 1879-520X (electronic)
Children's Well-Being: Indicators and Research
ISBN 978-3-319-18783-9 ISBN 978-3-319-18784-6 (eBook)
DOI 10.1007/978-3-319-18784-6

Library of Congress Control Number: 2015944113

Springer Cham Heidelberg New York Dordrecht London

Printed on acid-free paper

Springer International Publishing AG Switzerland is part of Springer Science+Business Media (www.springer.com)

Preface

This book was first suggested and started in 2004. It has taken 10 years to put together the chapter abstracts and notes, a structure, to work through a vast number of files in which cited material have been stored, books, online sources updating apace fast moving media reporting. In the end it was written from the middle of October 2013 through early September 2014. That was for a good reason.

This work is a follow-up to a joint publication, *The Next Generation: Lives of Third World Children*, written in 1987 through 1988 and published by Zed Press in 1989. In that book we looked at the ten rights principles described by the 1959 UN *Declaration of the Rights of the Child*. We were fully aware of the forthcoming convention and as well informed and up to date as probably most other people as drafting drew to an end (Ennew and Milne 1988: 14 and 200–216). Drafting finished soon after we had completed our work. In part one it looked at the state of children's right through the ten principles; in the second part it examined 12 country case studies. It was not written to criticise, advocate or predict but simply to look at what we had and what we hoped the new convention would move on to.

In many respects it is an extremely naive book looking back through it now. Yet one of the reasons this book came about is because whilst it never sold in vast numbers, it was much used, cited and enquired after for at least a decade. During that time we were often asked whether we would revise or update it and a new edition would appear. It was always a consideration. The commissioning editors at Zed also suggested a follow-up book.

In the fullness of time, there were less and less comments, but until very recently, it has been cited. Judith still received remarks and requests, including high praise for it as the best book of its kind at the time and even since. Looking back over it shows a starting point in our real involvement in children's rights rather than through single issues such as street children or child labour. The option of bringing it up to date became less and less attractive, and the first 10 years after the adoption of the *United Nations Convention on the Rights of the Child* was a defining moment because the century and millennium were close to ending and like everybody else we were curious about the future. Thus, after having occasional thoughts for five years, we decided to begin work on a follow-up; something like this has now shaped out in time for the twentieth anniversary of the adoption in 2009.

Changes in our lives and work made that difficult; thus, we snatched time when we met once or twice a year and exchanged ideas and materials electronically until we had a skeletal book with short abstracts below each chapter title. The entire book is very different to the work we set out to reprise without letting it become a polemical repetition of our 1980s points of view projected into the present. During 2013 Judith was saying that she would retire very soon after her seventieth birthday early in 2014, and then one of her priorities would be that we would begin seriously writing later that year. That was not to be. On 4 October 2013 she died. Within days I had decided all of our preparatory work would be compiled, the skeletal structure and abstracts fleshed out and a book begin to be written. By the end of October, I was giving every spare hour to working on it. I wanted to still be able to write it with my sense of how she would have approached some topics and specific issues had we been able to write together. I have done so to the best of my ability. Those chapters that were entirely to be written by her were naturally the most difficult, but she had left enough to work with to make it possible without too much deviation from her points of view. She had critically assessed the chapters I was to write alone, so she knew what she had thought was right, wrong or necessary to write about. Our planned joint chapters, only two, were perhaps the most difficult because we would have debated, 'juggled' and thoroughly dissected then reconstructed them, possibly several times. It is not easy to do that with oneself.

Nonetheless, her death triggered the start of a sometimes difficult effort to complete this book. I had been quite seriously ill myself, I was still taking medicines that often affected my memory and thought processes but the stimulation of writing and often at first forcing myself to remember made a major contribution to my recovery. At the time of Judith's death, I realised how low I was and find it almost ironic how somebody lived with diabetes which had been a serious problem for many years but had only begun to slow her down over the last two or so years of her life and had certainly brought about her end; it was exactly that which brought me back to where I am by showing me never to give up.

Thus, I wrote intending to be a co-author and at least a proxy. On the other hand, I learned that that is a great ideal but not a practicality. I can never write as she would have, nor can I devise a means of sharing thoughts that would have included hard debating. Therefore, I used what we had jointly prepared and injected what I could of her thoughts and way of thinking. I am satisfied with the outcome.

This book itself is not exactly a follow-up to the 1989 one. It bears it in mind and has been carefully reread for inspiration but does seriously allow for how naive we considered it had become since finishing writing in 1988. It was the age of the 1989 convention; we had great expectations but have been massively disappointed, irritated by narrow-mindedness, and yet we have retained great faith in what has happened. We saw the haste with which the first countries signed, that the first ratifications brought it into effect in 1990 and that, whilst vast political changes were going on worldwide, newly emergent and independent nations were signing and ratifying it faster than any other convention had ever seen. We saw what appeared to be extensive political goodwill. On reflection I can see how naive that was since despite ratification many nations have achieved only marginally more than nothing. That does not mean giving up on it as a failure but the incentive to find a solution. This book is not a defining explication of how that might be; it would be absurd to even try that but to contribute just the tiniest bit to a worldwide incentive to find a solution is all.

For the sakes of clarity and full explanation, there are appendices. They are lengthy but without comment, simply giving full texts of conventions, charters and treaties that are pertinent. They are intended to be used as required but not as 'obligatory' reading.

From the outset, we, Ennew and Milne, set out not to be judge and jury, thus condemning either the state of children's rights or any human contribution to its advancement or lack of progress. From the Introduction and eight chapters, we originally chose three each and shared two. I have closely adhered to Judith's notes for the three I wrote instead of her but had to entirely take on the two shared ones beyond the briefest abstracts we wrote together. Rather than becoming entangled in sometimes futile arguments, it was often far more useful to observe, consider and then take note of things. Of course there have been critical comments and disagreements on issues and with individuals or organisations but never heated nor enduring. It always seemed far better to draw the key observations together in this way. These are by no means all of them nor indeed is any individual or organisation being criticised. That names and titles are referred to in what appear to be critical contexts is inevitability that does not thrust blame or any other negative value on those named. They may, in fact, be critical only because some readers who feel implicated read them as being so. That was never intended. Nonetheless, many topics are approached in a critical manner in order to emphasise observations about them. Chapter five on the (mis)appropriation of language as a children's rights terminology is probably the most significant. Having acknowledged that, it is extremely difficult to do so otherwise although it is, as all else, simply a set of observations which are opinions about a particular phenomenon we recognised and wished to point out explicitly. Try as I may, I find no gentler way of taking a metaphorical bull by the horns.

It was always an attempt to keep our integrity by being honest about what we saw post-1989 and hoped would and could be done with our views. I found it very hard going since I do not like hurting anybody's feelings. Even so, I am quite certain that some people and perhaps a few organisations will feel attacked and expect some kind of apology or climb down on those matters. Since there are no attacks of this kind intended, I simply request people who may feel any kind of offence when reading to take it or leave it and not develop it into a debate which would be a distraction from the task actually in hand. It is this entire work that is intended to be read and not just parts with which people or organisations immediately identify. Disagreement and critique are as welcomed as positive reception in order to contribute to sustaining the advance of children's rights. Thus, there is no objective setting out a future, making plans and setting agendas for the future of that task here. It is a review of roughly a quarter of a century until the present, at least the most recent past, that does not set out criteria. It does, however, suggest that the present convention and all of the apparatus around it may need to be improved, given more powers to enforce and lead, but does not set out how that might possibly be. That is left to those who are willing to take in what they read here and the opinions of others with similar views.

It is, therefore, clearly a tribute to Judith Ennew, but it also pays homage to all of the people who have contributed so much to children's rights over the years and wishes to encourage others to take up the cause. Some years ago Judith suggested that we do not show other people this work until it is in the hands of publishers and at least at the stage of final edits. In fact her rationale was that we could eternally take in what other people said and develop it further but thus never finish. As with the first book it is also written from very personal perspectives. Nevertheless, I wish to thank some people for inspiration or at least support. Antonella Invernizzi listened, made suggestions and debated some ideas, Nigel Cantwell has always been an enormous inspiration, Henk van Beers and Manfred Liebel both consistently continue to work for children's rights in an opened-minded manner, Jasmin Lim represents a new generation that has much to offer and then there are far too many who shall remain unnamed because the list would be long. Rather than make omissions I have not attempted to write that list, but I know who they are.

Those named and myself were able to come together with several other friends and colleagues at the *Children Out-of-Place and Human Rights: International Symposium in Memory of Judith Ennew*, at the Freie Universität Berlin on 27 and 28 October 2014, thanks to the efforts of Manfred Liebel. We said 'goodbye' to her, but not her work and its influence which we wish to see developed and grow in the hands of a new generation of children's rights researchers and practitioners. I was able to gather some thoughts to round this book off from Alejandro Cussiánovich, Per Miljeteig, Michael Bourdillon, Sharon Bessell, Roxana Waterson and Bill Meyers who was too ill to attend but with whom I had been exchanging ideas, all of whom had a close working relationship with her.

Although earlier it was mentioned this book was finished in October 2014, in fact the Berlin Symposium and other important matters such as Somalia ratifying the *Convention on the Rights of the Child* in January 2015 have meant that up until submission of the manuscript, this was always a work in progress.

Thus, this is not a book by or about Judith, as much as a tribute to her as the original shared ideas, the discussions and disagreements en route to reaching what we had to say were as much hers as mine. Judith was an outstanding academic who only ever kept one foot in that world but commanded more respect than most other people who worked in the field of the human rights of children. It is a hard task to live up to her demanding standards. Nevertheless, the burden fell on me to assemble and write it; I have now done so; thus, as she and I would always wish, we now place the burden of taking it forward in the hands of the next generation.

Calès, France Brian Milne

Reference

Ennew, J., & Milne, B. (1989). *The next generation: Lives of third world children*. London/Philadelphia: Zed Books/New Society Publishers.

Contents

Introduction 1

This is an introduction I never wanted to write. At least I never wanted to write it alone. On the one hand, part of the overall work is a continuation of my work completed in 2012 (Milne 2013) and on the other of a work completed at the end of 1988 (Ennew and Milne 1989). Why I never wanted to write this is that rather than write alone, Judith Ennew had recently suggested that a planned revisit of our 1989 work was now very overdue and that some of what I would be writing in a follow-up to my 2013 publication should be included in it. She had just read my book.[1] We had, needless to say, been slowly but surely building up a set of notes for this book. Fortunately we kept our notes together as a single file, and it has been these notes I worked out of to write this book.

We both felt that the spirit of the years leading up to and particularly 1989 itself when the United Nations presented the world with the *Convention on the Rights of the Child* (UNCRC, henceforth CRC) had been lost. By 1 July 2014, the CRC had been ratified or acceded to by 195 states; at the time I am writing, only South Sudan and the USA have yet to ratify. The South Sudan National Legislative Assembly passed a bill during 2013 agreeing to ratify the treaty. Ratification has since remained pending during the ongoing armed conflict. Progress has been slow in the USA despite signing in 1995.[2] There are three optional protocols: the *Optional Protocol on the Involvement of Children in Armed Conflict*; the *Optional Protocol on the Sale of Children, Child Prostitution and Child Pornography*; and the *Optional Protocol to the Convention on the Rights of the Child on a Communications*

[1]That was part of a discussion with her during her final visit in the early summer of 2013 as to how we would proceed with this book after her retirement planned to follow her 70th birthday early in 2014. It was one of her priorities. However, fate decided otherwise. She died on 4 October 2013.

[2]Opposition has been concentrated among politically conservative and some religious groups who claim it conflicts with the constitution. Ironically, the USA played a very active role in drafting and commented on nearly all articles, even proposing the original draft of seven of them. If South Sudan ratifies, the USA would be the only member of the UN not to have done so.

B. Milne, *Rights of the Child*, Children's Well-Being: Indicators and Research 11,
DOI 10.1007/978-3-319-18784-6_1

Procedure. The first has 158 state parties to the protocol and 129 other states have signed but have not ratified, the second has 168 state parties and 121 others that have signed, whereas the third opened for signature on 28 February 2012, entered into force 14 April 2014 with the tenth ratification and currently (June 2014) has 46 signatures and 11 ratifications.[3] Given the number of signatories and ratifications of the CRC and its optional protocols, the CRC would appear to be one of, if not the most, successful international human rights instruments ever.

Both of us had been highly privileged to meet Professor Adam Łopatka (1928–2003), sometimes referred to as the 'Father of the Convention', who had served as the President of the Working Group on the CRC, and James P. 'Jim' Grant (1922–1995), a children's advocate who served for 15 years as the third Executive Director of UNICEF from 1980 onwards, thus was very actively involved in bringing the CRC to life. These people inspired us and infected us with their great hopes.

We were also interested in people who had been influential in children's rights becoming a reality. At the very beginning of the twentieth century, two sisters had the vision to realise the rights of children and offer them greater protection than hitherto at the end of the First World War. Thus, Eglantyne Jebb (1876–1928) and her sister Dorothy Buxton (1881–1963) decided to begin direct action and campaigning. The *Save the Children Fund* was launched at a public meeting in London's Royal Albert Hall in May 1919. Jebb wanted to make the rights and welfare of children a worldwide issue. Her *Declaration of the Rights of the Child*, also known as the Declaration of Geneva, was drafted by her in 1923 (Appendix 2). It was adopted along with some parts inspired by Janusz Korczak's version[4] (Appendix 1) by the League of Nations in 1924. The original document, which is now archived in Geneva, carries the signatures of a number of international delegates that include Jebb herself, Korczak and Gustave Ador, a former President of the Swiss Confederation. In 1959 the United Nations General Assembly adopted an expanded version as its own *Declaration of the Rights of the Child* (Appendix 3), which had ten principles in place of the original five. The Declaration in turn inspired the present CRC.

Adam Łopatka had been inspired by his countryman Janusz Korczak, the child welfare pioneer who died with orphans from the Warsaw Ghetto children in his care in 1942. Korczak was the penname of Henryk Goldszmit (1878/1879–1942), a Polish-Jewish educator, children's author and paediatrician also known by those in his care as *Pan Doktor* ('Mr. Doctor'). The importance of respecting children and their opinions was his main message and was to be an inspiration in the drafting and some of the articles of the CRC on the Rights of the Child. In his orphanage in the Warsaw Ghetto during the Second World War, Korczak, his colleagues and the children practised their rights in their daily lives. In the midst of the horrors of war

[3]Signatories and state parties to each optional protocol increase in number year-on-year; this was the situation in the third quarter of 2014.

[4]It is earlier than Jebb's version, but there is no exact date for when it was written. It is also far broader ranging and less practical, secular or legally and politically viable than her declaration.

in Europe, their small community in the ghetto developed a small democracy with an assembly and established rules of behaviour and a court.

Early in August 1942, German soldiers went to collect a handful less than 200 orphans and about a dozen staff members to be transported to the Treblinka extermination camp. Korczak had been offered safe haven on the 'Aryan side' by Żegota, also known as the 'Konrad Żegota Committee', the Council to Aid Jews (Polish: *Rada Pomocy Żydom*), an underground organisation of the Polish resistance in German occupied Poland that was active from 1942 to 1945. Korczak turned the offer down repeatedly, saying that he would not abandon the children in his care. On 5 August, he once again refused an offer of refuge, insisting that he would go with his children. When they went, the children were dressed in their best clothes, each carrying a blue knapsack and a favourite book or toy. They were marched to an *Umschlagplatz* (deportation point to the death camps). He boarded a train with the children and was never heard of again. It is highly probable that Korczak and the children were executed in a gas chamber immediately on arrival at Treblinka.

Janusz Korczak had demanded there be a 'Declaration of the Rights of the Child' considerably earlier than Eglantyne Jebb's version was drawn up and adopted by the League of Nations. His version had envisaged a demand for action rather than a plea for goodwill. It was left incomplete at the time of his death.

Jebb and Korczak were inspirations, in the former's case for her commitment and vision and in the latter's case for his courage and prototype model of children's participation in daily life as equals of their adult carers. We learned from these pioneers but never made the error, as we both believed, of 'canonising' them and holding them up as some kind of saints.

In the middle of 1987, the first words of *The Next Generation: Lives of Third World Children* were written in Selbu, Norway. That day was a deceitful reflection of the times we were living in: around us was a beautiful piece of the world, the sun was mostly shining and the temperature pleasantly warm, but there were a few rain showers. Those first words were written as one of us took part in a meeting while the other sat out in the sun and showers. There were several very young children investigating the stranger in the garden with a notepad. Writing began with their laughter within hearing distance. We were optimistic that the world would get even better than we thought it was just then. The world for children at that same time somehow reflected that day—sun and showers—often too many of the latter and too little of the former metaphorically speaking. Many things were improving; for instance, it was a world moving towards creating programmes to protect street children and child workers, child abuse in all forms was no longer a 'taboo' topic, the sexual exploitation of children had been acknowledged and there were plans to safeguard the lives of children in situations of armed conflict. Better still, there was a UN convention at a fairly advanced state of drafting. It would be the 'shining sun' in a previously overcast sky. We were optimistic.

In 1989 the book was published and the CRC was adopted by the UN. Since then many things have changed, some for the better and others for the worse, including us. Perhaps we were never swept headlong in the wave of euphoria that came with the CRC but held on to our reservations and room for doubts. We would hesitate to say that we could see what was coming, but at least never set our expectations too high. Both of us changed a great deal and have, perhaps, seen more than many other people would wish to see. If we did not see things ourselves, then one or both of us know people who have. It is implausible that we would ever have become cynical or disillusioned; however, more than a few individuals and organisations we had higher hopes for have let us down.

Since 1989 all UN member nations[5] except two in the world have signed and ratified or acceded to the CRC. However, the USA, who we are generally led to believe is the most democratic nation in the world, appears to have no intention of signing, let alone ratifying it in the immediate future. South Sudan is the newest recognised independent nation in the world and requires time to end internal conflicts before it can ratify. There have been three optional protocols to the CRC, one of them a somewhat 'diluted' version of what many of us had hoped to see that is specifically about child soldiers rather than all children in situations of conflict. The ILO has presented us with a convention on the worst forms of child labour and breathed new life into an earlier and originally unsuccessful one. Ironically the ILO's efforts come at a time when many of us who were once committed 'eliminationists' have thought again.

More nation states exist than back in the 1980s, and there are also many more national laws to protect children against a greater array of acknowledged tribulations than ever before. In general we were both more open about the situation of children and more concerned about their protection. There is a veneer of concern about children's rights. On the ground little has changed except that poverty appears to be hurting more children than ever before, and it would be callous to overlook the effect of, for example, HIV and AIDS on them. In many western countries, an almost obsessive fear of 'stranger danger' has consigned children to a life indoors where, ironically, most abuse and neglect occur anyway. That *angst* is gradually permeating other parts of our small world. Children's rights are becoming less and less realisable as children become less visible.

The analogy began with the sun rising and providing warmth and happiness. At present there is a cloud cast over that world, but as with the greyest weather in time, it should pass and better things come to pass. We hoped. Every child who survived the intervening years between beginning to write in 1987 and again in 2013 is now 26 years or more old. They are adults, that is to say, if they survived into adulthood rather than assuming some might have remained children like Peter Pan. One of the hopes of many people waiting to see the new CRC then anticipated that it would be a truly universal instrument of human rights that would serve us well by instructing children in ideals for a more equitable and peaceful world. For some of us, it was the convention that most adults did not and would probably never have but that bore universal ideals that transcended age. Today many of us would probably admit disappointment in the intention of universal knowledge of this wonderful instrument

[5]When UN observer, partly and non-recognised states are included, there are 201 countries worldwide as against 196 UN member states.

of law that would give access to its promises to all children. In all probability, we would admit, very few children know about it, let alone are real beneficiaries. We have seen cracks appearing in what is as patently fragile as fine porcelain through the CRC's imperfections and weaknesses. It was a starting point. Whilst discussing this book, we still shared hope. To be otherwise would have left us with nothing.

Thus, in and around 2007–2008, we already felt that the spirit that came with the adoption of the CRC in 1989 had faded and was perhaps all but dead in the case of many of the ratifying nations. We therefore began to think about what we had hoped in the 1980s and were seeing now in the 2010s and how we could speak out about that view.

We were pre-concerned with how the four influential figures, Łopatka, Grant, Jebb and Korczak, would have seen children's rights develop, become a universal principle and then begin to decline. Would they be disappointed or would they say that it was predestined to the state in which it is now? In the last decades of the twentieth century, a number of goals were set within the United Nations context, goals to be met by the year 2000: *Health for All* (1981), *Shelter for All* (1987) and the goals of the 1990 *World Summit for Children*, which were directly linked (by UNICEF at least) to the adoption of the CRC by the General Assembly of the United Nations in 1989. These goals have clearly not been met, even though we have the resources, especially research facilities and the technology which monitors and promotes the goals. And in any case, goals are not rights.

Goals are used to measure development, including the delivery of rights. There are eight *Millennium Development Goals* (MDGs) that include cutting extreme poverty by half, halting the spread of HIV/AIDS and the provision of universal primary education. The aim is to achieve all MDGs by 2015 that will be used as a blueprint that was agreed to by all the world's countries and foremost development institutions. They have stimulated extraordinary efforts to meet the needs of the poorest people worldwide. They were established subsequent to the *Millennium Summit of the United Nations* in 2000 that was followed by the adoption of the UN *Millennium Declaration*. All of the then 189 UN member states and over 20 international organisations committed themselves to making it a priority to achieve these goals by the year 2015. They are:

1. To eradicate extreme poverty and hunger
2. To realising universal primary education
3. To promoting gender equality and means by which to empower women
4. To significantly reduce child mortality rates
5. To raise the standard of maternal health worldwide
6. To combat HIV/AIDS, malaria and other diseases
7. To ensure environmental sustainability
8. To develop a global partnership for development

The subsequent set of development goals will be applicable to all countries and will be based on the principles of human rights, gender equality and rule of law. UN member states have agreed that the next set of goals will contain targets and indicators they will be required to work towards. The present UN Secretary General, Ban Ki-moon, has said that post-2015 development goals should above all focus on improving the lives of marginalised groups and empowering women. The framework 'must be bold in ambition yet simple in design, supported by a new partnership for development'. It must be universal in nature yet responsive to the complexities, needs and capacities of individual countries. Those goals should promote peace and security, democratic governance, rule of law, gender equality and human rights for all. The *Rio + 20 Conference* in 2012 set up an open working group that would report back to the UN in September 2014, whereupon intergovernmental negotiations on future targets would begin. A new set of goals would be presented to the General Assembly for adoption in September 2015. The high-level panel set up by Ban in 2012 that is chaired by Indonesia, Liberia and the UK devised 12 draft goals that include targets on health, education, the environment and women's empowerment, as well as access to justice, peace and security. The Beyond 2015 campaign of civil society groups has said that despite positive movements in the outcome document on human rights, peace and democratic government, it lacked real ambition necessary for bringing about change. Their co-chair, Neva Frecheville, said: 'Governments need to start listening to the people and to raise the level of ambition in order to ensure that no one is left behind. Civil society around the world will not accept a framework which does not deal with the structural causes of poverty and injustice. The global community gets one chance for deep thought every 20 years—and this is it'.[6]

Thus, it may be said that whilst the MDGs and the next set of goals include rights as a central target of their programme to achieve each of the goals, they are neither rights nor described as such. Now, in 2015, it would be very difficult to claim that the eight original goals have been achieved or will be by the end of this year. In that respect, it is difficult to claim that children universally have improved or more rights.

Therefore, this work sets out to be a realistic but not always critical review of two and a half decades of intensive activity in the field of children's rights worldwide, including not only failures but also examples of good practice and positive experiences. It is also a review of progress and lack of progress in child rights and welfare in the twelve countries used as case studies in *The Next Generation*. Finally, it considers the impact of current geopolitical and economic realities on children's rights in the early years of the twenty-first century.

It acknowledges that the world has changed a great deal since 1979. That is catalogued through children's involvement in each of the following topic areas.

Firstly, we saw changes in geopolitics: especially the Gulf and Balkan wars and how those countries have been reconstructed. The Gulf War was the first 'live broadcast' war ever. During the war the emphasis was very much on the weapons and 'sensational' coverage of actions such as air raids and hits by cruise missiles. There were some 'scandals' when civilians were killed or wounded, although those

[6]From the *Beyond 2015* press release of 25 September 2013 on http://www.beyond2015.org/news/beyond-2015-reaction-special-events-outcome-document-press-release

victims were also seen to be used as political collateral. It was no longer far away, since at the click of a key, we had live television coverage at our fingertips. When it came to the dispute with Iraq, children were occasionally presented as victims of Iraqi aggression when best media and political advantage could be gained. It was only once the war was over that the increasingly poor state of children in Iraq became news. They became 'pawns' in the negotiations with the international community: their health and welfare were a major reason for Iraq being able to trade some of its oil.

The Balkans took us through a similar passage in bringing the alien into our homes. As Bosnia moved on to be replaced by Kosova, weaponry diminished as a focus for newsmaking to be replaced by ethnic cleansing. Again children were news of the last resort, for instance, when children were amongst the victims of a bombing by other former Yugoslavians, it was important news; as victims of friendly fire, they tended to be less well presented.

Since then, the escalation of violence in Indonesia, beginning with East Timor, was similarly treated. Where children were part of forced migrations or victims of atrocities (especially when the elderly or Christian priests and nuns were also caught up in them), they made news in order to put an edge on the degree of violence. As I write, although it is no longer headline news every day, the same applies to Syria, Kurdish Iraq and the Gaza Strip.

Genocide, rape and torture are key themes, but what do we really know about the children? In stark contrast we are beginning to be informed about places and their regimes in greater detail than ever before. Where children do become central to these areas is in the aftermath when reconstruction draws in 'child savers' who busy themselves with the renovation of institutions full of neglected orphans, who are often in reality the physically and mentally disadvantaged ones who have been placed in institutions prior to the conflicts. However, they provide a very precise humanitarian face of aid and reconstruction.

Changes in global economics are a key topic. At present they preoccupy many of us in the wake of the events of the beginning of this century. The 2000s recession was a decline in economic activity that mainly occurred in developed countries. The global financial crisis of 2007–2008 has become a global recession. It has been the poorest of the poor who have been hardest hit and naturally include children.

There have also been changes in global environment: El Niño, global warming, pollution and HIV. In general, environmental problems have been viewed more in terms of other living species than as human problems. They have been expressed as damage done by our species or through our contribution to climatic change such as global warming brought on by pollution, deforestation, CFCs, etc. There has been some concerned expressed about where people live in lowlands such as on the Maldives and in Bangladesh, although little of it categorically referred to how that may affect children's futures.

Health has been affected by such pollutants as lead and mercury, where different forms of radiation occur and where chemicals such as those used in agribusiness have raised questions about deformity, cancer and other physical effects on children. These have been contentious in virtually every instance, whereby governments and corporations have very quickly had scientific research carried out to disprove or at the very least discredit the independent research. Where neither government nor business has succeeded has been in the wake of the direct outcome of climatic change as it has been manifested by heavy and long-lasting rains caused by El Niño; so that flooding in East Africa and even in the Bay of Bengal and the Yangtze Basin have been quickly explained away by describing the weather as simply 'extraordinary' or 'untypical'.

There is tacit denial of the possibility of a correlation between environmental change and the appearance and diffusion of HIV/AIDS. AIDS had, however, been used to good effect by media happy to exploit the suffering of AIDS orphans in much the same way as drought and famine provide pathos. Thus, it is the deprived, staring, hungry child, often with bloated belly and thin limbs, who calls for sympathy rather than the possibility that all children in the world may be affected by what is happening. What do people actually remember about events where children were severely affected such as Bhopal, Chernobyl, etc.?

There were also inevitable changes at 'the top' in the UN and its specialised agencies that had or are having consequences for children and children's rights. The people in those positions where any influence was imaginable, let alone possible, have more or less all moved on to be replaced by people with other important agendas. There is a UN *Committee on the Rights of the Child.* At first the Committee had a somewhat higher profile than at present. There have been some notable chairs, but it is sometimes slightly difficult to see why some of the members are there. Ironically, in some respects, one might argue that it is in fact the UN that has moved emphasis away from the human rights focus of the CRC towards it being an instrument used to justify and support an increasing number of protections. Those protections sometimes conflict with the notion of 'the best interests of the child' since they are imposed on children, usually with consultation with children, and may well have detrimental effects on their lives. Arguably, since a protection is essentially based on a benign concept, it must be in one sense or another 'enabling' for children, whilst in reality it may be 'prohibiting' from the point of view of children and their families. Also, in common with goals, protections are not rights which they are frequently misrepresented as being.

Changes in global information have had an enormous effect on children's lives. The Internet and media have moved forward at an ever-increasing rate since the generation we were looking at in *The Next Generation.*

Western politicians have occasionally proposed that every child in the world should have access to the Internet, World Wide Web and all other aspects of modern electronic communication and information.[7] It appears to be a high and worthy ideal but is actually mere rhetoric. It makes no account of resources such as the provision

[7]Bill Clinton's Vice-President Al Gore discussed his concerns with computer technology and levels of access in his 1994 article, *No More Information Have and Have Nots*, in Billboard, 22 October 1994. He was particularly interested in implementing measures, which would grant all children access to the Internet.

of hardware (the computers themselves), even electricity supplies and telephone connections. It also skates over the question of literacy—not only computer literacy but also the ability to read and write without which computers are virtually useless. Of course there are known to be Internet cafés in the remotest places which may be said to be leading the world in that direction, but that is the exception rather than the rule since it requires money to be able to use them. It is likewise a resource for the few who have time, money and the ability to use it.

Media, on the other hand, has expanded exponentially since the advent of satellite television transmission. Children and youth have been targeted through channels given over to their interests, hence Disney Channel, Cartoon Network, MTV and so on. The latter has particularly worked towards a globalisation of media and music, having begun at the time the vinyl record was being almost universally replaced by the tape cassette, very quickly by the CD, then minidisks and DVD and now download and digital technologies.

Popular music has itself shared the lead to a 'global villagisation' wherein fashion and language are led by dominant forces so that, for instance, North American black 'street language' has become the *lingua franca* of the young and designer trainers, baggy jeans and other clothes are becoming universal. It is what David Hesmondhalgh (1999 and 2007) calls a form of cultural imperialism, arguing that English is the predominant language of pop music and, as has been the case for many years, that industry is one of capitalism's most successful enterprises. Through this 'world bazaar', ethnic identity and popular culture are becoming intermingled. Thus, to use a simple example, in Brazil some Bahian black youth have abandoned samba in favour of reggae, rap, hip-hop and other black ghetto music, often adopting the dress of Rastafarians, US rappers and so on. When Bob Geldof put on the *Live Aid* concert in 1985, it fell almost immediately into place in the global aid arena and a little later when many people 'Ran the World' (*Sport Aid*, May 25 1986);[8] the interaction took from and fed such events into the so-called 'world bazaar'. It has been this interaction that has often fuelled the ambitions of western entrepreneurs to take the boundaries of media penetration even further.

Other things have happened that have shaped and reshaped the situation of children. For instance, in 1996 the United Nations General Assembly received a ground-breaking report on the 'Impact of armed conflict on children', written by Graça Machel. There were optional protocols to the CRC on sexual exploitation and child soldiers. Other actions such as *Comic Relief* in the UK have had significant influence to the manner and style of actions. Thus, we see a world in which children have, in some ways, become more visible.

[8] Sport Aid was the sporting event with the most participants in history and raised \$37 m to support famine relief in Africa. It was organised by Chris Long, Bob Geldof, Simon Dring and John Anderson. Paul Willies was coordinator for events in North America, also wrote the manual for the 10 k road race and help bring in UNICEF as the overall underwriter of the project. Sport Aid was supported by Band Aid and UNICEF. Sport Aid took place in 89 countries simultaneously.

Despite this visibility, whilst Judith and I talked about what we would be examining, each of the themes discussed above provided us with food for thought and consistently raised questions. We wanted to know whether or not these things were contributing to making the world better for children, not really making any change or might they even be making some things worse? Our first book included twelve country case studies that will be briefly revisited in this work; however, it also reminds that the full title of that book was *The Next Generation: Lives of Third World Children*. This work does not only examine 'third world' children, since too many of the changes we have seen affect all children; thus, I am at the least morally obliged to make it global.

Both of us profoundly disliked the way single issues are so often pursued. Not only that, but in general we found that within the single issues, only a single perspective was considered. Therefore, to take an example, we looked at research into child labour and saw that much of it use a few sketchy examples of what children were doing, but the main thrust of the research was to look for ways of eliminating it. Only a minority of researchers were examining how to improve children's working conditions, pay and all other aspects of employment. Fewer still were researching the legitimacy of work in order to support children's demands that they be allowed to work in the southern hemisphere. Everything appeared to be governed by people in the northern hemisphere whose goal was the elimination of all child labour. We recognised the folly of separating child and adult workers whose problems were frequently shared, but the people 'pulling the strings' in Geneva would not have it.

We also saw the 'discovery' of children's participation. In fact both of us already knew children's movements in Asia and South America. The people who believed they had discovered participation meant something else entirely. They created an environment in which children were hived off from adults in order to somehow sort the world out for children. Whilst they were mildly political in that most of them were encouraged to be anti-war and pro-environmentalist, the politicisation was discouraged from going further. They neither demanded the right to work nor did they overtly support or even acknowledge their counterparts in the South in any way. What was even more alarming for us was that children's participation in the North was proposing the agenda for the rest of the world to follow without any apparent acknowledgement of the experience of well-established children's movements in the South. Furthermore, participatory activities for young people were exclusively for them, usually set up and with an agenda created by adults, that had little and sometimes no linkage whatsoever with adults, therefore the rest of the world. We had both hoped that with the CRC and new concepts it offered, both single dimensions and age-related separatism would end.

We looked at the first 10 years with open minds. Then as the years increased, we saw more and more immovable positions developing. We were concerned that the recognition of children's rights that came with the CRC had become entrenched rather than move things forward. Rather than bring children into the mainstream of human rights, it had cut them off in a symbolically separate world, that of children as if they were not yet fully human beings. We recognised in that separation what Brennan and Noggle (1997) described as an *unequal treatment thesis* whereby children from specific age groups are legitimately excluded from doing many things adults are allowed to do. When combined with a single view of any observable aspect of being a child, rather than examining a whole picture, we realised how easy it is to naively accept childhood as a malleable mass rather than see children as individuals with unique identities, personal histories and futures who are social actors rather than merely would-be bearers of rights. Our expectation had been that with the basic structure on which to build the CRC would move things forward.

Our hopes were not exactly what we would define as unfulfilled but more like unreasonably slow in finding acceptance. We recognised fully the many differences there are in the world that would mean different stages of development and change at very different paces and beginning at numerous different times. However, we were not seeing a precedent that offered a broad-ranging example, more like a relatively few examples of parts of the comprehensive set of rights the CRC describes, often only one particularly, anywhere. It was not a case of children's rights not happening; it was beyond giving them a chance to become established and therefore find their own place or that despite concerted attempts nothing much was happening. It seemed more the case that recognition of children's rights justifies the unequal treatment of them by accepting them as separable. The world was therefore able to move on, leaving children with a set of rights in a niche of their own.

That niche was of different quality and size in each country and often within nations, in some almost indiscernible and in others at least visible but never too evident, although sometimes what there is appears to be rather ostentatious. Too many nations have ratified the CRC without reservations, yet there is no mechanism beyond the critical examination of the Committee on the Rights of the Child to take this to task. Indeed, the Committee's strong censure of the Holy See early in 2014 is proving the CRC to be a fantastically well-designed instrument but with no means of fixing what needs to be established as a priority. It is, in short, toothless. That, we felt, is where it falls at the first fence and why the commitment to fully adopt the CRC into national laws that comes with ratification is too high an ideal.

To cap it all, children's rights do not really exist in isolation as some people appear to think they do. They are part of all of human rights except that they focus on people under age 18 years. What we mutually questioned is the ability of those who work in the children's rights world who might appear to allow young people to fall into some kind of abyss called adulthood on reaching that birthday. Since life is a continuum, there is no legitimate reason to do that. Therefore, although our work looks at people below 18 years of age, we treated it as a stage in a whole life that had particular events and experiences in it that are carried over into adulthood. Children are born male or female; able or disabled; of many cultures, religions and language backgrounds; rich or poor; and in between. It is a far longer list in fact, but the basic point intended is that birth is the starting point of a life that may last moments or over a century; thus, those most recently born will also include the progenitors of the next generation and they, in turn, will do the same. Childhood is simply the preparatory phase for the rest of life, and those who have enjoyed delivery and observance of their rights are almost certainly in a better position than those who do not. Optimistically, one would see those who are aware of their rights as a child grows to be aware of their rights throughout their entire life and impart the message and ensure delivery of rights to following generations.

This book neither includes the word 'conclusion' in its final chapter nor attempts to reach conclusions. Since it is an examination of the progress of a human rights instrument and like all the others is part of an ongoing and perpetual process, there can be no conclusions. The past, present and all future generations will benefit or even suffer as part of that process, but those cannot be predicted; therefore, it does not project into the unknown. The emphasis is on reviewing the period after 1988 and commenting on what has happened.

Thus, our analysis was simply that we take a step or two back and look at what we have again, but do so objectively and thus accept it as imperfect and then think about how to take it forward. This book is our attempt to do so that I have accepted to write alone. It places Judith's share of the responsibility for what we had to say in my hands. However, I know she was willing to have borne her share of that responsibility herself and had she lived to see this work finished would have proudly said so.

This book is written primarily for academics working in human rights or specialising in the field of children's rights, or a related area, and, so often is the case, has a more active role such as occasionally working with UN agencies and NGOs. It is also for students, postgraduates particularly, and children's rights professionals. It is a work written neither for activists nor campaigners. Those people have their own ways of using information and acting on it and my own point of view is that I do not always agree with what they do and how and why they do it, and therefore, I would need to suggest on how they can change. I am not doing so here. I am writing a serious and principally scholarly work that, I hope, will inform towards critique and change that includes work by other authors, some taking these ideas forward and others proposing alternative or critical views. The basic principle is that even perhaps 2 weeks before she died, Judith and I had exchanged views on the changes worldwide and what we considered stagnation since we last wrote together. To follow up those discussions, I wished only to write openly and honestly about them.

Finally, the choice of title fell to me. Whilst there were still the two of us, we had thought of obvious ideas such as 'The Next Generation Revisited' or 'Beyond the First Generation'. We rejected our titles one after the other; thus, 'Changing Generations: The First Quarter Century of New Hope for Children' came out of notes on tentative sub-titles. Eventually with guidance from editors, the simpler *Rights of the Child: 25 Years after the Adoption of the UN Convention* was chosen. It says all that needs to be said, and the content of the book says the rest.

Finding the linkage between the quarter of a century since writing the first book and the present was the most important. We knew that the way in which the 1980s work was written reflected where we were then and also a pre-CRC picture. Case studies then served a purpose, but the world has changed and a global overview is far more important. Rather simply deserting our 12-country case studies, it was clear we would at least need to acknowledge them in the wider context of change.

Nonetheless, our then shared vision was that this would be a work that firstly linked the two works; secondly described change as we had observed it; thirdly included some kind of narrative that mapped the changes since, which if not at first apparent can be found; and finally would ideally require reading both books if at all possible but still be able to stand alone for those who cannot do so. In that respect we wished to put a great deal of seeing what this work merely outlines in the hands of the readers to expand on rather than claiming to be absolute, definitive or actually at all right. Taking on the flaws as well as what might be accepted without question became a hard task for a single author attempting to think for two, wishing to email her almost every day of writing to ask an opinion or how she would phrase something. It is nonetheless the best possible attempt at what was largely a shared vision and can also be considered to be part of a far wider set of tributes to Judith Ennew.

References

Brennan, S., & Noggle, R. (1997). The moral status of children: Children's rights, parent's rights and family justice. *Social Theory and Practice, 23*, 1–26.

Ennew, J., & Milne, B. (1989). *The next generation: Lives of third world children*. London/Philadelphia: Zed Books/New Society Publishers.

Gore, Al. (1994, October 22). No more information have and have nots. *Billboard*.

Milne, B. (2013). *The history and theory of children's citizenship in contemporary societies*. Stuttgart: Springer.

Signed, Ratified but Not Understood

2

There is probably good reason to look at how the world is changing every decade. The same could be said about children's rights, indeed the whole of human rights. However, this retrospective comes around quarter of a century after the first look at children's rights. Then, 1988, the idea was somehow 'fresher'. That is to say that it was still a year or so until the CRC was completed and presented to the world. The notion of children's rights and work in that field was in themselves not new, but the broader awareness was far less.

It is a very dangerous thing to do when somebody adopts a critical view of any single aspect of human rights. That seems to be especially the case when whoever does that appears to do so from within the field that is being questioned. It is a way of losing 'friends' and attracting criticism, which in both cases may be defensive or overtly embarrassed rebuffs. Nonetheless, it is a calculated risk that must be taken. If children's rights are to be realised, subsequently advanced and improved and to remain developing for all time, then what must be said simply should be said. The starting point here is that one of the issues that should be addressed is that child rights is part of the entire human rights agenda and not just a bolt-on to child welfare.

At present close scrutiny of children's rights would show that they represent an unfinished movement from the areas of needs, protection, welfare and services to an incontrovertible rights-based approach. Having looked at that question, it then looks at children's rights and cultural relativity and asks what relevance the CRC has. To do so demands examination of what cultural relativity is and where and how at all it fits into the human rights agenda and attempts to look at examples of its importance. This entails an examination of progress made in developing and implementing examples of regional or national instruments that may complement the CRC or provide an alternative in practice.

The first question that must be raised, therefore, is whether or not the CRC is seen as part of the human rights agenda and whether the notion of children's rights itself is recognised as part of human rights as distinct from it being an adjunct that

B. Milne, *Rights of the Child*, Children's Well-Being: Indicators and Research 11,
DOI 10.1007/978-3-319-18784-6_2

is age, 0–18 years, defined. It is by its nature a welfare instrument that mainly uses the word *rights* rhetorically, although some articles very clearly do set out some principles that are irrefutably intended to deliver rights. The CRC in fact cites the 1959 *Declaration of the Rights of the Child*, which it then makes part of the Preamble: 'the child, by reason of his physical and mental immaturity, needs special safeguards and care, including appropriate legal protection, before as well as after birth'. The emphasis is on health and welfare.

One need only carefully examine Article 3 as a good example of the language of welfare rather than what we may consider to be human rights terminology.

Article 3

1. In all actions concerning children, whether undertaken by public or private social welfare institutions, courts of law, administrative authorities or legislative bodies, the best interests of the child shall be a primary consideration.
2. States Parties undertake to ensure the child such protection and care as is necessary for his or her well-being, taking into account the rights and duties of his or her parents, legal guardians, or other individuals legally responsible for him or her, and, to this end, shall take all appropriate legislative and administrative measures.
3. States Parties shall ensure that the institutions, services and facilities responsible for the care or protection of children shall conform with the standards established by competent authorities, particularly in the areas of safety, health, in the number and suitability of their staff, as well as competent supervision.

Currently, children's rights represent an unfinished movement from needs, welfare, protection and services approaches to a rights-based approach. The best interests of the child are not necessarily the delivery of rights per se. Indeed, there is almost certainly justification in delivering child welfare rather than more ephemeral rights. It is, therefore, not so much a critical view here, as identification of the need to separate one from the other continues to deliver welfare but also to strengthen the rights. It is not enough to say that because children have a right to the things the CRC describes that whatever gives them other rights, for instance, political rights, can be excused for their absence. That makes the entire principle on which a framework of rights that should give children personhood is exposed as a fraud. In fact it objectifies them rather than giving them an identity comparable with but not identical to adults in the human rights environment.

Where this is different is where 'participation' is the object of Articles 12 to 15:

Article 12

1. States Parties shall assure to the child who is capable of forming his or her own views the right to express those views freely in all matters affecting the child, the views of the child being given due weight in accordance with the age and maturity of the child.
2. For this purpose, the child shall in particular be provided the opportunity to be heard in any judicial and administrative proceedings affecting the child, either directly, or through a representative or an appropriate body, in a manner consistent with the procedural rules of national law.

Article 13

1. The child shall have the right to freedom of expression; this right shall include freedom to seek, receive and impart information and ideas of all kinds, regardless of frontiers, either orally, in writing or in print, in the form of art, or through any other media of the child's choice.
2. The exercise of this right may be subject to certain restrictions, but these shall only be such as are provided by law and are necessary:
   (a) For respect of the rights or reputations of others; or
   (b) For the protection of national security or of public order (ordre public), or of public health or morals.

Article 14

1. States Parties shall respect the right of the child to freedom of thought, conscience and religion.
2. States Parties shall respect the rights and duties of the parents and, when applicable, legal guardians, to provide direction to the child in the exercise of his or her right in a manner consistent with the evolving capacities of the child.
3. Freedom to manifest one's religion or beliefs may be subject only to such limitations as are prescribed by law and are necessary to protect public safety, order, health or morals, or the fundamental rights and freedoms of others.

Article 15

1. States Parties recognize the rights of the child to freedom of association and to freedom of peaceful assembly.
2. No restrictions may be placed on the exercise of these rights other than those imposed in conformity with the law and which are necessary in a democratic society in the interests of national security or public safety, public order (ordre public), the protection of public health or morals or the protection of the rights and freedoms of others.

A great deal of emphasis has been placed on Article 12, a lesser extent on Article 13 and even less on Articles 14 and 15. However, participation at one stage began to shape how some people understood children's rights. The twentieth century was almost certainly the cradle of the notion of children's rights as we now understand them. It is, critically appraised, still a young reality and thus far has moved forward with a great deal of uncertainty. However, the reality itself is often a largely adult-made illusion of how we see lives of children should be. As much as we use the language of rights, we also abuse and misuse it, often saying what shall be right before it is tested and proven and rarely with either the collaboration or approval of children. Very early in the latter phase of the development of formalised children's rights through the CRC, it was said that the parts of the convention describing the actual 'rights' were made up of *protection*, *provision* and *participation*. It is a fait accompli that was achieved without consultation with those to and for whom those rights are addressed despite the enthusiasm for participation.

A great deal of stress has been placed on the importance of children's *participation* for roughly two and a half decades, yet the underlying trend has been towards increased *protection* and a disproportionately large part of that done under the guise of *provision*. Part of this predicament has been the prevalent use of the word 'participation' by large UN agencies such as the *World Bank* and its frequent use by politicians worldwide who use it generously and apply it sparingly. It has also become part of the language of the development world; parallel to this one often notes the tendency of children's rights issues to be associated with developing countries rather than in our midst or simply everywhere including in advanced industrial societies. It may be that there is a notion of there being no need for 'that kind' of participation since our children are so well protected they have no real needs; thus, it is easy to be dismissive. Of course, in better-off countries we do have children's organisations, municipal councils and parliaments, school councils, occasional conferences on environmental protection for young people and so on. There is no apparent universal discourse on their lives or rights. When questions periodically arise they are viewed as dissent and are seldom taken seriously.

Children who live in markedly difficult circumstances, thus including abused and neglected children and those who are sexually exploited, work, live on streets, become soldiers or are affected by conflict, juvenile delinquents and so on who attract attention, are those who have least access to any means of participation in any kind of political dialogue. A great deal is said about either improving their lives and greater protection being given to them or controlling them, occasionally punishing them. Their participation is also held to be a very important part of getting them out of their current situation and back into mainstream society. Ironically there is little concern with this ideal 'mainstream' anywhere. Used in such circumstances it is usually in the North and then a particularly western concept that is meant. It is attractive to acquire knowledge of what does not conform to the norm but very few people study what is 'normal'. Yet the final irony is that the children who do become part of parliaments, councils and child and youth conferences are often the good, clean and wholesome young people we consider normal.

Bill Cooke and Uma Kothari edited a book under the title *Participation: The New Tyranny?* (2002), drawing together the work of contributors to a conference of the same name at the Institute for Development Policy and Management at the University of Manchester. It critically emphasises the weight that has been thrust on participation in their world. One of the editors, Kothari (op. cit.: 139–52), draws attention to the work of Erving Goffman who very succinctly described one of the key ingredients of participation, namely, 'social interaction', in his *The Presentation of Self in Everyday Life* (1959). His work also examines the psychology of the individual, in which, given the relative importance that has been attached to individuation, the rights of individuals as distinct from those of the collective and so on over recent years cannot go unmentioned when discussing things done 'together'.

His approach used the theatrical stage as a metaphor to explain how we 'stage manage' images we try to convey to those around us which aptly describes much of what happens in children's participatory activities. The 'dramaturgical' approach is concerned with the mode of presentation used by the 'actor' and its meaning in a broader social context (1959: 240). Interaction is thus viewed as 'performance'. It is shaped by audience and environment so that it is constructed so as to provide others with 'impressions'. These are consistent with the desired aims of the actor (ibid.: 17). A performance exists regardless of the mental state of the individual, who as a character is often attributed to the individual in spite of his or her lack of faith in or perhaps unawareness of the performance. Thus, an individual develops a persona as a function of interaction with others through exchanges of information that allow for more specific definitions of identity and behaviour. Goffman also explores the nature of group dynamics through discussion of 'teams' and relationships between performance and audience.

The concept of the team demonstrates the work of a group of individuals who 'cooperate' in their performance, thereby attempting to achieve goals approved by the group (ibid.: 79). Cooperation might manifest itself as agreement on conduct and behaviour or taking on of various roles for each individual that are determined by the desired objective of the performance. The need of each individual to maintain his or her front in order to promote the team performance reduces the likelihood of dispute. However, Goffman does not provide a comprehensive description of interactive processes in this work. It is complemented by his work on the *Interaction Ritual* (Goffman 1967: 43–4) whereby he assumed a more abstract location in the communicative process that is a reconstruction of verbal prompts. The expression reflects a line suggested by others, regardless of awareness of its existence, to the actor that is based on the use of verbal and non-verbal symbols that either confirm or deny a social construct. By this means a process of locating the actor in the interactive process and broader society allowed Goffman to uphold George Herbert Mead's argument that identity is constructed through an understanding of the projection of the self onto others (i.e. see Morris 1934, or Miller 1982).

A significant connection can accordingly be made between Goffman and Durkheim in an inquiry into the concept of 'spontaneity'. The importance of spontaneity became an apparent aspect of performance in which an actor attempts to create a façade that does not appear to be affected. Spontaneity allows for the realisation of 'true' self which is an idealised type of interaction that allows an individual to accomplish a desired appearance. In *The Division of Labour in Society*, Durkheim described a macrosociological model of spontaneity that he said was a 'finely articulated organisation in which each social value . . . . . . is appreciated at its true worth' (1984: 313). Durkheim, though primarily examining labour, described a type of social interaction that reiterates the existing social environment through the notion of 'truth'. Each individual is bound to contemporary social organisation whilst attempting to achieve a sense of freedom in expression of truth.

Due consideration of Goffman's work shows just how authority provides a definition of 'idealised' performance and pressure to be consistent with the established definition. As a demonstration of what Marx termed 'the ideas of the ruling class' (i.e. Marx and Engels 1971: 106–118), a hegemony that '... creates a world after its own image' (op. cit.: 84), thus an authority that provides the mores, norms and laws to which stigma, ideology, character and also Durkheimian anomie can be applied. In this sense the hegemony provides a crucial link between the macrostructure of social institutions and the microsociological phenomena of head-to-head interaction. Whichever way we look at what Goffman, Durkheim or Marx may have been describing, we only find a form of 'participation' in which the aims and intentions of those who are overseeing the social actors from a position of power, patronage or perhaps as protectors are achieved. The impression of 'participants' having achieved certain outcomes is marked by approval or disapproval; thus, whether what has been achieved may be further acted on.

Naturally, such an examination of sociological analysis of human behaviour is as vulnerable to critique or reappraisal as it is to uncompromising acceptance of its validity. Yet it does say a great deal about where *participation* appears to be at present. It has become idealised and almost a doctrinal issue that influences which side we take on any question. There is no evident safe ground upon which to find a consensus on contentious ideas. Thus, what little discourse there is manifests itself as mostly bitter confrontation between representatives of either side of the conundrum.

Working children's movements have been almost inextricably drawn into this category of contention. Several points are overlooked in this argument. First of all, it is necessary to remember that those groups present different points of view. Some of them demand the right to work without compromise although they demand fair pay and conditions according to their own standards. Others have committed themselves to the elimination of what they consider exploitative whilst retaining the right to work. The variations go on in numerous permutations until we reach those organisations whose prime intent is to see the absolute elimination of child labour. The second point is that a few of those organisations precede the contemporary CRC lead version of what children's rights are. They may or may not have modified themselves to incorporate a notion of themselves as bearers of rights as described by the CRC. Their starting point was always a rights issue in the first place, and new ideas may simply be a case of 'moving goalposts'. The third and very important point is that there are degrees of how far children were ever initiators of those organisations and to what extent they are now 'in control' of them and also to what extent it is a shared task with adults. The fourth point raises a serious question about how genuine are some of those organisations as participatory bodies for children, or is it the case that some are political showcases for adult campaigners who occasionally appear to have recognised a wonderful opportunity for achieving their own ends?

The first point, where young workers are themselves calling for any kind of improvement of their working conditions, looks very much like demands early trade unions made and, in time, contributed to the creation of the ILO. It is now a specialised agency of the UN which seeks the promotion of social justice and internationally recognised human and labour rights and was founded in 1919 by the *Treaty of Versailles*. It became an agency of the UN in 1946. The ILO devises international labour standards in the form of conventions and recommendations, which set minimum standards of basic labour rights such as freedom of association, the right to organise, collective bargaining, abolition of forced labour and equality of opportunity and treatment and other standards regulating conditions across a broad range of work-related issues. It also promotes the development of independent employers' and worker' organisations and provides training and advice to those organisations. Within the UN system, the ILO has a unique tripartite structure with workers, usually represented by trade unions, and employers participating as equal partners with governments.

Extraordinarily, given their history, the ILO is far closer to elimination action groups and lobby organisations than to the young workers. They have aligned themselves with child protection organisations especially and child participation groups only a little. In fact, they quite rightly do not present themselves as a children's rights organisation even though IPEC tries to project itself into that mould. It is an organisation that has little in common with the children it sets out to 'liberate' from their work, rarely communicates directly with the children and apparently cares little for child participation. That is, naturally, unless it is the very demonstrative action of children demanding the elimination of child labour. Then, because it is the UN agency that creates and oversees labour standards, it is able to put conventions in place that ban children's work without consulting with them. They have as an agency or through conventions and recommendations, in fact, little in common with the sentiments and assertions of the CRC.

Then we may move to the second point. Ennew et al. (2004: 25) describe the CRC and where participation belongs within it; thus:

> The 1989 United Nations Convention on the Rights of the Child (CRC) is based on the recognition that children are human beings with the same rights as adults, rather than 'human becomings' who require socialisation before being regarded as full subjects of rights (see for example Qvortrup 1991; Van Bueren 1995). Sharing in the civil and political rights of all other human beings means that children have the right to participate in decisions made on their behalf, to freedom of expression and to peaceful assembly to represent their own interests (depending on their evolving capacities). The principles of participation were already in practice in some circles well before the drafting process for the CRC began in 1979; for example in organisations of working children, and even earlier in certain radical education and environmental planning activities as well as in the development of 'children's parliaments' in some European countries.

Yet, nowhere does the CRC advocate and demand a precisely spelled out collaboration between child and adult so that shared participation becomes an absolute. Instead it is a conditional participation for children but overseen and often manipulated by adults. The convention contains counterbalances in its Preamble and Articles 3 (best interests of the child) and 5 (direction and guidance in the exercise of their rights by adults) that are there to justify any or all of the superficially constructive participation rights being denied or withheld at any point in childhood and, indeed, with the possibility of entirely withholding them until majority is achieved. Despite what they say, 'the recognition that children are human beings with the same rights as adults', there is no benchmark against which to precisely measure adult rights. There is no equivalent convention. Thus, one may say that for lack of practice we do not actually know how to translate the principles of the CRC into action. However, even though the intention remains good, the counterbalances above are in place. They are, in Goffman's terms, very good for 'stage management' of how children use their rights.

The third point is a far more sensitive topic. We largely know to what degree children were initiators of children's organisations and the extent to which they are now in control of them. We often also know to what extent that is a shared task with adults. In reality nearly all have been initiated by adults. There is no serious reason to question the validity of that since it is quite apparent that without the organisational, lobbying, financial and other important tools for the sustenance of those groups they would not exist. That adults have engaged themselves to draw children together for altruistic purposes is hardly a bad thing in itself. Where some of those people have done so for their own ends is another matter altogether. One may also consider the question of this kind of 'participation' being far more a lobbying or action-oriented initiative that is shared by adults and children, thus less simple to dismiss as a 'children thing'. Where children act alone it will usually be inevitable that their activities are either considered 'childish', thus not taken seriously, or do not have access to the adult institutions they wish their message to reach.

There was an anecdote circulating some years ago that told the story of a street children's organisation in Brazil. It appears that the children had heard about the activities of the *Movimento Nacional de Meninos e Meninas de Rua* (MNMMR or National Movement of Street Boys and Girls) but wished to start a local action rather than join the national movement. They went to a number of adults for advice and finally set up a small organisation. They were not able to find a base, for instance, an office, because they were too young, not able to carry out financial transactions for the same reason nor had permanent addresses, etc. Consequently they found an adult who became a kind of manager. Once they had an office and a bank account, they needed a bookkeeper-cum-accountant, to keep themselves viable, and they needed someone with business and fundraising skills. Eventually there was an office staffed by six adults, one of them even became director. Soon the entire management of the organisation was governed by a council, at first a partnership of adults and children but quickly entirely adult. Although the organisation continued (perhaps even today still does) to work with street children, within 2 years it had gone from a children's organisation to an adult organisation working with child clients. Whilst being initiated by children, ultimately it was only nominally a children's organisation that had made a transition without stopping at the probably most important stage at which its entire operation would have been shared by adults and children.

Then we have the fourth question. Since the names of adults who represent 'children's' organisations have often become well known, but very few young people ever receive similar acclaim, the questions have been raised to ask: How genuine are some of those organisations as participatory bodies for children? Is it the case that some of them are little more than political showcases for charismatic adult campaigners who now and again appear to have recognised a wonderful opportunity for achieving their own ends? It closely correlates with the previous question, since adults tend to have access to important resources that children do not have. Child labour and the closely related street children area have seen affable figureheads whose very presence has occasionally overshadowed the children they were working for or with.

Nevertheless, as people working in the children's rights world are very aware, they are few in number. They have and do exist on both sides of the issue in the child labour world, those who would 'save' children from work and those who would fight to defend the rights of young workers. On the other hand, there are more than a few on both sides who become well known who are simply committed to what they are doing and we may consider real advocates for children. Reputations are as likely to be yet another 'stage-managed' construction of those who would like to see the suppression of those people's campaigns. In this situation it is the children who are the well-tutored actors in a 'play' that is shaped by its audience and environment in which it operates so that it is constructed in a manner that provides others with 'impressions'. That type of manipulation is especially favoured by powerful bodies such as the ILO or World Bank who can build up the persona of a well-known child campaigner who is in line with their policy and, by the same means, undermine the standing of somebody they do not favour. Again, we can do no better than turn again to Goffman to understand the dynamics of this dramaturgical construction of where children's rights may go.

Bill Cooke and Uma Kothari (op. cit.) include a paper by Harry Taylor (2002: 122–138) that challenges the optimistic slant of the 'rapid appraisal' school of thought's line on parallels between participatory development and management. His critique is that participation is part of an attempt to sway power relations between elites and less powerful recipients of programme work. This is an interesting point of view in terms of what has happened in the world of children's participation. Work with children that is very easily comparable to what Taylor refers to has frequently very deliberately chosen children in 'need' such as street and working children. This, needless to say, is the privilege of the participation programmes working in the south and appears seldom, if ever, to have been tried in the north. Poor, socially and politically weak people are accordingly visited by researchers and sometimes programme planners then later project workers. They appear to be offered something by the very presence of people from the rich north, at the very least the status of being chosen before people elsewhere. In effect they are told what to do and how to do it, and results and progress are duly measured before the project comes to an end. Children may well know how to conduct focus groups and role plays thereafter, but what is more certain is that they have the fact that they should not be working deeply ingrained into them. This, irrespective of whether work operates in line with local custom, economic survival strategy and so on, is the dogma that is almost certain to be left behind.

Of course, much of what is 'acted out' appears to collect data on what the needs of the programme beneficiaries are and examines what can be done to change conditions or one or more of several other possibilities. After the project goes usually no follow-up or support is left behind. People change or revert. Change can bring negative outcomes that are unpredictable and reversion can similarly be 'out of the frying pan into the fire'. However, the northern elite has done its participatory development work by showing the people the options and how to do them; the management of the thereafter particularly is what nobody in the north sees as a rule. At the same time, in the north there is very little happening. Children's participation is the privilege of the few who join school councils, children's local councils and parliaments and a very few other marginal activities. Adults seldom make big reputations in the north. Thus, how ironic it seems when one considers that the 'experts' are mostly from the north and go to the south to tell people what to do and how to do it and are then able to go back where they came from and not engage themselves with participatory work there.

Children's participation in development work using rapid appraisal methods particularly but latterly also in examining the authenticity of young people's roles in organised activities has been 'measured' against one standard. That is a ladder scale or variations on the same model. It was first used by Hart (1992: 9) to '... serve as a beginning typology for thinking about children's participation in projects' (op. cit.: 8), yet very few of the 'experts' who so slavishly adhere to the Hart version or one that is very slightly modified have contributed to development towards other and more appropriate models. In general, the people are development experts from the north who have little truck with anything that is not made and managed by them.

Working children's movements, it should be noted, tend not to suffer the same fate in the hands of foreign experts. Most of their adult 'activists' whether local or foreign tend to remain with them, both those who are genuinely engaged in their work and those who are opportunists. Whilst some of them may often travel the world campaigning and appearing only ever to be giving conference papers, the fact remains that they nearly all go back to 'their' children. There is long-term commitment.

Behind this are the real 'stage managers' who permit or prohibit what is being done and who also frequently hold the purse strings that all too often decide whether organisations will survive or fade away. Goffman, in following Mead's view that identity is constructed through an understanding of the projection of the 'self' onto others, is missing one component that redresses his more general idea to that of the specificity of children. That is to say that what we see when the 'self' in question is a child who may be poor, uneducated and working. How we view that child is partly what we are expected to see and has been given to us to understand by those who wish us to see things in particular way. Thus, the child activist is a potential threat to our way of life because the reality he is acting out is unlike the one the stage managers would have him or her act out. It is not the performance or persona we should see when we see a child. Who then are the 'stage managers' in this case? Most certainly they are identifiable as UN agencies or NGOs who have a particular slant on participation or certain aspects of the children's rights environment wherein child activism can be found. They are also the development 'experts', especially those working with rapid appraisal methods that require structured, preordained participation. Adults who lead supposed children's movements and organisations most certain stand accused although probably only a minority of them are as manipulative as we are sometimes led to believe. Above all else are those who make and uphold laws and moral leadership, in simple terms governments, civil servants, legal and police services, clerics and so on. In many senses the odds are heavily stacked against children to begin with.

Yet there is a note of optimism. Children's movements are like fleas that sometimes irritate almost invisibly, more so where they have strong collaboration with adult activists and advocates. They are the exception to the rule that reminds us that children potentially have more rights than the 'diktat' of a single convention. They are also beyond the dramaturgical performance of what is expected by the wider audience because they are demanding rights that they do not have and that it is morally very hard to justify denying to them because the CRC and ILO conventions may be attempting to stage manage another scenario. By using their right to have opinions, assemble freely and so on, they may also be defying the will of adults who believe their capabilities are not yet evolved to the point where their initiatives should be taken seriously or indeed happen at all. Subjective and selective views on best interests that are adult formulated do not always correspond with children's real needs. Rather than rights given, there are too many caveats that make them rights that can be withheld. If, of course, the preamble of the CRC is carefully read then we are minded of the fact that it bears reference to the *Universal Declaration of Human Rights* (UDHR) wherein Article 1 says:

> All human beings are born free and equal in dignity and rights.

and Article 2 reinforces that by saying:

> Everyone is entitled to all the rights and freedoms set forth in this Declaration, without distinction of any kind . . .

Thus, without further consideration of what written down rights are against the possibility of tacit, unwritten ones, we can simply ask, how stage-managed participation is the real McCoy? It seems inconceivable that in such an ostensibly egalitarian world, working children, as too all others who demand their rights, can be so blatantly told what they may and may not do and, indeed, whether or not grown-ups think they are capable. However, since the UDHR was presented to the world in 1948, there has been a proliferation of charters, declarations, conventions and treaties that are specifically made for classificatory minorities for reason of ethnicity, culture, belief, politics and so on and, almost demographically too absurdly, women, with the focus drawn back to children by the 1959 *Declaration of the Rights of the Child*, then the 1979 *International Year of the Child* and subsequent decade of drafting, the adopting of the CRC. It seems, although nowhere explicitly said so, that children have been rendered into a minority and thus, following the logic of all other minorities, require special forms of protection.

In real terms, since the CRC has achieved separation of children from the 'universal' standards of the UDHR, it no longer appears to need to include them under the collective terms 'all human beings' or 'everybody'. Instead they appear to need to be ranked under Jens Qvortrup's (1991; 1994: 18) suggested typology *human becoming* as Ennew, Hastadewi and Plateau suggest. It should be borne in mind that the focus of this essay is on child participation and that there is a clear differentiation between 'northern' and 'southern' childhood. It may also be, in the view of 'experts' in the north, that in the south they need special protection because of economic and social deprivation, exploitation and countless other hardships. The identity of 'the child' they have constructed comes not through an understanding of the projection of the self on to others, as Goffman or Mead would have it, but as an accumulation of perceived needs of vulnerable individuals for whom they choose modes of protection and provision. The means by which this is justified is found in the injurious things happening to those children. Each negative value would appear to further dehumanise children into victims and thus reinforce their argument.

Of course, it would be cynical to forget northern hemisphere children. Since the 'discovery' of child abuse and neglect, many have been more than generously assigned extra protection. The risk of 'stranger danger' justifies keeping them almost cotton wool wrapped away from harm. With the decreased visibility of children, those who are still in the public eye without adult accompaniment are increasingly viewed with suspicion as too those who are classified as vulnerable, for instance, those known to have jobs other than from a small catalogue of approved 'menial' tasks. It is essentially made very easy to justify exclusion from the CRC participatory rights everywhere given the already precarious position children generally appear to be in. The fact that almost as much thought most certainly goes into defining precariousness as protection itself is rarely discussed.

Earlier in this chapter the tendency of children's rights issues to be associated with developing countries rather than a universal value was briefly mentioned. Of course, since all countries but one have signed and all but three ratified the CRC at the time of writing this, then the reality is that it is a universal issue. In theory at least but also in practice in principle, all children should be treated uniformly if not equally. Needless to say, because the convention includes it, some allowance must be made for 'direction and guidance in the exercise of their rights by adults' and where extraordinary circumstances arise such as where children are exempted because of permissible exceptions or are mentally or physically unable to have any control over their own lives. The implications of this would be universally comparable levels of provision in childcare, education, juvenile justice and so on. Those provisions could imaginably, if ever they were possible, be devised with the participation and contribution of children. Nonetheless, the outcome would require political support in bringing them into legislation, presumably putting them entirely back into the hands of governments unless a suddenly enlightened world gave children a share in government of all nations. Of course, if we look at children's rights using the CRC as the locus of supporting arguments, then it depends entirely on interpretation and implementation of law which is the work of lawyers and administrators who inform those elected to govern nations. Those people are, as a rule, highly trained and experienced in the formation of the tools of governance. This is where popular opinion guides but seldom shapes legislation. That depends on the compatibility of any single law to all others for the structure and maintenance of a civil society through its legislation. Thus, the examination of the participation of children in civil society and protection of their rights cannot be rightfully examined primarily through social science or moral philosophy; thus, Goffman, Mead, Marx, Qvortrup and other authors cited in this essay could be considered to offer little more than tenuous notions that contribute to legal discourse in the formation and governance of a democratic state.

There is naturally every need for a big space for the disciplines that study and know the human condition. Whilst writing on the basis of work entirely carried out in the UK, Berry Mayall found that:

> Sociology also throws light on issues to do with respecting children's participation rights. For if we understand children not just as individuals but as members of a social group, then we are forced to reflect on that group's rights to participate in constructing the social order, social policies and practices. But sociology also reveals in stark form, the subordination of children as a group to adults as a group – a subordination that children themselves accept. This leads to difficulties. As a subordinate and marginalised group, children find they have dubious moral status. Adult visions of adult-child relations are built from the long history of developmentalism, intersecting with ideologies and policies which stress adult socialisation duties and responsibility for protection and provision; adult input rather than child agency are at the forefront of these visions. All these combine to foster adult suspicion of children – to disbelieve them, to blame them, to suspect their moral competence, to assign moral responsibility to adults rather than to children. Under these circumstances, it is hard for children to take the initiative and participate in social affairs, and it is hard for adults to permit them to, and very hard for children and adults to work together on anything like equal terms. (Mayall 2000: 256–7)

Her argument very helpfully places sociology as one of the several social sciences and moral philosophies that does clearly see where rights belong. Despite her data being drawn from her work in one country, her implications are universal. Law in itself is obviously only part of the equation since it is ideology and policy that drive and bring legal changes, and those come from mass public opinion which is still probably 99.9 % adult led and carries shadows of the time before the process of giving women 'equal' rights with men began. In only a few cases are children's participatory rights used in a manner that gives them a sharing decision-making, competence and responsibility status. It is and remains most frequently that which Roger Hart (1992) called 'tokenism'.

Education is very frequently proclaimed to be the pre-eminent route to some kind of 'liberation through knowledge' for children. The basic premise is good, but since education is largely adult made and organised, it is not achieving that. In many countries education is tied to curricula that are themselves designed for uniformity of outcomes through qualifications. The standards set and the examinations that bring qualification are scarcely if at all negotiable for the children and youth who are subject of them. To that extent the input of children into education is quite marginal and does not need to reflect children's rights standards. Participatory rights may be referred to as an incentive for councils but do not ensure their members a collective voice that has an input into education overall. Again reflecting on her work in the UK, Mayall noted that:

> As regards the education service, where children's participation rights are so woefully ignored, there is some pressure to take action, by, for instance, a statutory framework for school councils which give students a say (. . .) (ibid.: 257)

The question beyond whether or not a statutory framework is desirable for the adults who control education is what their function might be. Would it be possible for schoolchildren to contribute significantly to the content and structure of curricula or the aims, intentions and configuration of examinations and qualifications?

However, studentship does not end with school. Increasing numbers of young people are moving on from school to further and higher education where some are able to become active participant in processes immediately previously denied them. Student unions and representation on academic councils often consist of young people who have the recent experience of childhood behind them with its constraints and yet they are often very competent negotiators and spokespersons. In Europe particularly but probably in much of the world, these young activists become part of the political hegemony that ultimately restrains the movement of younger generations into sharing decision-making. In those same institutions it is highly probable that apart from the academic and intellectual minority who are engaged in issues pertinent to childhood in further and higher education, virtually nobody gives it much thought. Childhood is generally seen as a burden to be cast off as soon as one can, and after its end little consideration of the condition of having been a child is retained apart from a little bit of largely irrelevant nostalgia. Children's rights are thus something for children, and whilst they are children those rights are overseen and regulated by adults but do not unite all ages as a single society.

Indeed, it might possibly appear that 'participation' may be less viable as a way of bringing adults and children together than previously imagined. Children's participation has little to do with any level of governance of any nation, and even where well-established children's municipal councils exist, there is little evidence of significant input into any level of civil society between local and national. Extraordinarily enough it would appear to be children's movements such as working children's initiatives who appear to defy adult conventions that are making the most progress. They appear to be so effective because they are a 'thorn in the side' of the legal and political environments in which they are found. It is almost too ironic that they also often exist to represent children with less or little access (if any) to education than where there are large numbers of seemingly liberal education systems that advocate and maintain what appear to be active and successful school councils. To analyse that situation would be to more or less see the CRC as a raison d'être for tokenism that puts a perfect veneer on a less than shining reality in which children are no less subject to adult last words because 'they know best' than ever before.

Of course, we should not take such a cynical view and also one should not throw the baby out with the proverbial bathwater because at present the CRC is almost all we have. That is in part because, unlike the UDHR, it is a convention that does give us some kind of potentially enforceable standards. It lacks any kind of universal 'policeman' to oversee and enforce those standards or any real incentives to ardently assist ways of implementing them. It is perhaps at least a starting point and has all potential to progress so that the façade of participation we largely see today is as valid as the voice of any other lobby group or union of like people. As with them, given that there are least two sides but usually more to every issue we must resolve, once consensus is reached and with a fair starting point, children may in time come to share their rights with adults and thus treat us all equally as human beings to begin with. If they are ever allowed to share conditions and standards adults should enjoy, then the resultant partnership would even end another tension. They would cease to need the 'patronage' of apparent advocates who opportunistically build their careers and reputations in children's name. Likewise, adults who work together with children would cease to be diabolised for their efforts. There would be no need for such distinctions to be made. At present that appears a little too Utopian to take seriously but should despite that never be cast aside.

As long as children's rights are treated as the rationale for adult-directed, increased protection, it will never be possible since not only are there two or more sides to every argument but there also needs to be give and take. Perhaps one may imagine a situation in which the push for ever more protection is matched by the participation of children who have a say on their needs. Since protection is subjective and reflects perceived needs, they tend to be based on adult assumptions about what they should be. One example is clearly the attempt to eliminate child labour that generally ignores the possibility of considering the contribution working children and their organisations have to make. Who knows better what exploitation, abuse and everything else than working children? Morally should we not ask them what protection they need and how to apply it? This goes for numerous other domains where protection assumes children's needs irrespective of the enormous resource children have to offer to guide lawmakers and law enforcers. Having apparently given children a broad sweep of human and civil rights that many adults would themselves benefit from, the opportunity is there to share the responsibility for the realisation of the ideals on which they are founded.

If the 'stage management' of how children use their rights is more than a dramaturgical construction that depicts a well-staged 'make-believe world' in which children are simply the actors directed by, following the script and stage directions of adults, then the CRC has failed. It has limitations built into it that restrict assignation of what it appears to offer. At first what appears to be a manifesto for children's rights is as geared to taking or withholding than giving, and what appears to be given with one hand is effectively taken away with the other. The caveats in the CRC are in the hands of the stage managers. It is hard to imagine that they will let them go so easily. Thus, rights will be apportioned to children as judged appropriate to their age and ability to make decisions by adults. In other words, the real meaning of rights for children cannot be understood without first considering how they should be protected and what their needs are (provision). Thus, when considering whether children's rights represent an unfinished movement from a needs, welfare and services approach to a rights-based approach, we can only assume that progress is extraordinarily slow and that what we see is a very short step beyond the starting point.

The CRC came exactly 30 years after the *Declaration* with a 10-year drafting and refining process. We are now about a quarter of a century into the life of the CRC, and there are three Optional Protocols but further developments have neither happened nor are forthcoming. The 'three Ps' language of the CRC remains as it appeared very early, for the most part expressed in welfare terminology which is seldom questioned because the convention itself is still not understood other than as it was drafted as essentially a convention on the protection of children which allows it to remain untouched. As long, it would seem, as it offers children the right to be protected by adults and where adults identify the need for that, then its credentials as a human rights treaty will remain unquestioned.

References

Cooke, B., & Kothari, U. (Eds.). (2002). *Participation: The new tyranny?* London: Zed Books.

Durkheim, E. (1984). *The division of labour in society* (1893). Basingstoke: Macmillan.

Ennew, J., Hastadewi, Y., & Plateau, D. P. (2004). *Seen and heard: Participation of children and young people in Southeast, East Asia and Pacific in events and forums leading to and following up on the United Nations General Assembly Special Session for Children, 2002*. Bangkok: Save the Children Southeast, East Asia and Pacific Region.

Goffman, E. (1959). *The presentation of self in everyday life*. Garden City: Doubleday.

Goffman, E. (1967). *Interaction ritual*. New York: Pantheon.

Hart, R. (1992). *Children's participation: From tokenism to citizenship*. Florence: UNICEF.

Marx, K., & Engels, F. (1971). *The Communist manifesto* (1842). Harmondsworth: Pelican.

Mayall, B. (2000). The sociology of childhood in relation to children's rights. *The International Journal of Children's Rights, 8*, 243–259.

Miller David, L. (1982). *The individual and the social self: Unpublished work of George Herbert Mead*. Chicago: University of Chicago Press.

Morris Charles, W. (1934). *George Herbert Mead, mind, self and society*. Chicago: University of Chicago Press.

Qvortrup, J. (1991). *Childhood as a social phenomenon* (2nd ed.). Eurosocial Report 36/0. Vienna: European Centre for Social Welfare, Policy and Research.

Qvortrup, J. (1994). Childhood matters: An introduction. In J. Qvortrup, M. Bardy, G. Sgritta, & H. Wintersberger (Eds.), *Childhood matters: Social theory, practice and politics*. Avebury: Aldershot.

Taylor, H. (2002). Insights into participation from critical management and labour process perspectives. In B. Cooke & U. Kothari (Eds.), *Participation: The new tyranny?* (pp. 122–38). London: Zed Books.

Van Bueren, G. (1995). *The international law on the rights of the child*. Leiden: Martinus Nijhoff.

Signed, Ratified but Not Implemented 3

Having looked at the way children's rights is understood, or not as the case may be, in the previous chapter, this now turns to examination of the progress of children's rights since the adoption of the CRC. This is the paradoxical area. Ostensibly delivering children's rights is a worldwide issue, whereby, at face value, every country would claim to protect and provide for its children and see that as a right. Since September 1990 when it entered into force, implementation has been patchy if not simply forgotten in many countries. There are too many contradictory matters to go into entirely. With virtually all countries having already signed and ratified or acceded, one or two newly emergent countries that have still to sign and eventually ratify, one would expect better. However, that is proving not to be the case and, if anything, it is showing up how 'toothless' the means of overseeing this and probably any other convention or treaty is.

Early in the life of the CRC, a committee was created by the convention. After the 1989 ratification of the CRC, Poland proposed the implementation of a supervisory mechanism that would require each state party to submit regular reports to the UN *Economic and Social Council*. That proposal was not adopted as originally proposed but discussion began on the role of a *Committee for the Rights of the Child*. The CRC includes three articles, 43–45, which described the creation, composition, function and role of the committee.

At the end of February 1991, a *Committee on the Rights of the Child*[1] made up of 18 members from different countries and legal backgrounds, all of whom are of 'high moral standing' and acknowledged to be experts in the field of human rights, came into being. Members of the Committee are nominated by their countries and then elected by state parties to the CRC. They then act in a personal capacity as children's rights, or at least human rights, experts as part of the Committee. They

[1] The original proposition was translated as *Committee for the Rights of the Child*, but when the committee was set up, *for* was replaced by *on*, hence *Committee on the Rights of the Child* as it is officially known.

B. Milne, *Rights of the Child*, Children's Well-Being: Indicators and Research 11,
DOI 10.1007/978-3-319-18784-6_3

do not represent their home country's government or any other organisation they are associated with or introduce individual cases from their own country. They are elected for a 4-year term of office and may be re-elected. All state parties to the CRC are required to submit an initial and thereafter a periodic report on the national situation of children's rights for examination by the Committee. Its mandate did not originally allow it to consider individual complaints; however, children's rights could be raised before other UN committees that have the competence to consider individual complaints. Those could then be drawn to the attention of the Committee but would only exceptionally have been taken on by them. The third Optional Protocol[2] now allows children, groups of children or representatives, who claim that rights have been violated by their state, to submit a communication, or complaint, before the Committee.

The Committee examines the reports; if there are any issues of concern, it draws attention to them or makes recommendations to the state party. It also occasionally makes general comments on the interpretation of particular obligations the CRC places on state parties. The Committee submits an annual report to the Third Committee of the UN General Assembly; there is also a yearly statement from the CRC chair, and on the basis of the report and statement, the Assembly adopts a Resolution on the Rights of the Child.

The main problem with the reports and resolutions is that they do not have enforceable measures or mechanisms to support what they say. Typically, a Committee report will make up to around 20 points and then gives the state party a bit less than half a year to respond in normally 15 or 30 pages maximum. It lays down no methods for changing or is insistent on changes being made. It is simply asking for explanations and evidence of commitment to amend critical issues. Indeed changes do come about, but not always, and it would appear that reports are probably frequently more or less ignored. Similarly, the resolutions appear in a rather technical UN language and by and large seem to have brought about some change in a few countries but never universal change.

A UN *World Summit for Children* was held at the UN in New York on September 29–30, 1990, less than a month after the CRC entered into force. The summit was the largest ever gathering of heads of states and governments assembled to commit their nations to a set of aims and objectives to improve the situation of children worldwide by 2000. It was also the first time a UN meeting had set an extensive agenda for a broad range of objectives that included education, health, nutrition and human rights.

The foremost consequence of the World Summit was the *World Declaration on the Survival, Protection and Development of Children* and also a *Plan of Action* that consisted of a comprehensive set of child-related development goals by 2000. The World Summit set in chain a decade of high-level commitment to issues relating to children worldwide. The Summit had been proposed in 1989 by the

[2]Optional Protocol on a communications procedure, adopted in 2011 and entered into force on April 14, 2014; see Appendix 4c.

prime minister of Canada, Brian Mulroney, President of Egypt, Mohammed Hosni Mubarak, President of Mali, Moussa Traore, President of Mexico, Carlos Salinas de Gortari, prime minister of Pakistan, Benazir Bhutto, and prime minister of Sweden, Ingvar Carlsson. The six heads of state or government worked together 'to bring attention and promote commitment, at the highest political level, to goals and strategies for ensuring the survival, protection and development of children as key elements in the socio-economic development of all countries and human society'. The Secretary-General Javier Perez de Cuellar approved the project and gave it the full support of UNICEF and other UN agencies. One hundred and fifty-nine governments were invited to the Summit. Heads of state from 72 different countries and representatives of 87 other countries attended. The agenda was endorsed by three organisations, the *World Health Assembly* (the decision-making body of the WHO), *Education for All* (fronted by UNESCO) and UNICEF's Executive Board. UNICEF was a key contributor. Every year following the Summit, it issued progress reports on the implementation of its goals.

The *Special Session on Children* was a meeting the General Assembly held on May 8–10, 2002. It was held to review the progress made for children during the decade beginning with the 1990 Summit. It also served as a means of renewing commitments made in 1990 and committed the international community to particular actions for the next decade. Around 70 heads of state or government attended. Children from around the world were also invited to attend. They mainly took part in a wide range of supporting events rather than in the main assembly.

The, by then, Secretary-General Kofi Annan's report on children, 'We the Children', consisted of data collected in 135 countries that were based on reviews of the situation of children nationwide. It was the first and most comprehensive study of what was happening to the world's children at that time. It proved to be a statistical representation of minimal often negligible progress made over the decade. It states: '. . . the world has fallen short of achieving most of the goals of the World Summit for Children' (Annan 2001: 5). In other words, a few of the goals set could have been claimed to be successful, whilst others showed at least some progress. On the whole it showed that the majority of them had not been at all, partly or entirely achieved. The reasons why are given as:

> We have fallen short largely because the needed investments for children were not made. With limited support, even the poorest countries can afford to underwrite basic social services. But with few exceptions, developing countries devoted only about 12 per cent to 14 per cent of their national budgets to basic social services throughout the 1990s, while donors allocated only 10 per cent to 11 per cent of their aid budgets, which were already at a record low. These amounts fell far short of the minimum needed to meet the most pressing needs of children in primary health care, nutrition, basic education, safe water and adequate sanitation. (op.cit.: 5–6)

Despite the failure to achieve goals, the UN was at least critical and accepted its own failings in the process. The real problem is that in the wake of the surge of activity during the first decade of the CRC, we have seen no subsequent comparable follow-up. Instead we have seen the creation of 'ombudsmen',[3] 'specialised' areas of concern such as *CEDC* (children in especially difficult circumstances) or *CNSPM* (children in need of special protection measures) and monitoring which for some agencies has become the 'Holy Grail' of children's rights. However, with the lack of real follow-up and allocation of the responsibility passed on to ombudsman services, departments of UN agencies and NGOs that look at specific areas such as 'CEDCs'[4] and developing methods, indicators and targets for monitoring, the focus has more or less and almost certainly unintentionally seen them protecting children's rights, but not actually protecting children.

The ombudsman and similar services (see: Reif 2004: 289–332, or Tasca 2001: 150ff) have generally contributed very positively to overseeing the progress of children's rights in their countries and have also worked very directly with children in some countries thus delivering part of their reporting procedure from them. However, the UN itself has not been as successful in going directly to the source of information. Article 45 of the CRC describes the role of UN agencies in implementing it:

> (a) The specialized agencies, the United Nations Children's Fund and other United Nations organs shall be entitled to be represented at the consideration of the implementation of such provisions of the present Convention as fall within the scope of their mandate. The Committee may invite the specialized agencies, the United Nations Children's Fund and other competent bodies as it may consider appropriate to provide expert advice on the implementation of the Convention in areas falling within the scope of their respective mandates. The Committee may invite the specialized agencies, the United Nations Children's Fund and other United Nations organs to submit reports on the implementation of the Convention in areas falling within the scope of their activities;
>
> (b) The Committee shall transmit, as it may consider appropriate, to the specialized agencies, the United Nations Children's Fund and other competent bodies, any reports from

[3]There is a Children's Ombudsman, Children's Commission, Child Advocate, Children's Commissioner or equivalent in over 40 countries at this point in time. The number is still growing. Each one is a public office given responsibility for overseeing the protection and promotion of children and young people's rights. Their mandate is either to look at society in general or in specific groups such as children within the care system. They usually have a considerable degree of independence and mostly exist as specialised ombudsman offices or as national human rights institutions. They examine and act on individual complaints and intervene in the activities of other public authorities. Some conduct or commission research. If their mandate allows, they are also active in advocacy such as promoting children's rights in policymaking and both lawmaking and enforcement as too general practice. Their creation has been promoted by the Committee on the Rights of the Child and other bodies such as the Council of Europe.

[4]When the first commonly used acronym, CEDC, emerged, it was used as a collective term to cover street children, child workers and others in comparably 'difficult circumstances'. Unfortunately it became a dehumanising substitute for the actual term and one commonly heard children referred to as a CEDC. As other acronyms appeared, children began to be known as them too. Eventually the situation had arrived in which some people talked (and occasionally wrote) in jargon rich in acronyms. Some of us who were critical of the use of acronyms were known to amuse ourselves by asking so-called 'experts' to tell us what they meant. It was not all uncommon for these people not to know what the acronym was in fully expressed words.

> States Parties that contain a request, or indicate a need, for technical advice or assistance, along with the Committee's observations and suggestions, if any, on these requests or indications;

UNICEF has assumed the role as the UN agency with special responsibility with almost minimal cooperation with other agencies or organisations such as NGOs working on the ground. They began to measure the situation of children and map out progress through data collection and analysis. They began to keep and continually update databases and encourage dissemination of what they consider to be evidence-based data for planning and promotion of the CRC. UNICEF thus assumed the position as the lead UN agency with responsibility for monitoring child-related *Millennium Development Goals* (MDGs).[5] They also began to develop indicators to aid countries to monitor progress in implementing children's rights. They created several databases that look at the lessons learned at all levels and in all places. Additionally they collaborated with *Childwatch International,*[6] and UNICEF field offices also began to take part in different stages of the research process by assisting countries to organise major consultations before drafting reports and also contributing to the Committee's review of country reports. They then work with those countries to develop implementation strategies in response to the recommendations made by the Committee.

UNICEF supports countries' collection of data through *Multiple Indicator Cluster Surveys* (MICS). MICS is a household survey programme developed after

[5]The MDGs are eight international development goals established following the UN Millennium Summit in 2000 that followed adoption of the UN Millennium Declaration. The MDGs are:

To eradicate extreme poverty and hunger
To achieve universal primary education
To promote gender equality and empowering women
To reduce child mortality rates
To improve maternal health
To combat HIV/AIDS, malaria and other diseases
To ensure environmental sustainability
To develop a global partnership for development

[6]The Childwatch International (CI) Research Network is a group of NGOs that conduct research on children and their rights, in order to engage governments and civil society in the process of monitoring, implementating of the CRC, giving priority to balancing universal rights with national and cultural concerns, promoting children's rights and improving their well-being worldwide. CI was founded in 1993 in response to an enquiry from the research community working on the CRC. CI works to change the focus of research and ensure that the perspectives of children are heard and included. The CRC is the basis of the CI's common agenda. CI links local, regional and national research to international research which is based on knowledge, practice and policy on children's issues. It thus looks at more effective and strategic approaches to child research everywhere. CI encourages multidisciplinary research, policy development and training that promote the well-being, rights, civic and social participation and development of children. Judith Ennew who would have been the co-author of this book was a preliminary board member of CI from 1993 to 1995. She was also designer and international coordinator of their Monitoring Children's Rights Project, which was then based in the Centre for Family Research, University of Cambridge.

the World Summit. Since the mid-1990s MICS have made it possible for many countries to generate statistically valid and cross-country comparable estimates of a range of indicators in areas of education, health, child protection and HIV/AIDS. Findings have been used as a basis for policy decisions and interventions as well as influencing public knowledge and opinion on the situation of children. They have put a great deal of effort into researching in the health and related fields, developing new methods for keeping track of estimates on child and maternal mortality, low birth weights, antenatal care and vitamin A deficiency. Malaria, iodine deficiency disorder, pneumonia, female circumcision (genital mutilation), HIV/AIDS, sanitation and water along with other priorities make it an ambitious and full research programme.

The data assembled is used for planning and monitoring. The key data appear in publications such as the annual *State of the World's Children* and in reports such as *Diarrhoea: Why children are still dying and what can be done*; *Pneumonia: The forgotten killer of children*; *Tracking progress on child and maternal nutrition – A survival and development priority* and *Countdown to 2015*. They also aid data dissemination through DevInfo, a database system that tracks progress towards the MDGs; monitors commitments to constant human development that generates tables, graphs and maps and shows trends.

Whilst the general principle is highly creditable in its own way, what it does not tell us is a great deal about delivery and protecting children's rights and how children are enjoying and living out their rights. In fact, it is an ambitious child protection research programme which links more comfortably with UNICEF's welfare-based origins than a bona fide human rights approach. To an extent UNICEF's role blocks progress by providing a great deal of quantitative rather than qualitative data and analysis. Changing the focus to the inclusion of qualitative data to support quantitative is exactly what Childwatch International set out to do originally but appears not to have achieved. Instead we see children's rights to health, education and other key elements of improving standards of life and well-being without children themselves being treated as bearers of rights with the ability to determine and choose by free will, their own actions, beliefs, etc.

Sometimes UN agencies and NGOs have organised gatherings such as national and international children's 'parliaments' and 'councils'. NGOs in developing countries particularly, but also a few in the North, have involved children at most levels of decision-making up to what are as a rule thought of as 'adult' activities. Thus, some of them share a role in fundraising, policymaking and project administration and supervision. Young people, the majority of whom appear to be at the end of childhood, represent children and youth at high-level international conferences on a number of key issues that affect them including the environment, human rights and child labour that attract a lot of media attention. Those children normally attend those meetings with adult escorts who give the impression they are there solely as 'observers' in many cases. The young representatives frequently prepare their own presentations and speeches, albeit they often have adult guidance. However, it is often open knowledge that the children are selected by adults rather than as their representatives by peers. At times it would seem that because the meeting is hearing a child's voice, it can be accepted as authentic. Many of these conferences are held publicly in front of an audience of adults who respond with tumultuous applause. It is essential that even the most dedicated children's rights advocates realise that because children are made visible, that is not the same as participation on an equal footing (Woollcombe 1998).

Thus far there is little evidence to suggest that the views of young people have had any real influence on any kind of policymaking. In fact, when we look at the representatives of child workers' organisations and movements from the South who wish only to be respected and their plaintiffs for their need to work to be understood and accepted, we repeatedly see the best examples of this. Their appeals are recurrently dismissed as the misguided views of misled children by adults with a single track view of the world which is for the elimination of child labour without actually listening to what is being said. Those children are like actors in a scene staged for an audience that wants to believe.

Childhood is the most thoroughly overseen part of anybody's personal existence. The contemporary child is the focal point of numerous endeavours that are claimed to protect him or her from all forms of danger, physical, sexual or moral, to make certain that child goes through a 'normal development' (Rose 1989: 124). Moreover, the protection of children is also frequently linked with a kind of trepidation with regard to how they are controlled and supervised; thus, it is assumed they need to be subject of instruction in order to grow up to be valuable citizen. Instruction is often in reality discipline, so that any deviance from the supposed norm can be punished. Discipline is a series of methods by which an individual's actions and behaviour can be controlled. It works by controlling and supervising an individual's actions and how he or she is able to use space and time within set parameters. Observation and supervision are the key instruments for the exercise of power. Therewith the notion of the 'normal behaviour' developed. It is what Foucault (1995) was describing when he argued that discipline creates 'docile bodies' that are ideal for the times we live in; thus, it is somebody who functions as they should in the environment in which he or she belongs, for instance, in the school classroom. Discipline, the force that creates docility, must come about without excessive force through vigilance and forming individuals into how they 'should' be through constant observation and supervision of their actions. It does not concur too well with autonomy which is one of the things that most disturbs those who cannot accept the ability of children to have any degree of self-determination. The belief is that this threatens the moral fibre of society because it will inevitably lead to deviance.

Child welfare involvement is thus intended to be a means of protecting children's innocence and from the pitfalls of inexperience. At the same time, it sets out to correct behaviour that does not conform to normative concepts of childhood as it is approved in local morality (Platt 1969). Child protection intercession not only provides support and protection, it also instructs the observer how to observe and supervise and thus correct children's behaviour whenever it strays from what is considered to be normative. In fact this almost always restricts children's autonomy.

An abundance of articles and books over the diverse areas of the social sciences has launched the search for what agency is. Agency refers to the capability of individuals to act independently and thus make free choices and, thus, be autonomous. In contrast, structure refers to factors such as age, gender, social class, customs and other contributory factors that influence what determines or limits an agent and his or her decisions. The relative divergence in influences from structure and agency is unsettled. It is by no means clear to what extent an agent's actions are constrained by social systems, for instance, the culture he or she belongs to. An agency-centred paradigm has appeared in childhood research that is much discussed but little analysed. In fact, the notion that children and young people have agency has become a something that some social scientists working in the field of childhood feel they must include (Vanderbeck 2008: 396; Jeffrey 2012: 245). There is a great deal of difference between agency and the right of autonomy when it is approached theoretically and the maintenance of moral standards that govern children's conduct. Durham asked:

> ... what kind of agency do youth have? And what does it mean for us as anthropologists to go out and seek to identify youth agency in various places around the world? (Durham 2008: 151)

What this asks is whether the form of agency children and youth have is the same as adult agency. Since the notion of agency first appeared in childhood studies (e.g., James and Prout 1990), both practitioners and theoreticians have undertaken all manner of approaches to find evidence of agency and therewith reach a definition. These studies have often targeted street and working children (e.g., see Rizzini 1996; Hecht 1998; Panter-Brick 2002). The propensity of social workers and programmes working with these children has been to pour scorn on the idea of children's autonomy, agency and capacity of resistance by viewing them as victims (Aptekar 1991; Beazley 2003). In contrast, it has been shown these characteristics of such children which were classified as forms of deviance (Kovats-Bernat 2006) should be dealt with by programmes that teach authority, respect and rules, often using disciplinary methods such as closed institution those children are 'rescued' into. Thereby, child-focussed intercession into their otherwise autonomous lives is assessed and supervised to conformity with expected 'conventional' children's behaviour and thus objective consistent with standards and moral notions of childhood and youth defined by adults. Those adults far too often work with organisations that import those principles from the North and attempt to implant them in the South where cultural values are usually entirely different.

It is this question about children's agency that leads to the next area of concern with this convention that appears to have been signed and ratified but not implemented. There have, of course, been all manner of situations in which children have been involved in a way that allowed them to describe their lives through participation in children's movements and projects, interviews, focus group discussions, written work and filmed events. For all of that we still know very little about most children, particularly those who are not in the position to be part of the examples just mentioned. We see some of them in the media when they are so often seen used as the victims of natural disasters, war and other extreme events that totally wipe out family, friends, community and way of life as it was, leaving them as pathetic objects of pity. As a rule there is no real insight into their feelings, what individuals are suffering, their present state of mind and what they think should happen for and with them. They are simply part of a single situation that can be photographed, written about and quantified to satisfy those looking for information. One of the problems that come with that is that such children are seen as a virtually homogeneous group. For instance, children affected by war in Syria and seen as being much like children in Iraq at the time of the war or more recently Afghanistan. Hungry children looking skeletal but with a swollen, bulbous belly and large pleading eyes attract exactly the same compassion wherever they are although the reasons they are starving may be very different. The image belies the reality of the many differences in where, why, how and what the people affected are ethnically, culturally and linguistically and many other unasked questions. Thus, a question of cultural relativity arises.

The image of the starving child is almost iconic. It encourages people to make donations to organisations making appeals that use the image without exactly saying what that money will be used for. The information provided is minimal; it will tell of famine, war or any other reason for the fundraising drive. It may give numbers of starving children, perhaps of all ages or not at all. It does not usually give any details about the people. We know of them but not about them. That there are almost certainly cultural aspects of the situation in which a child or group of children was photographed is not raised. Indeed, we cannot be sure that what we see is not a library picture from somewhere else entirely that a person from where the emergency is would be taken aback by.

It is this point magnified into a world in which every state in which people are found in great affluence and comfort to the poorest and most precarious lives needs to be looked at each in its own context. We need to do so culturally relative to the lives of those we bracket within one mental image. Cultural relativity has two meanings, the first is moral and political and the second methodological. Morally and politically, it means that we must respect other cultures and treat them as one should one's own. That is not as easy as it may seem. Our views tend to originate within one of two points of view. The first is an 'own culture' or almost nationalistic position in which cultural relativity might appear to pose a threat, that is to say, that may penetrate one's own culture, identity and nation. The second is from a universalist point of view whereby that version of cultural relativity makes us reject all notions of intervention that might cause change and avert us from being critical to the point that we tolerate the intolerable in some kind of faux gesture to prove how much we respect the 'other'. Indeed this is often done to the point that we sometimes tolerate the most shameful violations of human rights thus ignoring such instruments as the UDHR or CRC because we 'accept' that is what people do.

Thus, the ethics of how we view cultural variance create an ethical dilemma in which we are led by our own moral and aesthetic judgements which need to be scrutinised, the latter being since what we see we believe we should not criticise. This entails sometimes capricious degrees of 'empathy' with unfamiliar norms and habits. In fact, it would be different if we were able to contain our own values and be in command of our spontaneous reaction to 'alien' phenomena. Without a great deal of informed understanding, it is more or less impossible to either comprehend what we see or establish mutual trust. Both are preconditions for entering into the dialogue through which change through any kind of intervention may be attempted and eventually achieved.

Douglas and Sebba (1998) compiled a collection of essays written by legal scholars in Ireland, Israel, Palestine and the UK that explore the degree to which recognition of the concept of children's rights is affected by deference to cultural, ethnic and religious traditions. The book sets out to examine two points. Firstly it sets out to elucidate the 'interface' between norms that are internationally established which describe conduct towards children, examining national and cultural resolve of people to preserve their traditional approaches. Its second aim is to consider conflicts that occur within societies when different cultural and religious groups attempt to establish whether liberal and predominantly secular or conservative and chiefly religious norms prevail in attitudes towards bringing up children. It reaches conclusions that are more heavily weighted towards the conservative, religion-orientated tendency to preserve traditions rather than be drawn into the modern 'liberal' world which would entirely reshape their societies. Brittany Kühn examined this question in sub-Saharan Africa and sums it up very fittingly, thus:

> ...children's rites of passage encounter overwhelming international dissent. Although there is strong international condemnation of practices that are harmful to children, many rites continue to hold significant meaning among indigenous populations. These cultural customs, such as ritual circumcision, symbolic cuts to the body, tests of endurance, and extended periods of isolation, are viewed as vital steps in the transition into adulthood in many indigenous communities. (Kühn 2009: 60)

In short, rather than accepting the images presented to us and statements that inform us of the need to change, we need to acknowledge that there are significant differences in attitudes that inhibit just how far new, imposed standards can be effective. The human rights world is, in that sense, no different without us going beyond reason and accepting deliberate and avertable breeches of those rights. Children's rights are no different. That is where the CRC is flawed and there is great need to look at its relevance globally.

The solutions are not simple. Each situation requires detailed examination in context. That would take an extremely long time to achieve, but at this point in time with the CRC a quarter of a century old, it has not yet made any noticeable progress. There also probably needs to be a step-by-step entry into this matter. A starting point may be regional instruments. Thus, the question arises whether or what progress has been made with them, if any. The *African Charter on the Rights and Welfare of the Child* (ACRWC) followed close behind the CRC.

The ACRWC came about because the member states of the African Union (AU) believed that the CRC missed important sociocultural and economic realities particular to Africa (Gose 2002 and Himonga 2008: 73–90). The Charter emphasises the need to include the vast variety of African cultural values and experiences when considering the rights of the child. To begin with it has a clearer definition of a child as a person aged less than 18 years. It expressly states that it has a status higher than any custom, tradition and cultural or religious practice that does not fit with rights, duties and obligations in the Charter (Olowu 2008: 13–32). For instance, the CRC challenges traditional African views which are often in conflict with children's rights issues such as child marriage, parental rights and obligations towards their children and the status of children born outside of marriage. Nonetheless, it prohibits marriage or betrothal of children, grants girls the right to return to school after childbirth, includes particular reference to the care of the child by extended families and encourages state parties to provide support for parents 'in times of need'. Furthermore, it seeks to promote positive action for the education of girls, protect handicapped children, internally displaced and refugee children and engage in specific African issues that affect children such as confronting and achieving the abolition of *apartheid* and similar systems. Whilst *apartheid* has ended, this provision in the ACRWC still applies where children live under regimes that practise ethnic, religious or other forms of discrimination or violence against children (Kassan 2008: 165–82). What it shares with the CRC are the best interests of the child, the importance of the life, survival and development of the child, non-discrimination and children's participation.

There has naturally been some critique of the ACRWC in that unlike the CRC that categorically assigns rights to children of minorities, there is no comparable provision in the Charter, although many countries on their continent have considerable populations of minority and indigenous groups. There is also confusion with regard to Article 31 that covers children's responsibilities. They are required to respect parents, superiors and elders at all times. That could come into conflict with a child's right to participate in decisions that affect him or her, and also Article 20 could be interpreted as allowing physical punishment by parents because it is unclear what 'domestic discipline' means. Furthermore, it makes provision for special protection measures for the disabled yet omits to explicitly include disability as a prohibited ground for discrimination (Combrinck 2008: 299–322). Looking at child and youth criminality, it makes no provision for alternative measures such as community-based rehabilitation and does not protect children from life imprisonment without the possibility of early, conditional or even eventual straightforward release, and there is no article describing rights such as to be able to remain silent, be protected from retroactive laws and challenge being kept in custody or giving compensation for miscarriages of justice.

Above and beyond its good and bad qualities, there are other issues hindering the progress of the ACRWC. Although it was adopted and opened for signature and ratification in 1990, there was only the required number of ratifications for it to be put into force at the end of 1999. Since progress has continued to be slow, advancement of the Charter has been slow. As yet not all of the 54 members of the AU have ratified. There are also reservations by some that do not sit comfortably with other state parties. There are also the states that have not ratified who have been suspected or proven to be gross violators of human rights. They include the

Democratic Republic of the Congo (DRC), Sahrawi Arab Democratic Republic[7] and Somalia. The violations range from early child marriage, harmful cultural practices such as female genital mutilation and male child preference, sexual exploitation, trafficking and enslavement, drug abuse as users or 'mules', child labour and recruitment of child soldiers. Thus, within Africa as a single continent, there is a vast range of differences of cultural, legal and political practices and values that justify what is allowed or shunned as bad practice, within which there is a whole array of those ranging from traditional to modern values. Thus, no single context describes or can define children as bearers of rights.

At present Africa is the only continent with a region-specific children's rights instrument and at present there appear to be no others forthcoming or even proposed. Thus, most continents, despite the enormity of difference between the many cultures, their traditions, beliefs and legal systems, have only the CRC. Since Africa therefore has two unlike all other regions and the progress towards real implementation has been slow at best, the example it sets the world does not encourage new regional instruments.

This brings us back to our starting point, the title of this chapter 'Signed and Ratified but Not Implemented', the final words at least, 'not implemented'. Thus far the UN, CRC itself, the Committee, NGOs and individuals working in the sector appear to have looked at it as an instrument that protects children's rights, but does not actually protect children. Monitoring has been consistent, and indicators developed for 'measuring' the delivery of rights and the Committee alone have often proved the value of having a panel of independent experts instead of government-appointed functionaries who would have been bound far more by diplomatic niceties. UN agencies, NGOs and all manner of individuals have engaged themselves in the field. The third Optional Protocol now allows children or their representatives to file individual complaints for violation of the rights of children. It may change things significantly but is still not enough to enforce implementation of the CRC as a whole.

When a country ratifies and thus becomes a state party to the CRC, they become bound to it by international law. National governments are committing themselves to protecting and guaranteeing children's rights within their borders and any territories they govern and have thus agreed to hold themselves accountable for their country's commitment before the international community. State parties to the CRC are furthermore obliged to develop and undertake all actions and policies in the best interests of the child. Thus, Article 4 states:

> States Parties shall undertake all appropriate legislative, administrative, and other measures for the implementation of the rights recognized in the present Convention. With regard to economic, social and cultural rights, States Parties shall undertake such measures to the maximum extent of their available resources and, where needed, within the framework of international co-operation.

[7] At present only around 45 UN member states recognise SADR. They have acceded to the ACRWC but are not able to sign or ratify the CRC since they are not a UN member state.

Articles 43 to 54 describe those obligations and how governments and international organisations have the responsibility for ensuring children's rights are delivered and protected. However, Article 41 says that if the laws of a country provide better protection of children's rights than the articles in the CRC, those laws should apply. With regard to engaging the entire in principle, Article 42 places responsibility on governments to make the CRC known to adults and children. The principle is that adults should help children learn about their rights too although it might have been a little more insightful and encouraged a view that children could also help adults to learn about and understand their rights.

Viewed through the lens of the pertinent articles and placed in an ideal world, the existence of the CRC for a full quarter of a century, the actual need for monitoring and scrutiny by the Committee could theoretically be by now unnecessary. That is far from the case. Upholding the commitments made by state parties is reflected in a few examples of the treatment of children that cannot be hidden from governments but no concerted effort to end them has been made. The first is female genital mutilation and cutting (FGM) which is a traditional practice that often has severe health consequences for girls and women. It is reported in all parts of the world but is prevalent in 28 countries in West and Central Africa and the Middle East (UNPF, 2008). It is estimated that approximately 100–140 million women have already undergone FGM worldwide, usually before their fifth birthday but also up until early teens (UNICEF, 2005). Estimates of around three million girls and women are cut annually. In sub-Saharan Africa it was usually performed by traditional practitioners but a more recent 'medicalisation' of FGM, whereby girls are circumcised by trained personnel, is increasing in some countries (Johansen et al. 2013). In Guinea where as many as 96 % of women are cut, younger generations are almost three times more likely to be cut by trained people of older generations. Nearly all countries throughout the entire world where this is practised have ratified the CRC should by now have ended it.

The second is the problem of 'child soldiers'. The internationally agreed definition of a child soldier, a child associated with a governmental or nongovernmental armed force or armed group, refers to any person below 18 years of age who is, or who has been, recruited or used by an armed force or armed group in any capacity. That includes but is not limited to boys and girls used as combatants but also as cooks, messengers, porters, spies or as 'sex slaves'.[8] It therefore does not only refer to children who are taking or have taken part in actual conflict (see: *Paris Principles and Guidelines on Children Associated with Armed Forces or Armed Groups*, 2007.[9]).

---

[8]The expression 'sex slaves' is rather blunt. However, given the nature of recruitment for sexual purposes and irrespective of whether they are boys or girls, it is enforced sexual exploitation or prostitution and therefore is probably as appropriate as any other choice of description.

[9]The version used here was downloaded from UNICEF: http://www.unicef.org/emerg/files/ParisPrinciples310107English.pdf

Exact figures and other details are not known; thus, estimates and what is known about them are taken from any available source such as children who have escaped, been liberated or rescued, families of children recruited or taken for military use, former combatants, journalists and others who have seen or been with them. The estimates used here are based on those used by four organisations[10]; thus, there is sometimes a measurable degree of variance.

There are estimates of between 250,000 and 300,000 child soldiers in the world at present.[11] Most of the ones under 15 years of age are found in nongovernmental military organisations. However, many child soldiers under 18 have been recruited into governmental armed forces. For instance, in the UK the minimum recruitment age is 16 although young soldiers are not allowed to take part in operational duties if they are below 18 years old. At present, over 50 countries recruit children under age 18 into their armed forces. Since the year 2000, the involvement of child soldiers has been reported in most armed conflicts and in almost all regions in the world. Although no exact figures can be quoted, and with numbers constantly changing, hundreds of thousands of children under age 18 continue to serve in government forces or armed opposition (rebel) groups. Some of the children involved directly in armed conflicts are under 10, with the youngest said to be about 7 years old. Additionally, estimates show that around 40 % are girls. Many of them are used as 'sex slaves' by male combatants. It has also been alleged that when some children are recruited, they are forced to injure or kill a family member in order to break ties with their communities, thus making their return home impossible or at the least difficult. The UN General Assembly adopted the first optional protocol, the *Optional Protocol on the Involvement of Children in Armed Conflict to the Convention on the Rights of the Child* (see: Appendix 5a), in 2000. It entered into force early in 2002. It requires state parties assurance that although armed forces may accept volunteers below 18, they may not be conscripted and that 'States Parties shall take all feasible measures to ensure that members of their armed forces who have not attained the age of 18 years do not take a direct part in hostilities'. At the time of writing just over 150 countries have ratified the protocol and around 20 further ratifications are pending. Despite that, children still serve in armed forces in a considerable number of state parties.

The third example is trafficking. Again there was a second optional protocol to the CRC, at precisely the same time as the 'child soldiers' one: the *Optional Protocol to the Convention on the Rights of the Child on the Sale of Children, Child Prostitution and Child Pornography* (see: Appendix 5b). It too entered into force early in 2002, and at present there are 166 state parties with others pending. Despite

[10]Warchild: http://www.warchild.org.uk/issues/child-soldiers, Child Soldiers International: http://www.child-soldiers.org/, Human Rights Watch: http://www.hrw.org/news/2008/12/03/facts-about-child-soldiers and UNICEF: http://www.unicef.org/emerg/files/childsoldiers.pdf

[11]There are definitional problems regarding who and what a child soldier actually is since not all members of any kind of army are combatants. Activists in this area have generally included all children who are immediately involved but conventional definitions do not include all of those.

that, child trafficking is a global phenomenon. UNICEF's website still uses the ILO's 2002 estimate of 1.2 million children trafficked each year as its benchmark, whereas in 2012 the *United Nations Office on Drugs and Crime* (UNODC) reported that the percentage of child victims had risen over a 3-year span from 20 to 27 %. From every three child victims, it was calculated that two are girls and one is a boy. Of all people trafficked 17 % were girls and 10 % boys. If internal trafficking victims are included in estimates, the number is in the range of between two and four million, of whom 50 % are estimated to be children. So there are between one and two million and at present said to be rising. There was said to be approximately 20.9 million victims of trafficking worldwide by 2012. Using the combined girls and boys of 27 % estimate of all victims, that would make around 5.65 million, or on the basis of 50 % per annum being a constant, it would be 10.45 million. According to the *Protocol to Prevent, Suppress and Punish Trafficking in Persons, Especially Women and Children (2000)* to the *United Nations Convention Against Transnational Organised Crime* (ICAT 2010), child trafficking is 'recruitment, transportation, transfer, harbouring or receipt of children for the purpose of exploitation. It is a violation of their rights, their well-being and denies them the opportunity to reach their full potential'.

Whilst Article 35 CRC covers the abduction, sale and trafficking of children, specifically a rather lengthy list of other articles similarly covers different aspects of the entire trafficking issue. It is a major matter in children's rights terms since it deprives them of many of their ascribed rights and protections. Bearing in mind that almost all nations are state parties to the CRC, in theory trafficking should not happen as too neither of the two preceding examples.

The three examples are just that—examples. There are others that could be used in the context of implementation. They suffice to show the impotence of the UN to do anything about it, let alone any other international and, in many cases, national bodies to do so. The simple reason why is that there is no possible way of enforcing the commitments made in any form of convention, its protocols or any other form of treaty.

The newer optional protocol, the *Optional Protocol to the Convention on the Rights of the Child on a Communications Procedure* (see Appendix 5c), addresses all of those issues. As with the two other protocols, it is open to state parties to the CRC, was adopted by the UN General Assembly at the end of 2011 and entered into force in April 2014 after the tenth ratification. The protocol allows either individuals or groups of children or their representatives to submit complaints for violation of their rights. This protocol enables the Committee to examine all such complaints and decide whether or not the CRC has been violated in each case. They may then request that the state against which the complaint has been made enforce 'interim measures' (Article 6) to prevent any further harm to the complainant. According to Article 9, priority is given to whoever filed the complaint and the government reaching a 'friendly settlement' or resolution everyone is happy with. If a friendly settlement is reached, the complaint procedure will be closed. There is, as all other aspects of the CRC and its optional protocols, no way of enforcing the outcome of the complaint other than the agreement of a state party to resolve the matter.

Even attempts to take actions to any international human rights court seem to suffer the same. The *International Court of Justice and Human Rights* (ICJ) in The Hague, the *International Criminal Court* (ICC) in Geneva, the *International Court of Arbitration* (ICA) in Paris and regional courts such as the *European Court of Human Rights* (ECHR) in Strasbourg all have different roles. They are all able to examine cases between or within states. In most of the courts dealing with international law, thus worldwide, individuals have no right of direct access, whereas the ECHR mainly receives individual complaints. In all cases their verdicts can only seek to ask nations complained against to redress violations without any guarantee of enforce, although most states usually do try to resolve them. Similarly, whatever comments the Committee may make after examining country reports and calling representatives of state parties to answer for their countries' failings tend to achieve little or even nothing. The Secretary-General may make some scathing comments in his or her annual speech to the General Assembly but action all too frequently follows those words.

The world is, unfortunately, not (yet) able to police itself and enforce even basic national laws, let alone as treaty signatories and state parties in order to be, at least nominally, part of the acceptable and respected international community. Without any form of sanctions or means of enforcing laws, they simply cannot be implemented. Until there is unanimity in the world and cross-border cooperation becomes the norm, it will never happen. In the present world that common ground does not exist. To truly implement children's rights using the CRC or any other approach is and shall for the foreseeable future be and remain an ideal.

References

Annan, K. A. (Secretary-General of the UN). (2001). *We the children*. New York: UNICEF.

Aptekar, L. (1991). Are Colombian street children neglected? The contributions of ethnographic and ethnohistorical approaches to the study of children. *Anthropology and Education Quarterly, 22*(4), 326–349.

Beazley, H. (2003). The construction and protection of individual and collective identities by street children and youth in Indonesia. *Children, youth, and environments, 13*(1), 105–33.

Combrinck, H. (2008). The hidden ones: Children with disabilities in Africa and the right to education. In J. Sloth-Nielsen (Ed.), *Children's rights in Africa: A legal perspective* (pp 299–322). Farnham: Ashgate.

Douglas, G., & Sebba, L. (1998). *Children's rights and traditional values*. Farnham: Ashgate.

Durham, D. (2008). Apathy and agency. The romance of agency and youth in Botswana. In J. Cole & D. Durham (Eds.), *Figuring the future. Globalization and the temporalities of children and youth* (pp. 151–78). Santa Fé: School for Advanced Research Press.

Foucault, M. (1995). *Discipline and punish: The birth of the prison*. New York: Vintage Books.

Gose, M. (2002). *The African charter on the rights and welfare of the child – An assessment of the legal value of its substantive provisions by means of a direct comparison to the convention on the rights of the child*. Belleville: Community Law Center.

Hecht, T. (1998). *At home in the street: Street children of Northeast Brazil*. Cambridge: Cambridge University Press.

Himonga, Chuma. (2008). African customary law and children's rights: Intersections and domains in a new era. In J. Sloth-Nielsen (Eds.), *Children's rights in Africa: A legal perspective* (pp. 73–90). Farnham: Ashgate.
ICAT. (2010). *An analytical review 10 years on from the adoption of the UN trafficking in persons protocol*. Vienna: Inter-Agency Coordination Group Against Trafficking in Persons.
James, A., & Prout, A. (Eds.). (1990). *Constructing and reconstructing childhood: Contemporary issues in the sociological study of childhood*. London: Falmer Press.
Jeffrey, C. (2012). Geographies of children and youth II: Global youth agency. *Progress in Human Geography, 36*(2), 245–53.
Johansen, R. E. B., Diop, N. J., Laverack, G., & Leye, E. (2013). What works and what does not: A discussion of popular approaches for the abandonment of female genital mutilation. *Obstetrics and Gynecology International*, Volume 2013, Article ID 348248, https://biblio.ugent.be/record/3203741
Kassan, D. (2008). The protection of children from all forms of violence – African experiences. In Julia Sloth-Nilesen (Ed.), *Children's rights in Africa: A legal perspective* (pp. 165–182). Farnham: Ashgate.
Kovats-Bernat, C. J. (2006). *Sleeping rough in port-Au-prince: An ethnography of street children and violence in Haiti*. Gainesville: University Press of Florida.
Kühn, B. (2009). Universal human rights vs. traditional rights. *Topical Review Digest*: *Human Rights in Sub-Saharan Africa*: 59–73.
Olowu, 'Dejo. (2008). The regional system of protection of human rights in Africa. In Julia Sloth-Nielsen (Ed.), *Children's rights in Africa: A legal perspective* (pp. 13–32). Farnham: Ashgate.
Panter-Brick, C. (2002). Street children, human rights, and public health: A critique and future direction. *Annual Review of Anthropology*, *31*(1), 147–171.
Platt, A. M. (1969). *The child savers: The invention of delinquency*. Chicago: University of Chicago Press.
Reif, L. C. (2004). *The Ombudsman, good governance, and the international human rights system*. Leiden/Boston: Martinus Nijhoff Publishers.
Rizzini, I. (1996). Street children: An excluded generation in Latin America. *Childhood, 3*(2), 215–233.
Rose, N. (1989). *Governing the soul: The shaping of the private self*. London: Routledge.
Tasca, E. P. (2001). Human rights and the child: From the New York convention to the institution of the Ombudsman. In K. Hossain, L. F. M. Besselink, H. S. G. Selassie & E. V. Edmond (Eds.), *Human rights commissions and Ombudsman offices: National experiences throughout the world* (pp. 147–155). The Hague: Kluwer Law International.
Vanderbeck, R. (2008). Reaching critical mass? Theory, politics, and the culture of debate in children's geographies. *Area*, *40*(3), 393–400.
Woollcombe, D. (1998). Children's conferences and councils. In V. Johnson, E. Ivan-Smith, G. Gordon, P. Pridmore & P. Scott (Eds.), *Stepping forward – Children and young people's participation in the development process* (pp. 236–240). London: Intermediate Technology Publications.

'It's a Lie. They Didn't Ask Us' 4

There are some flaws in the principles of children's rights that are mainly ignored because of the truth they may expose. That is the role of children in the drafting of the CRC, their views about and ways of approaching participation, being protected without asking them whether they need to be or not and having a real say in the reporting to the Committee. The title of this chapter is in fact a quotation of the response made by a child taking part in a discussion about the report to the Committee by his country at which Judith Ennew was present. He was a working child, and he had read the comments on child labour and seen the drive towards eliminating it, despite that fact that he knew many children like himself who were proud of what they did. Of course they would have liked to go to school instead since they knew that education offered the possibility of a better future. What was more important for him was that he contributed to the day-by-day struggle for survival with the rest of his family. He was a member of a working children's organisation and grateful for their existence. Whilst the organisation offered solidarity with fellow working children, he felt strongly that adults, particularly those reporting on the situation in their country, had not consulted children like him. From that position, irrespective of whether his words were right or wrong, he considered the pertinent part of the national report regarding working children a lie.

The point the boy was making about his own but ultimately all children's exclusion from the creation of children's rights generally, the CRC specifically, the reporting process likewise and outlawing children's work very personally. He saw all of this as the 'mischief' of adults who believed they knew all about children that was made by strange people in countries he had never in heard of. Judith Ennew drew similar conclusions:

> As if to illustrate the axiom that history is always written by the 'winners', the heroes and heroines of the history of children's rights are adults. Indeed, this history narrates how and why the CRC was written, rather than the development of children's rights. It is also essentially grounded in the histories written by the dominant nations of the North.
>
> Early European notions of what would now be recognised as children's rights emphasised both children's need for special protection and their place in society within families

B. Milne, *Rights of the Child*, Children's Well-Being: Indicators and Research 11,
DOI 10.1007/978-3-319-18784-6_4

> and schools, but not in the workplace. Although these ideas were current throughout the nineteenth century (in child labour reform for example) the first identification of children as subjects of rights, rather than objects of concern, is usually associated with the work of Eglantyne Jebb. (Ennew 2000: 44)

Eglantyne Jebb's role in developing the concept 'children's rights' is looked at in Chap. 6, but the real matter to be considered here is that of the role of children themselves in delivering, protecting and choosing whether they accept all, some or none of children's rights as we adults accept them at this point in time. Children were not included in the 10-year-long drafting process. It came largely from the nations of the North. The outcome was allegations of having been cultural bias, as well as drawing the notion of rights specifically for children into long-standing debates about whether human rights can ever be applied universally. Those arguments inevitably included the notion that universal delivery of these rights would be driven by globalisation. Jo Boyden (1990) drew attention to the fact that globalisation is not simply an economic concept. It also refers to the cultural imperialism that is the foundation of those economic structures. Thus, the images of childhood preferred in the North have been exported to the South. What nobody has spoken out about is that in all cultural, economic and globalisation discussions, children have been continually excluded. It is as if their world, the one they will grow up in, needs to be shaped for them as preceding generations see fit and not as children might choose. In that sense one might accuse children's rights of being biased against children and favouring the adults who determine what is good for them. Indeed, with that in mind Eugeen Verhellen (1997) considered the thought-provoking possibility that it often seemed as if there is more concern about a need to protect children's rights than protect children themselves.

When the 1924 *Declaration* was being drafted by Eglantyne Jebb in 1923, it was based on the notion of child welfare rather than children's rights. Indeed, at that point in time, human rights in general were still more commonly associated with the American and French revolutions, which in turn launched a period of democratic change throughout the northern hemisphere during the nineteenth century. It heralded the struggle for, and in turn, eventual arrival of universal suffrage. That was an entirely adult matter that still meets strong resistance whenever it is proposed that it goes a step forward to the inclusion of children. As it was, the question of children's rights was no kind of concern for revolutionaries and was certainly not included in the French *Declaration of the Rights of Man and of the Citizen* (*Déclaration des droits de l'homme et du citoyen*) in 1789. Children were merely considered to be a minor category of person who had absolutely no need of human rights. Those were endowed on their parents, at least fathers since at that time only men had citizens' rights at all, or other adults with responsibility for them. Children were simply seen as the property of their parents with little real value. However, at that time it was assumed that children required adult protection in order to safeguard the exercise of their rights. The original perception that children should be beneficiaries of welfare continued to be upheld through the redrafting of the *Declaration* by the League of Nations, then into the 1959 UN and, in turn, the CRC. Children continue to be viewed as *objects* of international human rights law and not as *subjects* of rights and it is always their welfare that is the first consideration. Childhood is a fixed concept that is defined by biological and physiological characteristics rather than the culture or society a child belongs to and that is unambiguously expressed in international children's rights laws. Human rights activists have simply taken on board the models of childhood that are fundamental 'facts' carried over in the history and culture of the northern hemisphere and all countries that belong culturally to its sphere of influence.

However, the changes of attitude in the social sciences have drawn people working in the field of childhood studies to conclude that children have agency (for instance, see Berthelsen and Brownlee 2005; Lister 2007 and Redmond 2009) and they are human beings rather than 'human becomings' which the older notions at best held them to be, if they had either status or value at all. The child is now seen as a social actor in his or her own right, somebody who is actively constructing his or her own childhood. He or she has opinions, experiences and a set of values attached to being a child. Thus, the 'becoming' child is considered to be an adult in the making who is as yet deficient in the common skills and characteristics of the adult he or she will eventually be (for instance, see Brannen and O'Brien 1995; James and James 2004; James and Prout 1990; James et al. 1998; Jenks 1982, 1996; Qvortrup 1991, 1994; Uprichard 2008). Thus, we have the recent perception of a child as a full human being rather than him or her being a 'human becoming' that brings with it conflicting assumptions about what it means to be a child. Who and what is the child then, given that he or she has yet to develop the traits that will make him or her and adult? These views are simply theory that are very rarely taken to children in order to gather from them their perceptions of their humanity rather than that seen by adult 'experts'.

The exclusion of children from the compilation of established versions of recent and contemporary history that partly formed the basis of an argument for children to have rights is more often than not based on what adults have done or what it is believed they should have done for children. In general they give little information about actions children have carried out for others or have taken in attempts to assert self-determination. Since the compilation of history is in the hands of adults, this comes as no surprise. Where and when children arise it is often to portray them as exceptional heroes; thus, military actions and wars crop up frequently. Today children's roles in political actions such as active roles in wars or industrial actions alone or with adults whereby they are there of their own choice and have contributed to bringing about change tend to be frowned upon in not meeting with outright disapproval or even punishment.

Examples of children's 'exploits' beginning with premodern events can therefore easily begin with the Children's Crusade. It is the appellation attached to a catastrophic crusade by young European Christians to expel Muslims from the Holy Land. It was said to have occurred in 1212 but is probably more than a single event, if either really happened as some accounts would have them. Raedts (1977: 279) said of it that: '. . . the historian is forced to resort to *ex post facto* narratives which at times seem imaginative if not completely fanciful'. The popular versions tell of how Nicholas, a young shepherd from the Rhineland, set out to lead a German group across the Alps into Italy during the spring of 1212. He promised the sea would part before them, allowing his followers to cross the Mediterranean into the Holy Land. Two groups formed and took different routes through Switzerland. Two out of three of the 'crusaders' are said to have died. Many others returned to their homes rather than continue their journey. Some of them are supposed to have reached Ancona and Brindisi in Italy although none ever reached the Holy Land. Nicholas appears to have led a second attempt which failed to even cross the Alps.

The second movement was led by a 12-year-old French shepherd, Etienne de Cloyes. In the summer of 1212, Etienne led his followers from Vendôme to Marseilles. They lived on food they begged for along the way. The overwhelming majority appear to have been discouraged by the hardship of their journey and thus went home to their families. Of the people who reached the coast, purportedly free passage was offered with boats to all children who were still wanting to go on, but they were said to have been either taken to Tunisia to be sold into slavery or had perished when shipwrecked off the small San Pietro to the southwest of Sardinia during a storm. Nobody knows when it actually happened or if indeed all of the crusaders were actually children (see Dickinson 1992: 83–105, 2008; Gray 1870; Raedts 1977: 279–333; Scheck 1988: 176–182).

Jeanne d'Arc lived from circa 1412 until her execution aged approximately 19 in 1431. Little is known about her prior to the siege of Orléans in 1429. She would have been 18 years old and thus already an adult in our terms, but then accounting for her rise to become the symbolic leader of the French army, she must have done so during the latter part of her childhood (Brooks 1999). She is one of the most highly considered heroes in France but is rarely if at all ever seen as a child who led an army.

In more recent times, the UK has awarded young combatants the Victoria Cross, the highest military award, for gallantry in action. John Travers 'Jack' Cornwell was awarded the VC for gallantry at the Battle of Jutland during the First World War. During the battle in 1916, he was serving on the Chester which came under intense fire from four German ships. The gun mounting where Cornwell was serving was hit at least four times. All of the gun's crew except Cornwell were killed. Although he was seriously wounded, he remained at his post until Chester retired from the action. When the ship's medical crew arrived on deck, they found Cornwell the sole survivor at his gun. Although he reached shore and was taken to hospital, he succumbed to his wounds (Anonymous 1918).

Thomas Flinn was a 15-year-old drummer serving in the British Army during the Indian Mutiny in 1857. He was awarded the VC when he engaged in hand-to-hand combat with two rebel soldiers and was wounded. Andrew Fitzgibbon was the youngest combatant to receive the VC. He was just over 15 years old, serving as a hospital apprentice with the Indian Army during the Third China War in 1860. Under heavy fire, he went attending a dhoolie bearer, and having been ordered to bind his wound then whilst the British and Indian troops were advancing under enemy fire, he crossed open ground to attend to another wounded soldier. He was seriously wounded. Each of the three boys is recognised as a hero. Jack Cornwell has been particularly often picked out as the model of military heroism (Brazier 2010).

We do not know how any of these young people saw themselves. Were they just children out of place or were they individuals serving what they thought of as more noble causes for country or beliefs? Such notions of the possibility of children independently asserting their views and rights through actions are not only normally belittled by adults but also aggressively restrained or forbidden. This has most often been seen in countries of the South where the concepts adults and children are far more indistinct than in the North. Children were in the vanguard of the fight against *apartheid* in South Africa until it ended. They were very present in the *intifada* in Palestine. In both they died and were wounded, maimed and disabled, and some were imprisoned along with adults. By taking part in the two examples here and others, they were often also at the 'pit face' of activating political protest and action. However, once peace processes began in the wake of such conflicts, we usually see a revival of the predisposition the international community has to fail to appreciate their involvement. UN agencies, NGOs, antiwar activists and all other people concerned with war consider young people who had chosen to be combatants anything other than heroes. Normally the preferred attitude is to view them as victims, traumatised rather than being allowed to be proud of what they have done, thus concluding that their future role in the society they helped to change or establish can only be detrimental.

The pathology of those who have taken part in war means they must be damaged and therefore pitied rather than praised. They are allowed to help effect change, to contribute to history, but will then be excluded from the democratic processes they have helped shape by not having political franchise or even being consulted about future policy for their peers in new-found peace. They can be very insightful into ways adults choose to use them, and where a Jack Cornwell can become a useful piece of adult propaganda, another child who began his or her role in a conflict by being branded a terrorist, then share gaining victory and positive change, will see their participation negated. They become forgotten heroes and should they then become resentful and angry adults will put that down to the effect of war on them. On the contrary, they will have seen themselves as contributors to a democratic process for which they could potentially have given their lives and probably saw others go down but who adults show no gratitude to when they reassume control over them.

They can also be effective political activists. Sometimes that is deliberate, other times it was never their intention. Children went on strike in 1889 in New York. They were newsboys, the main sellers of newspapers to the public from the mid-nineteenth to the early twentieth century in the USA (Nasaw 1985). They reduced Joseph Pulitzer's *New York World* circulation from 360,000 to 125,000 and caused similar drops in sales of William Randolph Hearst's newspapers. They were striking because they were underpaid. Their strike was successful. The amount of money newsboys received for their work was subsequently increased. They then formed a union for children selling newspapers. In England in 1889 and 1911 children went on strike for better education and less discipline (Baker 2010). Many of the children involved in those strikes came from areas already affected by industrial unrest and some were from families heavily involved in the trade union movement, particularly in the north of England (Marson 1973).

In 1902 in the USA, children went on strike together with adults to draw attention to child work in mining. The *Great Coal Strike* had considerable impact on the society of the USA for two main reasons. Firstly, the workers wanted a pay rise in order to pay debts and get their children out of the mines. Secondly, they wanted a shorter work day in order to be able to rest before the next day's work and spend time with their families. The strike had limited success, although hours were shortened, pay improved and children were eventually able to stop working in the mines (McKechnie and Hobbs 1998).

In 1903 Mary Harris 'Mother' Jones was a prominent labour and community organiser. In 1901, workers in Pennsylvania's silk mills went on strike, many being young female workers demanding to be paid adult wages (Stepenoff 1997: 446). She became involved and continued to include children in her campaigning for improvements in conditions for all workers. In 1903 she was angry about the sloppy enforcement of the child labour laws in Pennsylvanian mines and silk mills. She organised a children's march from Philadelphia to the home of President Theodore Roosevelt in New York that came to be known as the 'Children's Crusade'. They carried banners proclaiming 'We want to go to School and not the mines!' (Bartoletti 1999). The march brought the issue of child labour to prominence in the public examination of child labour at that time. Mother Jones had noticed that many of the children at union headquarters had missing fingers and other disabilities. Despite thwarted attempts to gain newspaper reportage, mines often being owned by the same proprietors as mines, it reached the attention of the government and contributed to eventual change.

Again in the USA in 1911 the *Ludlow Massacre* was an attack on strikers by the Colorado National Guard and Colorado Fuel and Iron Company camp guards. There was a tent colony of approximately 1,200 striking coal miners and their families at Ludlow, Colorado, on April 20, 1914. The militiamen went into the camp, set fire to tents and killed two women and 11 children who had taken shelter from shooting in a pit below a tent. The children had been active participants in an otherwise perfectly peaceful protest (Zinn 2005: 34–49). The purpose of the raid was to force men back to work in the mines without consideration of their demands for better pay and safer working conditions.

In England a school strike in Burston, Norfolk, was part of the longest-running strike in British history that lasted between 1914 and 1939. It began when two teachers at the village school, Annie and Tom Higdon, were dismissed after a disagreement with the area school management committee. Schoolchildren went on strike in support. Sixty-six of the school's 72 pupils went on strike and marched around the village waving flags. None of the pupils ever returned to the school and instead had lessons in a tent on the village green. The tent school was well equipped, kept a full timetable and observed normal school regulations with full support of parents. The authorities took 18 parents to court, and they were fined for their children's nonattendance at school. Money was collected outside the court to pay the fines. Because parents were sending children to the school of their choice, the authorities were soon forced to concede defeat. The tent school that eventually moved to a permanent building was renamed the Burston Strike School. The strike continued until 1939 when Tom Higdon died (Edwards 1974; Scobie 1991; Zamoyska 1985).

Coming closer to the present, in South Africa, the Soweto Uprising was a series of protests led by high school students in 1976. Students from the township's schools began to protest in the streets of Soweto against the Afrikaans Medium Decree of 1974, which forced all black schools to use only Afrikaans and English fifty-fifty for teaching. An estimate of 20,000 students took part in the protests (Ndlovu 2006: 331–32). Early in March 2011 sprayed slogans began to appear on walls in Daraa on Syria's border with Jordan. Secret police arrested 15 boys aged between 10 and 15 years. They were held in an interrogation room where they were beaten and burned and had fingernails pulled out by government officials (CBS News 2011). Later the same year, child protesters were reported to have been tortured and killed. Two teenagers died after being beaten and shot. Fifteen-year-old Thamer al-Sahri had been taken several days before his body was returned to his family. His body was reported to have been punctured by bullet wounds and was missing an eye and several teeth. His neck and one leg were also reportedly broken. Thirty-two children, aged between 12 and 17, remained in detention at that time in connection with the protests and were considered to be at risk of torture or other ill-treatment. Other reports said that at least 82 children had been killed (Amnesty International 2011).

In Nepal in 2010 demonstrations and a general strike reportedly brought about cases of children's rights violations. Children both participated in and were adversely affected by the protests. Several incidences of injured children were reported including the death of a 3-year-old as an outcome of the actions (CWIN-Nepal 2010). In 2012 UNICEF reported about 250 children in school uniforms marching stridently around the central market of Biratnagar, in the east of Nepal, following a banner that declared 'Allow us to study'. They were shouting slogans, blowing whistles, banging together metal objects and ringing bells and carried signs reading 'Let schools remain as Zones of Peace', 'We are not just the future, we are today' and 'Search for alternatives to closures'. The protesting children were members of the Network of Working Children's Clubs in Morang District and Biratnagar Municipality. They were protesting because of attempts to close schools during *bandas* or political strikes that had shut down roads and businesses all over Nepal as groups had attempted to persuade the government to draft a new national constitution.

When children's actions are less proactive but nonetheless aim to give them a well-defined place in society, it is often seen as delinquent rather than rational behaviour. Thus, schoolchildren who formed unions in France and the UK, reflecting conduct more closely associated with the student movements of 1968 that took part in massive protests which also included large number of workers and poor people who felt they faced increasingly violent state repression throughout the world, were very critically appraised. They were dismissed and shunned as attempting the ridiculous and their protests unnecessary rather than expressing anything of real use by the authorities. Very much in response to 1968, two Danish teachers, Søren Hansen and Jesper Jensen, wrote 'Den Lille Røde Bog For Skoleelever' (The Little Red Schoolbook (for Students)) in 1969. It was a small red volume that was approximately the same size as 'Quotations from Chairman Mao Tsetung' (Mao 1977) that was more commonly known as the 'Little Red Book' and was considered the 'gospel' of revolution at that time. The Little Red Schoolbook included details on striking and demonstrations (Hansen and Jensen 1969: 50–54). Over its 200 pages, it included 20 very detailed pages about sex and 30 about drugs that also described the pros and cons of alcohol and tobacco use and abuse. Although teachers themselves, Hansen and Jensen, questioned the responsibilities of teachers, school discipline, critically looked at examinations, looked at what intelligence is and the structure and methods of different kinds of school. The book was either assumed to be encouraging schoolchildren to copy university students' behaviour or advocating bringing about the end of stringent adult control. Worldwide politicians, educationists and other members of the establishment criticised the book, fearing that it would lead to an erosion of the moral fabric of society and incite anarchy in schools. It was banned in several countries but nonetheless reached young people with a backlash that included the ruin of political careers in some cases. It was an example of how much fear there is of independent political action by children that still survives until the present although the anticipated schoolchildren's anarchy and rebellion never came about.

Since the mid-1970s, there have been activists and groups who took up the fight for the rights of street and working children. They were mainly NGOs or members of organisations with backgrounds in trade unionism and workers' rights rather than in the child protection field. Those activists encouraged the development of self-determination through political and organisational skills among those children. The earliest initiatives were self-help groups and unions, often called children's movements; some were formed and well established before the adoption and entry into force of the CRC. They are also unmistakably true to the intended purpose of Article 15, which describes the children's right to form associations, particularly bearing in mind the universal prohibition of children joining trade unions:

Article 15

> 1. States Parties recognize the rights of the child to freedom of association and to freedom of peaceful assembly.
> 2. No restrictions may be placed on the exercise of these rights other than those imposed in conformity with the law and which are necessary in a democratic society in the interests of national security or public safety, public order (*ordre public*), the protection of public health or morals or the protection of the rights and freedoms of others.

However, when looking at the recent history of children's rights, we find that they are regarded recipients of rights in the discourse that is almost entirely about their welfare far more than recognising them as individuals who themselves possess a set of rights that allows them the kind of self-determination the new groups offered them. Whilst the CRC is a ground-breaking treaty that proposes that children are active agents with rights in accordance with international human rights law, the world is not yet able to move away from the notions that children need protection. Furthermore, not only do they have need of particular forms of protection above and beyond those given to them by human rights law, but they also need specific kinds of protection since they are considered to be vulnerable in legal and in the development of their growth and acquisition of rights as they become adults. The establishment sees their role as the duty to protect, although children have the right to have their opinions taken into consideration when decisions are made on 'for' them (Article 12), to express views (Article 13), to have to the freedom of thought, conscience and religion (Article 14) and to be members or set up associations that represent their interests (Article 15). Whilst there is almost universal ratification of these articles without reservation, it is difficult to see whether these articles mean much at all in many states parties.

Thus, children's organisations, whilst almost always set up by adults, tend to carry some of the stigma attached to The Little Red Schoolbook, where they appear to be anarchic and subversive. The oldest of these, *MANTHOC* (*Movimiento de adolescentes y ninos trabajadores, Hijos de obreros cristianos*), was set up in Peru in 1976. It was specifically for working and street working children who needed an organisation to offer them protection through solidarity and self-representation of their needs as young workers. It became exemplary throughout Latin America where there are now numerous working children's organisations, many of them closely collaborating within an international movement. In Brazil in 1985 the MNMMR was formed by activists working together with street children. The MNMMR gained an international reputation for its marches and demonstrations for the rights of street children. In India in the same year, activists with a trade union background helped children set up *CWC* (the *Concerned for Working Children*). In turn, in 1990, CWC helped set up *Bhima Sangha*, the union of working children, which was also one of the founding member organisations of the *International Movement of Working Children* in 1996 and the *National Movement of Working Children* in 1999. In 1995, Bhima Sangha was the initiator of forming the first *Makkala Panchayats* (children's councils) and *Makkala Grama Sabhas* (children's village meetings) which now exist throughout India. *ENDA TM Jeunesse Action* (Environnement et Développement du Tiers Monde, Jeunesse Action) was also set up in Senegal in 1985 with the main purpose of providing an organisation for street and working children. In Nepal, *CWIN* (*Child Workers in Nepal*) was set up in 1987 and was the first of several similar organisations in their country. Each of these organisations precedes the

CRC by several years. Each was also received badly by national and international communities. IPEC with its mandate to progressively eliminate child labour has always stridently opposed them. Each organisation has withstood the challenge. The child members stand up in defiance of all efforts to prevent them working and proclaim their right to work and demand protection of that right. It is the children, they are helped to learn how to organise and speak for themselves, the principles of democracy and political action, who form the walls of solidarity against efforts to destroy their organisations proclaiming their rights under the CRC.

Although the organisations were set up by adult supporters, often needing to register as charities or formal associations which only adults can do anyway, they have always very quickly passed the main responsibility for activity over to their child members. Other supporters, activists for human rights, with trade union backgrounds, sympathetic international NGOs, academics and researchers among them, have also helped expand them. In the 1990s such people set up *Niños y Adolescentes Trabajadores* (NATs) that originally focussed on the Spanish-speaking Latin American region but has become an integral part of the International Movement of Working Children set up in 1996, the model in which many national movements have come into being. Adults pass on the greater part of the activities to children, but whilst national and international movements allow children to have exchanges in order to learn from each other and engage against opposition such as the ILO, the structure of organisation has also taught them how to enter into dialogue with adults. This, in turn, has shown the way for children representing themselves in all situations, not being thwarted by attempts to be heard by adults, and has seen them received by politicians and national and international bodies who are in principle against their existence and actions. It was a member of one of those organisations who gave this chapter its title. Whilst Article 12 has been in many ways hijacked (see Chap. 2) to conform to adult and global agendas, it also illustrates how well children can and do use this part of the CRC, thus providing sound evidence that children can be agents for change and bearers of human rights in their own right rather than simply subjects of protection.

The third *Global Conference on Child Labour* was held in Brasilia in October 2013. It looked back over progress made since the *Hague Global Child Labour Conference* of 2010. It considered remaining obstacles and agreed on measures to strengthen actions to eliminate the worst forms of child labour by 2016 and also the eradication of all forms of child labour in the too far distant future. The *Brasilia Declaration* at the conclusion of the conference summed up determination to encourage greater efforts to promote social change by addressing attitudes and practices that contribute significantly to ignoring or tolerating child labour which included abuse of and violence against working children. It restated the significance of promoting the universal ratification and effective implementation of ILO standards, CRC and its Optional Protocols. It also called for the establishment and further development of legal and institutional frameworks to prevent and eradicate child labour. Furthermore, improved and more national statistics and data and additional measures to extend and improve access to free, compulsory and high-quality education for all children were backed up by advances in making the social protection of children a global standard. In the 24 closing comments of the Brasilia Declaration not once is dialogue with children and their organisations or representatives ever mentioned. Article 12 CRC would imply that this is neither possible nor permissible, yet the UN itself and its agencies remain blind and deaf to the lobbying by working children themselves. Among the lobbying efforts of the international working children's movement, the fact that despite children's rights laws they are excluded from having their demands and opinions heard is one of their most commonly restated pleas. From 1989 until the present, they are not heard.

Judith Ennew and I always maintained a close relationship with the children's organisations, were privileged to have seen many of them in their home countries and met many of the children, and both of us learned an immense amount about what the real message of children's rights should be from the young members we met. A familiar request would always be their desire to be genuinely included rather than ignored, except when the ILO or another unsympathetic organisation tells them what they think they should or should not do.

The basic tenet of children's organisations has grown, and whilst some pre-existed the CRC, the number of children's municipal councils and school councils has flourished in many countries. Whilst many genuinely do have a degree of impact, particularly in allowing children to have dialogue with adults and be influential in reaching decisions, others are entirely tokenistic (see Hart 1992) and set up to give children 'their own' groups who discuss largely uncontroversial matters that have little or no impact in the settings in which their meetings are held. There are exceptions. In Wales, *Funky Dragon* (*Draig Ffynci*)[1] was set up by a partnership of children and the Welsh Assembly. Their efforts feed into the country's policies on children and youth and to some extent to other areas. *Mousedeer Msia* was set up in Malaysia in 2012 with the specific purpose of collecting children's inputs for their country's first children's report to the Committee on the Rights of the Child. In both cases these children's organisations are contributing to the delivery of their rights and beyond. They are neither at odds with the aims and objectives of the CRC nor at risk of confrontation with adult organisations who oppose their claim to the right to work. They are part of what is considered a respectable face of children's search for their place in the world, not defying the 'rules' such as child labour laws that determine what they should and should not be and rejecting their campaigns without needing to see or hear what young people have to say about their lives, choices, needs and priorities.

There are some extraordinary perceptions of how children's voices should be heard. In 2002, over 7,000 people took part in the biggest international conference on children for over a decade, a *Special Session of the UN General Assembly on Children*, at which representatives of a large number of nations committed themselves to a string of goals that set out to improve the situation of children.

[1] At the time this book was being completed, they had closed down with exception of some ongoing projects because the Welsh Assembly had not granted them further funding.

It was unique in being the first ever Session devoted entirely to children and include some as official delegates. The Session was held primarily to review progress since the *World Summit for Children* in 1990 and refresh international commitment to children's rights. Around 70 heads of state, prime ministers or deputies, with many high-ranking government delegations, went to New York for the Session. NGOs and academic, business, cultural and religious groups plus distinguished personalities, such as Nelson Mandela and Bill Gates, attended. Four countries, the Netherlands, Norway, Sweden and Togo, took youth representatives to address the General Assembly for their countries.

It was said that the participation of young people at the Special Session represented a breakthrough at the UN. Children and youth met before the Session in a Children's Forum to discuss issues and come up with suggestions for governments, civil society organisations and children themselves to work together to make the world a better place for all ages. Their views were presented in a statement, *A World Fit for Us* (UNICEF 2002), at the opening of the General Assembly debate, thus officially addressing it for children for the first time ever in the history of the UN. A large number attended the Special Session as delegates from NGOs or their countries. Others were also actively involved in several official meetings and supporting events; some took part in three high-level round-table discussions where they were able to speak directly with heads of state and country representatives. The young delegates were divided into groups to discuss things that mattered to them: children's rights and participation, exploitation, health, education, poverty, HIV and AIDS, the environment and war. Four hundred and four children between ages of 7 and 18 attended the *Children's Forum*. Of those, 242 were girls and 162 were boys, all selected by governments as members of official delegations from 142 countries. A further 140 children came as members of 106 NGO delegations. All together, children represented 154 countries. All participants had been selected at national or regional level through competitions in schools and communities, membership of youth parliaments, involvement in the *Say Yes for Children* campaign or association with NGOs. The young people had participated in national or regional preparatory meetings at which they are selected to be delegates. The Children's Forum statement drawn up from their discussions was read out to the Special Session by two delegates, Gabriela Azurduy Arrieta, 13, from Bolivia and Audrey Cheynut, 17, from Monaco.

One of the critical views of the Special Session was that although the ages of children were from 7 to 18 years, a disproportionate number of them were actually youths, including a number of 18-year-olds, thus no longer children in the sense of the CRC. It was also said that the selection process had favoured children from mainstream society who did not represent a true cross section of the world's children. There was no representation from children who had chosen to be combatants in conflicts that set out to change their countries for the better. No children from street and working children's organisations were chosen, and indeed many would not have had the chance since they did not attend formal schools or were part of the kind of forums those selected belonged to. Those children had no opportunity to present their arguments for respecting their organisations, their aims and objectives and also their real needs. Furthermore, once the Special Session was over, apart from UNICEF publishing *A World Fit for Us*, which only reached a very limited audience, there was no real follow-up.

Whether or not the allegations are true, the fact is that despite the uniqueness of the event and the fact that there was child and youth participation, it is a largely forgotten event that has never been repeated although regular international, political and economy reassessment of the situation of children was always foreseen. That has been left to UNICEF's annual *World Fit for Children* which is a mainly quantitative review presented in statistics but with little qualitative contents that describe the actual situation of children.

Much of what could be considered at all 'follow-up' has been left in the hands of the Committee on the Rights of the Child. They permanently have a considerable list of reports to read, plus the meetings at which reporting countries are discussed, but no real working time to supervise their task or any tools for the enforcement of their findings. More or less none of what they do is contributed by or done in any form of direct consultation with or in the knowledge of the children. Whilst a few NGOs have attempted to be child inclusive, work with them to produce children's national reports and attempt to send delegations to the Committee, the overall outcome is almost too small to measure. Some more influential NGOs or groups of NGOs have produced alternative reports, some of them in collaboration with governments. However, the guidelines for the Committee give them no mandate to take account of those reports. In fact they hardly ever have time to take them into account and have imposed a limit on the number of pages, no more than 30, only one per country and in one of the three languages the Committee works in, English, French or Spanish, with the first preferred so that all members can read it. If it is written in the country's own language, it is recommended it is given to UNICEF to translate (Dimmock 2011: 40). Again, there is no real space for children's movements to raise their own arguments in detail and present them to perhaps the only possible route where they may be seriously considered. It was on the presentation of their country's national report that a young member of a working children's organisation spoke the words that gave this chapter its title.

This has contributed to what Judith Ennew (2000: 47) described as a 'crisis of identity' supporters of children's participation have been becoming ever closer to. Children have been as a means to their own ends by some ambitious, lucid and often self-proclaimed experts on participation through training courses, public presentations, books and articles that have promoted their careers but do not very often represent what children would define their participation in civil society as themselves. They prescribe participation according to their interpretation and often redefinition of Article 12 and very often use Roger Hart's ladder (Hart 1992: 8) as a model of how it proceeds (see van Beers et al. 2006: 22–33). Careers have built on often quite superficial examination of what participation means. Adults have been trained to train children using narrow parameters of what their role in civil society is and have generally implanted a select few established and assumedly successful models. Those models have often reproduced ones started by NGOs working with street and working children and often predate the CRC by a number of years.[2] In fact, some of them have drawn on the experience of children's movements of the kind already described that are generally 'outlawed' by participation experts. There has also been a proliferation of projects whereby NGOs send in 'experts', mostly white Europeans, who have set up participatory research and training in what are sometimes almost inaccessible parts of developing nations. The experts leave when the project or training ends leaving no kind of permanence or follow-up that would provide a rationale for its continuation. Apart from the occasional children's council, they all too often cease to exist soon after.

There has been scant in-depth examination of what participation in civil society really means for children and their citizenship, national and political identities, beliefs, culture or economics (Milne 2013). Participation is neither precisely defined but usually presented as models that are designed for children and thus are often little more than play instead of activities that would help impart their role in their society and are frequently imposed on them without asking what their real needs are. The question thus arises whether those methods applied by experts who tend to be inflexible in their approaches at all represent a meaningful sector of activism within children's rights that still remains to be heard. On the other hand, they may be all that children have as yet to use as the most efficient mean of having their voices heard. Whatever the conclusion may be, there are now 'myths and legends' (Ennew, op.cit.) about what participation is and how it reproduces democracy for them, although it never appears to enter into more complicated questions such as the differences between nationality and citizenship (Milne, op.cit.). Thus far no organisation such as UNICEF or NGOs working on children's participation, developing programmes and projects or funding research has entered into these more comprehensive issues. In contrast, the working children's movement has a history that often considerably predates the CRC; thus, their activities not being based on what Article 12 describes have often gone far beyond the ideas and approaches of most well-known 'experts'.

Since this narrowing down of one part of the children's rights agenda has generally been practised to the exclusion of organisations with extensive experience in children's participation and rights in general, the integrity of those defining what and who belongs within their environment is called into question. The nature of the CRC, as with all human rights instruments, is the inclusion of all children without exception, bias or other reasons for any form of exclusion.

Thus, the exclusion of the street and working children's organisations along with their national and international movements essentially goes against the grain of children's rights. However, international organisations such as the ILO and UNICEF are committed to ending their reason for being. Articles 32, 34, 35 and 36 CRC all directly or indirectly aim to end child labour and particularly protect children against

[2]The original participatory work of street and working children's organisations is rarely, if it can be avoided, mentioned by 'mainstream' organisations although their methods have been closely examined and replicated, often badly, as the basis on which career experts have constructed 'their' models.

the more detrimental issues that are often associated with their work. From the point of view of working children, the elimination of the worst forms of child labour is a highly acceptable proposition. On the other hand, they defend their right to work where it is necessary. This plaintiff is usually derided as the word of children too young to understand their situation or decide for themselves. If one looks at the many forms of work children do, the diversity is itself vast. It is necessary to look at what they are briefly to have any idea of the range. Almost any compilation will give a broad overview; the description of jobs done by children following is based loosely on that of the *International Trade Union Confederation* (ITUC 2008). Some are very visible, whilst others are not. There are also other forms of work, including those very easily dismissed through to some of its worst forms.

Domestic work is probably the most common and often considered quite acceptable. It is most likely to be found in the family home but also very often outside the home. When it is outside their home, children, generally more girls than boys, commonly work long hours. Where they live at their place of work rather than home, they are often unable to go to school and may be cut off from family and friends. Many working children are found in agriculture. They often work on family smallholdings or farms or with their entire family for an employer. Their work is sometimes seasonal, for instance, picking particular crops or on plantations, or may be permanent if they are looking after animals. Industrial work may be regular or casual and legal or illegal. Some children work alone and others as part of a family. Sometimes their work is unpaid when they are working alongside parents who are paid by piecework or depend on rapid outputs. The work ranges from small-scale production, which may be within the family only, to large-scale industries. Children are exposed to hazards ranging from accidents with tools and machinery to harm caused by dangerous materials to serious beatings by supervisors. Some die as a result of their work. They also work in mines and quarries: particularly in small mines in many countries, even some small enough to be a family enterprise. They usually work long hours without adequate protection and are exposed to risks and health hazards that may result in long-term health problems or death. Work in the informal economy includes a whole range of activities including shoe shining, begging, selling newspapers and other forms of street vending, as porters and collecting rubbish. Some forms of informal work are easily observed, whilst others are often hidden from view. Children are found in pornography, prostitution and other forms of sexual exploitation. They are exposed to sexually transmitted diseases (STDs) including HIV and AIDS which may lead to their death, as well as many forms of physical and mental harm. Then there are children forced to become soldiers or do some of the other military-related tasks previously mentioned in Chap. 3. There are other forms of forced labour, slavery and trafficking whereby children are abducted, given away, bought or sold for their use in many kinds of work including those already mentioned.

According to ILO some years ago, 56 % of 10–14 year olds estimated to be working in developing nations are boys. It was possible to measure numbers of girls doing unregistered work as domestic servants, whether at home or for an employer, and it would show more female child workers than male. Girls usually work longer hours on average than boys. This is especially relevant in the case of girls who have employment outside of their home but must then carry out domestic duties after work (UNICEF 1996). A great deal of evidence shows that whilst great emphasis is placed on ending child labour in the developing world, there is probably no country in the entire world that is without.

IPEC was after all said and done, created with the ultimate goal of eliminating all forms of child labour, with the initial undertaking to be elimination of the worst forms of child labour. Its priorities for immediate action are defined in the *ILO Convention on the worst forms of child labour, 1999 (No. 182)* as:

> all forms of slavery or practices similar to slavery,
> such as the sale and trafficking of children,
> debt bondage and serfdom and forced or compulsory labour, including forced or compulsory recruitment of children for use in armed conflict;
> the use, procuring or offering of a child for prostitution, for the production of pornography or for pornographic performances;
> the use, procuring or offering of a child for illicit activities, in particular for the production and trafficking of drugs as defined in the relevant international treaties;
> work which, by its nature or the circumstances in which it is carried out, is likely to harm the health, safety or morals of children.

It is sometimes ironic that it is the ILO that seems to be most concerned with child labour. It was formed in 1919 to reflect the belief that universal and lasting peace can be accomplished only if it is based on social justice. Its constitution was drafted in 1919 by the *Labour Commission* which first met in Paris and then again in Versailles. The Commission was composed of representatives from nine countries: Belgium, Cuba, Czechoslovakia, France, Italy, Japan, Poland, the UK and the USA. The outcome of the first meetings was a tripartite organisation that brought together representatives of governments, employers and workers in its executive bodies. The Constitution contained notions already tested within the *International Association for Labour Legislation* that had been founded in Basel in 1901. Advocacy for an international organisation that dealt with labour issues had started in the nineteenth century at the behest of Robert Owen from Wales and Daniel Legrand from France who were both industrialists with philanthropic views of the nature of employment. In 1946, the ILO became a specialised agency of the recently founded United Nations. In 1948, the *International Labour Conference* adopted *Convention Number 87* on the freedom of association and the right to organise (Alcock 1970).

The irony is that the ILO was effectively born out of philanthropy and trade unionism. Both played a significant role in ending child labour in its most hazardous form in advanced industrial societies. However, by adopting Convention Number 87 and supporting Article 15 CRC, it should respect those values as much for children as adults. This is not the case. It has adopted a position that contradicts the underlying principles of both conventions. It is, on the basis of its historical background that included ending child labour, between a rock and a hard place as one might say. To begin with, perhaps by bearing in mind the examples given here already, what is it? Are shared tasks within the family or community work or a simple contribution to the common good of those people? Is work that children choose to do, especially where there is little, poor quality or no formal education available, justifiably a target for elimination? That gives children no learning opportunities whatsoever, has anybody ever thought about that or the logistics of changing it? Why do elimination focussed organisations, groups and individuals not enter into a meaningful dialogue with children who need or want to work or are contributing to their social group?

Thus, street and working children whose movements have attempted to attain some form of representation that would recognise children to be organised in unions and similar groups remain muted. They have a valuable contribution that it is their right to give but yet still largely denied. Organised street and working children have answers to the conundrum of solving the dilemma that is often unpalatable for those with the inability to define what child labour actually is and what its benefits are. Yet no dialogue seems to meaningfully develop or when it does last long enough to reach any solutions. That is a denial of what CRC defined rights set out to incorporate.

Street children in such organisations are well aware that it can be harsh and risky for them, jeopardise physical and psychosocial development and often have a negative influence on the rest of their lives. Most of them invest great effort to find lawful work on the street for their own or families' survival. Those children shine shoes; carry luggage and goods; wash and guard cars; sell flowers, cigarettes and every imaginable kind of small thing they can afford to stock; collect recyclable rubbish at landfill sites; and have many other, often very ingenious ways earning small amounts of money. Most of them go home to their families in shanty towns and squatter settlements every day. They are children *on* the streets as against *of* them. Children who only beg are far more often only able to do so because they have no money or other collateral for materials or stock for street vending, at least minimal protective clothing for other tasks, tools and materials for others and are frequently found to be those without homes and families to return to, often without anywhere where they have proper protection and shelter to live (Ennew and Milne 1989, 1996). Those are children *of* the streets. They are children who rarely have a voice. They also need to be heard.

Working children engaged in agriculture, small-scale industries and sometimes mines and quarries are very often working within their family unit. Likewise in domestic work, although to have a wage to take home is invariably for an employer. Otherwise, children who have jobs outside of their families usually work to earn money for their families. Paramount in all cases where a wage is taken home or a contribution to family members' work is that they are contributing to family survival. In an ideal world they would not work but would prefer to enjoy school and free time in which they play or take part in sports and activities that most children would follow rather than need to work.

There is a tendency to forget advanced industrial nations, and despite the fact that there are working children in more or less all of them, there are also homeless and street-living youth in too many of them, but they lack the kind of organisations and movements who are active for and with them in developing nations. There are also 'personalities' in perhaps most countries to whom a blind eye is turned. They are film and stage actors, singers, musicians, fashions and photographic models, athletes and others who are professionals in these and comparable occupations. Nonetheless, they often work extremely hard from a very young age. Thus far country reports to the Committee have largely overlooked these and other issues such as trafficking, child laundering, involvement in pornography and prostitution, child poverty, lack of access to proper medical services and several other equally controversial areas. Developed nation children are as likely as their peers in the developing world to be deprived and unaware of their rights and most certainly not be included in any kind of consultation when data for country reports is being collected. It is highly likely the children of the 'North' would agree with the child in the 'South' who was given his first insight into his country's report and said 'It's a lie. They didn't ask us'.

References

Alcock, A. (1970). *History of the International Labour Organisation*. London: Macmillan.

Amnesty International. (2011). *Fears for Syrian child protesters amid fresh reports of deaths*. http://www.amnesty.org/en/news-and-updates/fears-syrian-children-detention-amid-fresh-reports-torture-death-2011-06-09

Anonymous. (1918). *Jack Cornwell: The story of John Travers Cornwell, V.C., 'Boy – 1st class'*. Toronto: Hodder and Stoughton.

Baker, W. (2010). Explaining the outbreak and dynamics of the 1911 school strike wave in Britain. *Reflecting Education, 6*(1), 25–38.

Brooks, P. S. (1999). *Beyond the myth: The story of Joan of Arc*. New York: Houghton Mifflin.

Bartoletti, S. C. (1999). *Kids on strike!* Boston: Houghton Mifflin Harcourt.

Berthelsen, D. C., & Brownlee, J. M. (2005). Respecting children's agency for learning and rights to participation in child care programs. *International Journal of Early Childhood, 37*(3), 49–60.

Boyden, J. (1990). Childhood and the policymakers. In A. James & J. Prout (Eds.), *Constructing and reconstructing childhood* (pp. 184–215). London/New York/Philadelphia: Falmer Press.

Brannen, J., & O'Brien, M. (1995). Childhood and the sociological gaze: Paradigms and paradoxes. *Sociology, 29*(4), 729–737.

Brazier, K. (2010). *The complete Victoria Cross: A full chronological record of all holders of Britain's highest award for gallantry*. Barnsley: Pen and Sword Military.

CBS News. (2011). *How Schoolboys began the Syrian Revolution*. CBS News Global Post. http://www.cbsnews.com/news/how-schoolboys-began-the-syrian-revolution/

Child Workers in Nepal. (2010). *Child Rights Monitoring Report*. Kathmandu: CWIN-Nepal. http://www.respond.org/data/files/nepal_child_rights_monitoring_report_by_cwin.pdf

Dickson, G. (1992). Stephen of Cloyes, Philip Augustus, and the Children's Crusade of 1212. In B. N. Sargent-Baur (Ed.), *Journeys toward God: Pilgrimage and crusade* (pp. 83–105). Kalamazoo: Medieval Institute Publications.

Dickson, G. (2008). *The Children's Crusade: Medieval history, modern mythistory*. Basingstoke/New York: Palgrave Macmillan.

Dimmock, S. (2011). *My pocket guide to CRC reporting*. Geneva: Child Rights Connect.

Edwards, B. (1974). *The Burston school strike*. London: Lawrence and Wishart.

Ennew, J. (2000). The history of children's rights: Whose story? *Cultural Survival Quarterly, 24*(2), 44–48.

Ennew, J., & Milne, B. (1989). *The next generation: Lives of Third World children*. Philadelphia: Zed Books: London and New Society Publishers.

Ennew, J., & Milne, B. (1996). *Methods of research with street and working children: An annotated bibliography*. Stockholm: Rädda Barnen.

Gray, G. Z. (1870). *The Children's Crusade*. New York: Hurd and Houghton.

Hansen, S., & Jensen, J. (1969). *The little red schoolbook*. London: Stage 1.

Hart, R. (1992). *Children's participation: From tokenism to citizenship*. Florence: UNICEF.
ITUC. (2008). *Mini action guide: Child labour*. Brussels: International Trade Union Confederation.
James, A., & James, A. (Eds.). (2004). *Constructing childhood: Theory, policy and social practice*. Basingstoke: Palgrave Macmillan.
James, A., & Prout, A. (Eds.). (1990). *Constructing and reconstructing childhood: Contemporary issues in the sociological study of childhood*. London: Falmer Press.
James, A., Jenks, C., & Prout, A. (1998). *Theorising childhood*. Oxford: Polity Press.
Jenks, C. (1982). *The sociology of childhood: Essential readings*. London: Batsford Academic and Educational.
Jenks, C. (1996). *Childhood*. London: Routledge.
Lister, R. (2007). Why citizenship: Where, when and how children? *Theoretical Inquiries in Law, 8*(2), 693–718.
Marson, D. (1973). Children's strikes in 1911. In *History workshop pamphlets* (Number 9). Oxford: Ruskin College.
McKechnie, J., & Hobbs, S. (1998). *Working children: Reconsidering the debates*. Amsterdam: International Working Group on Child Labour.
Milne, B. (2013). *The history and theory of children's citizenship in contemporary societies*. Stuttgart: Springer.
Nasaw, D. (1985). *Children of the city: At work and at play*. Oxford: Oxford University Press.
Ndlovu, S. M. (2006). The Soweto uprising. In *The road to democracy in South Africa, Volume 2, 1970–1980* (pp. 317–368). Pretoria: South African Democracy Education Trust.
Qvortrup, J. (1991). *Childhood as a social phenomenon* (2nd ed.). Eurosocial Report 36/0. Vienna: European Centre for Social Welfare, Policy and Research.
Qvortrup, J. (1994). Childhood matters: An introduction. In J. Qvortrup, M. Bardy, G. Sgritta, & H. Wintersberger (Eds.), *Childhood matters: Social theory, practice and politics*. Aldershot: Avebury.
Raedts, P. (1977). The Children's Crusade of 1212. *Journal of Medieval History, 3*, 279–333.
Redmond, G. (2009). Children as actors: How does the child perspectives literature treat agency in the context of poverty? *Social Policy and Society, 8*(4), 541–550.
Scheck, R. (1988). Did the Children's Crusade of 1212 really consist of children? Problems of writing childhood history. *The Journal of Psychohistory, 16*(2), 176–182.
Scobie, P. (1991). *The school that went on strike*. Oxford: Oxford University Press.
Stepenoff, B. (1997). Keeping it in the family: Mother Jones and the Pennsylvania Silk Strike of 1900–1901. *Labor History, 38*(4), 432–449.
Tsetung, M. (1977). *Quotations from Chairman Mao Tsetung (Little red book)*. Beijing: Foreign Languages Press.
UNICEF. (1996). The shapes of child labour. In *State of the world's children 1997*. New York: United Nations Children's Fund.
UNICEF. (2002). *A world fit for us*. New York: United Nations Children's Fund.
Uprichard, E. (2008). Children as being and becomings: Children, childhood and temporality. *Children and Society, 22*(4), 303–313.
van Beers, H., Invernizzi, A., & Milne, B. (2006). *Beyond article 12: Essential readings in children's participation*. Bangkok: Black on White.
Verhellen, E. (1997). *Expert evidence, report: First public hearings of the International Tribunal for Children's Rights*. Montreal: International Bureau for Children's Rights.
Zamoyska, B. (1985). *The Burston Rebellion*. London: Ariel Books.
Zinn, H. (2005). *A people's history of the United States* (pp. 346–349). New York: Harper Perennial Modern Classics.

5 Hijacked Agendas

The argument that any agenda has been hijacked is, of course, a very contentious assertion that many children's rights activists would very strenuously deny. However, critics would remark on how little change has occurred since the CRC entered into force in September 1990. One of the most compelling arguments is that it is on the whole a very western convention that by its nature unintentionally contributes to a North–south dichotomy because it is expressed in a language that generally does not reflect the cultural diversity of the nations who have signed and ratified it but have done little to implement it nor does it realistically take into account significant social, economic, cultural and religious variants that will almost unquestionably raise accusations that it is not written for 'others', thus pointing at the UN as though it genuinely only represented the interests and values of the northern hemisphere.

The CRC has nevertheless been described as reflective of a cross-cultural perspective on children's rights (Walker et al. 1998: 43). That perspective has been described as having been developed out of the international discussion throughout the years of drafting and thus written in a language carefully pulled together from many cultural perspectives. Where there has always been a pronounced difference that one can very quickly recognise is in the area of street and homeless children.

'Street children' is a generic term for young people who spend much of their time and work on the streets of towns and cities. The definition of street children is contentious; however, many practitioners and policymakers use UNICEF's concept of boys and girls less than 18 years old, for whom 'the street' has become their home and their normal source of income and who are insufficiently protected or overseen. 'The street' is also a generic term that includes derelict and vacant buildings and empty plots of land. Some children and youth, particularly in developed nations, are often classified as 'homeless children and youth'; they are also referred to as 'runaways', and there is a subcategory that refers to them as 'throwaway children' who have been forced to leave home. Throwaways are statistically more likely to come from working class and single-parent homes than settled, economically viable

B. Milne, *Rights of the Child*, Children's Well-Being: Indicators and Research 11,
DOI 10.1007/978-3-319-18784-6_5

homes. In the USA, Covenant House[1] is the largest national organisation working with homeless youth who take refuge in the streets. It was founded in 1972 and has centres in over 20 countries throughout the USA, Canada and Central America. They are the largest privately funded charity in the Americas providing services for homeless, abandoned, abused, trafficked and exploited youths. According to their estimates, each year in the USA, up to two million youths experience a period of homelessness. Every year, more than 5,000 of them lose their lives in the streets. At the time of writing, they claim to be working with about 50,000 at-risk and homeless children across their entire programme. Whilst there are not only children and youth from the lower strata of society, the majority comes from homes where economic reasons may force young people to leave or be rejected or abuse and exploitation give them little option. These young people are particularly vulnerable to abuse and exploitation, including the risk of being trafficked (Colby 2011) (see also Chap. 5). However, in the USA, as typically most of the North, they are not called 'street children'. That is a category almost exclusively reserved for the young of the South whose lives are conventionally seen to be far more economically hazardous to begin with. Essentially, the differences may be that the proportions of reasons for leaving home are different but on the whole remain part of the same list.

Thus, the homeless, runaway and throwaway children of the North are the same as street children when the euphemisms are cast aside. What then are street children? A variety of categories is used. Three main typologies predominate: children *of* the street, children *on* the street and children who are part of a street-living family. Those definitions do not generally reflect cultural diversity in and across countries as well as fluctuations in the situation of children and families. The variables also do not take into account socio-economic and cultural contexts between countries, thus allowing the North–south dichotomisation to continue largely unquestioned.

The UN does not make that distinction. They define the term 'street children' to include every boy or girl for whom the 'street', using the broadest sense of that word, has become his or her everyday place of residence and/or is their source of earnings, who is insufficiently or not at all protected, supervised or under the charge of adults who carry the responsibility for them. There is no division between 'homeless' children in the North and the 'street children' of the South, thus rejecting the otherwise accepted dichotomy.

Looking at the phenomenology of living on or spending a great deal of time on streets, particularly those who work, those who go to the streets during the day but return to their family or group at night and those who live permanently on the street without family connections, there are always common traits. All of them are at risk of abuse, exploitation and violence. The most vulnerable of them line and sleep on the streets, go to abandoned and derelict buildings at night and hide under bridges, in sewers or on the concourse of railway stations among the many different places where they can conceal themselves. Some have semi-permanent jobs such as shoe shining or street vending, often newspapers, tourist trinkets or loose cigarettes,

[1]http://www.covenanthouse.org/about-homeless-charity

in order to survive. Some ultimately die on the street or in their hiding places as victims of disease, drug abuse, inter-gang rivalry and violence or malnutrition. Their life expectancy is often very low, even after they have left the street. They lack even the most basic education, although they may have started school and attended for a few years, or any kind of training for future occupations. There have been many very good studies of all kinds of street children; there has also been a plethora of bad ones.

Where the bad studies, reports and journalism use street children to their own end is intended to make the phenomenon into a vehicle for amazement and disbelief that there are so many children living that way today or, alternatively, to go to the worst extreme to warn the world of the scourge of dangerous beggars, muggers and killers. One of the means of making most impact is by using numbers. The principle used is 'the larger the number, the greater the impact'. A good example of that is the enormous variance in estimates for Brazil.

One Brazilian government estimate shows that the number of children and adolescents in 2012 sleeping and working on the streets was approximately 23,973. The estimate was based on figures returned by a national census ordered by the *Human Rights Secretariat of the Presidency* (*SDH*) and the *Institute for Sustainable Development* (*Idesp*).[2] Another government statistic gives an estimate of around 200,000.[3] In 2005, a NGO, *Children of Bahia*, gave an estimate of between 200,000 and 8 million.[4] Roslyn Mickelson (2000) gave a further estimate of five million. Inciardi and Surratt (1997: 1) say that: 'Estimates of their numbers in Brazil have ranged from 7 to 17 million, but more informed assessments suggest that between 7 and 8 million children, ages 5 to 18, live and/or work on the streets of urban Brazil'. As too often the case, they do not give the source of those 'informed assessments'. According to an unnamed source, in 1994, Lewis Aptekar cited an estimate of 30 million mentioned by Sanders (1987). Another NGO, *Brazilian Street Children*, claimed in 2010 that 17 million children aged 5–18 years live on the streets of two cities, São Paulo and Rio de Janeiro, which would make a projection of the actual statistic for Brazil phenomenal.[5] In 2013, the population of São Paulo was 10,021,295 and Rio de Janeiro 6,023,699. In other words, the NGO's figures are so grossly representative that there would be more street children than the entire population of the two cities combined. Whilst probably a misuse of statistics by people who lack the skills to use them and having chosen words wrongly, the national projection has been assigned erroneously to the two biggest urban centres in Brazil.

[2] 'Street Children in Brazil', Consortium for Street Children, 2012: http://www.streetchildren.org.uk/_uploads/publications/Street_Children_in_Brazil_-_Briefing_to_IPU_2012.pdf

[3] http://www.brazil-factoid.com/crisis-of-street-children-in-brazil.html

[4] http://www.childrenofbahia.com/childpoverty.html

[5] http://brazilianstreetchidren.webs.com/

The present population of Brazil is 194 million, of whom 60.13 million are aged 0–18 years. The range of proportions of street children as a portion of their entire peer age group would vary between 0.04 % (±24,000), 11.6 % (±7 million) and 28.6 % (±17 million) to just under 50 % (±30 million). More realistically, there is somewhere between 0.33 % (±200,000) and 13.3 % (±8 million), probably towards the lower rather than higher end would be approaching any kind of accuracy. As Hecht (1998: 99) draws attention to whenever numbers are cited in a book or article, it is often using, or is based on, somebody else's estimates, and all too often, there is simply no reference in order to find any kind of substantiation for the claimed numbers.

It is this grossly distorted use of 'guesstimates' rather than substantiated estimates or relatively useful census and survey data that has allowed street children to be 'hijacked' for sensationalist journalism, for shock tactic NGO propaganda and for impressive client figures for fundraising efforts. During the 1980s particularly, UNICEF was saying there were 40 to 50 million street children in Latin America alone (Ortiz and Poertner 1992). These guesstimates would have meant that more than 45 % of all Latin America's children were street children (Ennew 1986: 10–11). Worldwide numbers of street children are similarly disparate. In 1989, UNICEF estimated that 100 million children were growing up on urban streets worldwide (UNICEF 2002: 37). Fourteen years later, UNICEF again reported: 'The latest estimates put the numbers of these children as high as 100 million'. More recently, UNICEF has stated: 'The exact number of street children is impossible to quantify, but the figure almost certainly runs into tens of millions across the world. It is likely that the numbers are increasing' (UNICEF 2005: 40–41; Thomas de Benítez, 2007: 64). The 100 million estimated number is still frequently cited, but there is no evidence to support it (see Ennew and Milne 1989: 54–59; Hecht 1998: 99). Sarah Thomas de Benítez of the *Consortium for Street Children* described estimates ranging from 30 to 170 million street children worldwide. On the other hand, she explained that it is difficult to keep track of them, especially given that they are not included in censuses and surveys. Numbers are essentially estimates. It is always contentious whether or not numbers of street children are increasing worldwide or merely that awareness of young people living on street has grown (Thomas de Benítez 2007: 64).

It is thus that one can refer to the street children topic as having been hijacked. It has clearly served as a means to an end, at international and local levels, by UN agencies and NGOs and was mainly able to do so because nobody can exactly refute those numbers. However, there are other aspects of the lives of street children that add 'gloss' to their image and that have historically allowed the choice of whether one considers them a scourge or a pitiable figure.

In *The Next Generation*, one section of Part One goes under the heading 'Separation from Parents: The Urchin Rascal' (Ennew and Milne 1989: 54–59). It begins by looking at the romanticism and sentimentality so often attached to them: 'Some writers give children of the street, who live outside family and state control on the urban streets of the world, the free, the bandit status of modern Robin

Hoods' (*op.cit.*: 54). Like Robin Hood, they are dangerous but alluring, perhaps even seductive or sexy. Working children and those living in unattractive poverty of economically depressed rural and urban areas do not present this element of adventure and excitement.

It is notable that it tends to be exceptional but also repeatable situations such as street children living in sewers, the *Candelária Massacre*-type events, systematic murders and semi-political marches that make news. Eight street children and youths aged between 11 and 20 were killed and several others wounded when a group of policemen shot at a group of about 70 street children as they slept beside the Candelária church in Rio de Janeiro in 1993 (McQueen 1998). One of the children who survived the Candelária attack was shot several other times before he could testify against the military policemen who eventually went on trial. Many people in Brazil demanded the prosecution of those who shot the Candelária children. Only two were ever prosecuted (See also Chap. 7 for more detail).

That event brought with it outrage. Then it showed street children as innocent victims of the most violent injustice. Normally, they are seen as young criminals, outside of society. Brazil has often provided the setting for the image of street children as both victims and illustrious characters (for instance, see Scheper-Hughes and Fishel Sargent 1998: 352–388). They are often extraordinarily adapted into fiction, often coming out like a latter-day Huckleberry Finn who first appeared in *The Adventures of Tom Sawyer* in 1876 (Twain 2011).

Huckleberry 'Huck' Finn is the son of the town's itinerant drinker, 'Pap' Finn. Huck sleeps on doorsteps when the weather is good and in empty barrels during storms and essentially lives off of whatever he is given. He lives the life of an impoverished drifter. Twain used him as a metaphor for the stereotypical 'juvenile pariah of the village' (Twain 2011: 41) and described him as 'idle, and lawless, and vulgar, and bad' (*op.cit.*), although it is these the children in the village admire whilst their mothers 'cordially hated and dreaded' (*op.cit.*) Huck. He is a good example of an unfortunate innocent who is always able to determine the right thing to do despite the conventional moral philosophy and narrow-minded attitudes of the southern American states at the time. A good example is his decision to help his Afro-American friend Jim escape from slavery, although he believes he will probably be damned for doing it. Huck wears castoff grown men's clothes which he in all probability received as gifts. Twain described him as 'he was fluttering with rags', hat torn and broken, whilst his trousers are supported with a single suspender. He lives a carefree life free of societal norms or conventions; he steals chickens and watermelons and 'borrows' boats and cigars. He has had almost no education. His 'salvation' comes towards the end of *The Adventures of Tom Sawyer* when he is adopted by Widow Douglas, who then sends him to school because he saved her life. Many street children are portrayed comparably.

A modern-day Huck Finn image can be seen in the main character of the Brazilian film *Pixote: A Lei do Mais Fraco* (Pixote: The Law of the Weakest) (Pixote means 'small boy') which is directed by Hector Babenco in 1981 and based on the 1977 book *A Infância dos Mortos* (*The Childhood of the Dead Ones*) by

José Louzeiro. It is a story about the lives of marginalised children on the street and in detention. The film was made at the end of military dictatorship showing children abandoned by 'economic miracle' of the 1970s. For many years following the military dictatorship of 1964 until1985, the situation became worse (Scheper-Hughes and Hoffman 1998: 352). Thus, this storytelling of life for these children in the late 1970s becomes almost part of history rather than fiction. Pixote is a young boy who is involved in mugging and drug trafficking. When police round up a number of street children, Pixote is sent to a detention centre. There he begins to sniff glue in order to emotionally get away from the constant threat of abuse and rape. The story tells how young criminals are only pieces in the illicit, callous games prison guards and the commander play out on the children. A boy dies of abuse by guards who then frame a transgendered boy known as Lilica for the murder. His lover then dies, implicating the guards.

A short time later, Pixote, Lilica and his new lover Dito have the chance to escape. After hanging around in the city, Pixote and friends go to a club to do a drug deal. Pixote finds a showgirl who has cheated them out of some cocaine whom he stabs. The boys begin pimping for Sueli, a prostitute who is no longer young and probably ailing after a bungled abortion. The group conspires to rob her customers, but Lilica's lover Dito falls in love with Sueli and Lilica leaves them. Then their robbery plan fails when an American retaliates, who they then shoot. Pixote also unintentionally shoots and kills Dito as well. Pixote tries to gain consolation from Sueli by treating her as a mother figure. However, she rejects him. The film ends with him leaving, walking down a railway line, with the gun in his hand. He disappears in the distance, out of the camera range, thus symbolically out of the unfinished story.

Huck Finn and Pixote share the same kind of swagger: both are 'deviant' and both have mother figure saviours, although in Pixote's case, she rejects him. It is the kind of representation of marginalised children that has superseded that of the street child as the victim, the helpless impoverished casualty of the brutality of poverty, neglect and abuse.

The pathetic image is historically that of the kind of character Charles Dickens created in his works that depicted the situation of those lost even to the lower echelons of society (Ennew and Milne 1989: 55). Jo the crossing sweeper from *Bleak House* (1853) portrays such a dismally displaced character:

> Jo sweeps his crossing all day long, unconscious of the link, if any link there be. He sums up his mental condition when asked a question by replying that he "don't know nothink." He knows that it's hard to keep the mud off the crossing in dirty weather, and harder still to live by doing it. Nobody taught him even that much; he found it out.
>
> Jo lives—that is to say, Jo has not yet died—in a ruinous place known to the like of him by the name of Tom-all-Alone's. It is a black, dilapidated street, avoided by all decent people, where the crazy houses were seized upon, when their decay was far advanced, by some bold vagrants who after establishing their own possession took to letting them out in lodgings. Now, these tumbling tenements contain, by night, a swarm of misery. As on the ruined human wretch vermin parasites appear, so these ruined shelters have bred a crowd of foul existence that crawls in and out of gaps in walls and boards; and coils itself to sleep, in maggot numbers, where the rain drips in; and comes and goes, fetching and carrying fever

> and sowing more evil in its every footprint than Lord Coodle, and Sir Thomas Doodle, and the Duke of Foodle, and all the fine gentlemen in office, down to Zoodle, shall set right in five hundred years—though born expressly to do it. (Dickens 1985: 160)

Jo is wretched and pitiable, a child made entirely compliant to his circumstances but has no other part in the affairs of the world. He has none of the negative connotations associated to a Huck or Pixote; he is the street child of the NGO fundraising booklet whose situation requires intervention before detention. Yet there is another Dickensian character, Jack Dawkins, the Artful Dodger in Oliver Twist (1838), who is neither fish nor fowl, perhaps more the child who can go either way but is at least pure of heart in his idiosyncratic way:

> He was a snub-nosed, flat-browed, common-faced boy enough; and as dirty a juvenile as one would wish to see; but he had about him all the airs and manners of a man. He was short of his age: with rather bow-legs, and little, sharp, ugly eyes. His hat was stuck on the top of his head so lightly, that it threatened to fall off every moment—and would have done so, very often, if the wearer had not had a knack of every now and then giving his head a sudden twitch, which brought it back to its old place again. He wore a man's coat, which reached nearly to his heels. He had turned the cuffs back, half-way up his arm, to get his hands out of the sleeves: apparently with the ultimate view of thrusting them into the pockets of his corduroy trousers; for there he kept them. He was, altogether, as roystering and swaggering a young gentleman as ever stood four feet six, or something less, in the bluchers. (Dickens 2003: 59)

There is some of the Huckleberry Finn character written by Twain four decades later in the Dodger, but none of the slightly more malicious streak; Jack Dawkins is more of a trickster, someone living on his wits who does not intend to draw too much adult attention to himself. Although he is a pickpocket, he is not a callous character. Eventually, he is caught in possession of a stolen silver snuff box, and it is left open for the reader to understand that he is sent to a penal colony in Australia, although only that is hinted in the novel when the judge says: 'Transportation for life. Take him away.' (Dickens 2003: 254). He considers himself a 'victim of society' when he shouts to the jailer 'I'm an Englishman, ain't I?' and asks 'Where are my privileges?' (*op.cit.*). It even seems unjust that this good-hearted, even dependable youth is treated so harshly. Again, the line between good and bad becomes blurred, as so often is the ambiguousness of the 'typical' street child's character. Whilst his outcome is not as brutal as that of the Candelária children, it appears that when retribution is served on street children, it is done so as if they have lost their childhood; thus, severity and sometimes outright brutality are justifiable in the interests of seeing justice done.

In 2007, the *European Observatory on Homelessness* produced a report on child homelessness in Europe. How they define that emphasises the difference between the developing and developed world:

> There are very few international or European comparisons on child homelessness which provide any clear definition. FEANTSA carried out research on youth homelessness in Europe in 1998, but this analysis rather covered young people under the age of 30 without a specific focus on children. There are a number of existing international terms which refer to children such as "unaccompanied minors", "separated children", "street children", but these are rather used in relation to children seeking asylum or children living in developing

> countries, and not specifically in relation to children experiencing homelessness in the more economically advanced countries of the EU. (FEANTSA 2007: 8)

They took it further to make that more explicit:

> It is especially important to distinguish between homeless children and the concept of street children since the term "street children" is used in very different ways, most commonly to describe children in developing countries who live on the street permanently and earn their living from working on the street (UNESCO, European Foundation of Street Children Worldwide). In Europe, the term is used for children spending time on the streets with different levels of connection with their family (connected, partially-disconnected, and disconnected). (*op. cit.*)

The definitions outline the differences of the approach that set apart the North and South although they possibly lack only the sensationalism of Candelária-type incidents to make them more visible generally, since those would raise consciousness of the importance of the 'at-risk' situation of those young people. There are also very few studies that attempt to compare the two spheres, and when they do, they have tended to be weighted towards the developing world (for instance, Williams 1981). If the USA's two million young people spending at least some time homeless each year (Colby 2011) is used to show that it is not because of lower numbers, then the question remains open why this is the case. One may be led to assume that it is political expediency that, on the one hand, saves the face of nations considered 'rich' and, on the other, neither morally nor socio-politically forces them to spend public money on attempting to resolve the 'problem'. Thus, the illustrious characters created by Dickens or Twain can be considered part of the past rather than the present, still having them in the midst of what are thought of as generally affluent societies. Nonetheless, a Huck Finn-type character is ever present as one of the children who spend time on the streets with a limited amount of connection with at least one family member. The Artful Dodger represents the pathetic child who has nobody but his pride, something popular images of street children in the developing world tend to refute, but is less explicitly said when looking at the homeless children and youth of the North.

As already said at the beginning of this chapter, there are perspectives that have been expressed as developing during the international discussion during the decade of drafting the CRC that is phrased to draw together the many cultural perspectives. Article 20 describes a child's need for protection when the alternatives to his or her biological parents are in the child's best interest in which culture is taken into account:

1. A child temporarily or permanently deprived of his or her family environment, or in whose own best interests cannot be allowed to remain in that environment, shall be entitled to special protection and assistance provided by the state.
2. State parties shall in accordance with their national laws ensure alternative care for such a child.
3. Such care could include, inter alia, foster placement, *kafalah* of Islamic law, adoption or if necessary placement in suitable institutions for the care of children.

> When considering solutions, due regard shall be paid to the desirability of continuity in a child's upbringing and to the child's ethnic, religious, cultural and linguistic background.

In other, simpler words, a child who cannot be looked after by their own family has a right to special care and must accordingly be looked after properly. That applies very much to children separated from families who are on the streets of any country. That must be done by people who respect their ethnicity, religion, culture and language, thus in a culturally and religiously sensitive manner. In the North where cultural and religious detail is far more blurred than in the South, in fact placement should be easier. In practice, it appears not to be since in the North the 'problem' is not really visible enough to attract attention and the kind of action required, whereas in the South the numbers are so great and resources so scarce that it is at the very least difficult to implement.

Thus said, Article 20 is used here as an illustration of where there appears to be no real understanding of what it says, part three particularly, when bearing in mind the intent that it is a child's right to have whichever parts of this article are relevant to him or her is not only respected but also protected. In other words, all children have the right to their own sociocultural environment. Thus, it is in the hands of those who make and uphold laws to ensure that all children in their country, as a state party to the CRC, enjoy that right. Irrespective of whether they are 'street' or 'homeless' children, what state parties have committed themselves to is not being implemented.

Another example of where Article 20 clearly does not work as intended is found in human trafficking which is considered to be one of the fastest-growing criminal industries. Many of the people trafficked are children. Whereas poverty and lack of educational and economic opportunities may force people to voluntarily migrate in search of work, it also creates the situation in which they can be exploited (Weitzer 2007: 447–75; Berger 2012: 523–70). Some of those are street and homeless children and youth. Globalisation has opened borders to a greater trade in commodities and capital, with which labour migration has also increased. Less well-off countries are generally less able to offer opportunities for people to earn adequate living wages. The economic impact of globalisation has forced people to consciously decide to migrate and has made them vulnerable to trafficking. Traffickers offer assistance in reaching countries where good incomes will be assured; instead, those individuals become the property of the people who buy them. In other words, they become slaves. Large numbers of trafficked persons are children. Their parents or carers may be persuaded to 'sell' them so that they can be taken to a country where they will have a better life or they may be induced or even kidnapped by traffickers. Runaways and throwaways are highly vulnerable to becoming victims of enticements of finding a 'better life' in the sex industry, by selling drugs or by being lured by traffickers (Colby 2011). Trafficking has become a major concern globally, with very open revulsion shown for children bought and sold in almost every country in the world.

Some of the more fortunate children are trafficked for adoption. According to UNICEF in 2012, tens of thousands of babies, toddlers and young children are also adopted across international borders every year. The largest number goes to the USA and Western Europe. Numbers began to decline after 2004; however, according to UNICEF in 2009, which was the last year for which reliable figures were available, 24,839 children were taken from their home countries to the top five adopting countries. The numerous media reports would suggest those numbers are considerably higher. They also spell out more explicitly than UNICEF the fact that those children are sold for adoption. With the exception of the USA, the receiving countries are all state party to the CRC and will mostly be members of the *Hague Adoption Convention* of 1993[6] and the *Hague Convention* of 1996.[7] At present, there are 93 contracting parties to the former and 41 to the latter. The Russian Federation has signed the 1993 convention but has yet to ratify or succeed; Italy and the USA have signed the 1996 convention but have also neither ratified or succeeded to either.[8] There are other nonmembers who have either only signed or have ratified or succeeded in both cases.[9] The countries in which children are sold will be in all cases, whether for adoption or other purposes, state party to the CRC. Where adoptions are sanctioned and formalised despite the adoptees having been sold to their future parents, this is in spite of the commitment those countries have made.

Whilst precise data are difficult to confirm and are often contradictory, the ILO (2005: 6) reported that there were at least 600,000 children involved in forced begging (Craig, 2010: 29). That problem might well be far more prevalent. In 2012, ILO reported that 'The trafficking of children appears to be increasing. Of the detected victims whose age profile was known and reported in the period 2007–2010, some 27 % were children' (ILO 2012: 10). In China, the Ministry of Civil Affairs reported that up to 1.5 million children had been forced into begging (Pumin 2011: 18–19). The probably most reliable but not necessarily the most precise statistic is that provided by the ILO who estimated that at least 1.2 million children are being trafficked each year which includes both cross-border and internal trafficking (ILO 2002: 10). There are more recent figures from the *UN Office on Drugs and Crime* reports (UNODC 2009, 2012); the percentage of child victims rose over a period of 3 years from 20 to 27 %. The gender and age profile of victims identified worldwide showed that 59 % were women, 14 % men, 17 % girls and 10 % boys. From every three child victims, two were shown to be girls and one a boy. A US government source quoted by UNODC stated that an estimated 600,000 to 800,000 men, women and children are bought and sold across international borders each year to be exploited for either some kind of forced labour or commercial sex.

[6] www.hcch.net/index_en.php?act=conventions.text&cid=69

[7] www.hcch.net/index_en.php?act=conventions.text&cid=70

[8] This is as of the beginning of September 2014.

[9] The *Hague Conference on Private International Law* currently has 77 members: 76 states and the European Union. There is a difference between 'members' and 'parties' (or nonmembers) who sign, ratify, accede or succeed to its conventions.

With internal trafficking victims added to estimates, the number of victims each year comes to an estimated two to four million, whereby 50 % of the victims are estimated to be children. The range of average ages of victims is said to be 11 to 14 years. Supporting statements explain that estimates now show that human trafficking has overtaken the illegal sale of weapons and will almost certainly exceed the sale of drugs over the next few years.

The rationale for this is shown in that children used as drug mules are normally used once and are thereafter gone, whilst victims of child trafficking can be used and abused time and time again. Thus, UNICEF is able to estimate that there are some two million children who have been forced into prostitution in the global commercial sex trade (UNICEF 2012). The average range of life spans of people forced into prostitution is three to seven years, whereby they may be found dead after a violent attack or suffer extreme abuse, starvation, accidental or intentional drug overdoses or means of committing suicide, HIV/AIDS and other STDs.

The UN *Global Initiative to Fight Human Trafficking* (*UN.GIFT*) was created to promote the worldwide fight against human trafficking using existing internationally agreed and adopted UN agreements and conventions. It was launched in March 2007 by UNODC and is managed in cooperation with the ILO, the *International Organisation for Migration* (IOM), UNICEF, the *Office of the High Commissioner for Human Rights* (OHCHR) and the *Organisation for Security and Co-operation in Europe* (OSCE). By October 2013, the *Protocol to Prevent, Suppress and Punish Trafficking in Persons especially Women and Children*, which supplements the *UN Convention against Transnational Organised Crime* and is overseen by UN.GIFT, had been ratified by 158 states. Of the conventions taken into account by the Protocol, the CRC is naturally included. However, much effort is being put into stopping all trafficking but particularly focussing on children as the most vulnerable victims; a number of questions appear not to be asked. Several of them are very clearly related to the sale of children, mainly by parents, other relatives or carers or those who thereafter become their masters or owners. Subsequent to a sale, when the ensuing relationship with the child is in effect a non-exploitative one rather than for any kind of servitude, the usual intention of the sale is to make the child available for adoption. Many of these children are sold through child laundering rings.

The child laundering rings are often large, international organisations that consist of numerous people in different positions of power and rank whose main objective is to benefit from large profits to be made as part of the black market that exists for overseas adoption. There is usually a complicated hierarchy within those organisations which may include government representatives or employees, orphanages some children are purchased from, go-betweens, the birth families or carers and the eventual adoptive families. People operating these international child laundering businesses are said to make anything between $2,000 and $20,000 for each adoption. In order to run such a business, it is very useful for the people directly involved to have language and social skills that enable them to work closely with western adoption agencies, particularly officials such as those in passport offices and parents and carers in countries of origin. Go-betweens are essential for finding and purchasing children; thus, their main role is particularly to find and determine which particularly poor families may be willing to hand over their children because of sheer necessity (Smolin 2005: 115–59). The people concerned in engaging and running the adoption ring are often local middle or upper class people who have a particularly negative view of poorer members of their society. It is therefore very easy for the people recruiting these intermediaries and the go-betweens themselves to rationalise taking these children away from their biological families and cultures on the basis of a belief that they will be better looked after in the wealthier countries.

Adoptions are also a front for other uses of children. In China, for example, considerable numbers of children are thought to be bought and sold. A 2007 book tells how low-income families and unmarried mothers sell babies, usually girls, through the underground market in China. Some of the sales are for adoption by families who want children whereas others are to 'adoptive parents' who want servants or prospective brides for their sons (Raymond 2007: 246–7, citing a report in *China Daily*). It has also been argued that child laundering in China is the outcome of the one-child policy that brought about a surplus number of children who could be adopted. Demand for Chinese children has increased; therewith, sales of children and also kidnapping have grown in order to meet the demand as well as make an easy profit (Custer 2011). This point of view has been criticised since the organisation of international adoptions has created a system whereby poor families have been abused in order to satisfy Western demand for children for adoption. Furthermore, ethnocentric rationalisation for adoptions put forth the argument that these children have better lives when connection with their biological family is severed. This is also very often irrespective of how the adoption was made possible. However, there are others who believe that the family should be kept together and protected at all costs (see, for instance, Smith-Gary 2009). In their 2011 figures on international adoption, the US Department of State reported that between 1999 and 2011, there had been 66,630 adoptions of Chinese children. That is to say, known adoptions, those sold through laundering rings, are generally outside of any official figure unless a child, a number of children or the laundering ring itself is found. Of course, China is only one of the considerable number of countries of origin. Similar accounts from other countries can be described; however, whilst often smaller in numbers, the basic message is precisely the same.

Without considering laundering for adoption, the details of trafficking alone make dismal reading. In UNODC's *Global Report on Trafficking in Persons* (2012), sexual exploitation was described as undoubtedly the most commonly recognised outcome of human trafficking (79 % in a sample of 52 countries) followed by forced labour (18 %). Whilst the largest number of trafficked persons was women, 17 % were girls and 10 % were boys (*op cit*, 2012: 10). One million two hundred thousand children were estimated to have been trafficked worldwide in 2000 (ILO: 2002: 25); there have been no comparable estimates since, but it has been said trafficking of children is still increasing. 50 % of international victims are estimated to be minors (US Department of State 2007: 8); thus, the proportion of children in national trafficking is far lower. According to UNICEF in 2010 (US Department of State

2010: 12), in the international commercial sex trade alone, two million children were being exploited. There may of course be some statistical biases that distort these estimates, but by all standards, they are quite stunning numbers. In contrast, other types of exploitation are under-reported including forced and bonded labour, domestic service, forced marriages, their organs for transplants, begging and civil and military conflicts.

Naturally, where children are trafficked for any exploitative purpose, their placement in an appropriate social environment is most certainly the last consideration the traffickers think of. Where they are taken from their 'homes' for adoption, it is far easier to put Article 20 into context. It appears that at present, children and adoptive parents are encouraged to carefully consider and understand the origins of children's birth countries. That is to say, the situation of birth parents and their cultures are more or less expected to be examined in depth. That brings with it a number of difficult questions. How do adoptive parents deal with a bi- or even multiracial family when they are of one racial origin and the child or children from another? Of course, the new parents may be of mixed race themselves, so does the addition of other ethnicity work? Is a child's well-being harmed by keeping them 'ignorant' of their birth origin? Conversely, does encouraging and agreeing to foreign adoptees finding out about their birth culture do damage to them in their adoptive world? These are among many questions being asked by experts in cultural diversity such as anthropologists who have recently begun to look at international adoptions. Some have only recently begun to study the outcome of breaking kinship ties. How, they are asking, does that affect their sense of belonging, cultural and national identity? Pauline Turner Strong contributed a chapter to a book edited by Sarah Franklin and Susan McKinnon, *Relative Values: Reconfiguring Kinship Studies*, in which she says: 'Adoption across political and cultural borders may simultaneously be an act of violence and an act of love, an excruciating rupture and a generous incorporation, an appropriation of valued resources and a constitution of personal ties' (Franklin and McKinnon 2001: 471).

Furthermore, lawyer Elizabeth Bartholet (1996: 264) says, very much in line with Article 20 and in differently chosen words, that:

> Adoption regulation is premised on an understanding that adults and adult communities have rights in children, and that children 'belong' either to their birth parents or to their racial or religious or ethnic or national communities. Birth parents are given powerful, constitutionally protected fights to hold onto their children. And children are regularly talked of as 'precious resources' belonging to their racial group, ethnic community, or country of origin.

Thus said, where does Article 20 CRC stand in this set of questions? Here, one must bear in mind that the emphasis is on trafficking and laundering with a particular focus on adoption, although other outcomes of the illegal trade in children must be similarly borne in mind since 'legitimate' adoption is also implicated to some extent. Part three includes 'due regard shall be paid to the desirability of continuity in a child's upbringing and to the child's ethnic, religious, cultural and linguistic background'. In the case of the illegal movement of children from one country to another, the very last thing that would be on the minds of the people buying and selling them would be placing them appropriately because it is their right to any or all of those things.

Commercial sexual exploitation as an outcome of the sale of children can never be reconciled with any ethnic, cultural or belief background, yet they are bought and sold for sex with adults. Child prostitution is commercial sex offered by persons of any age under majority. In most countries, prostitution of or by a person under 18 years old is illegal, even when he or she is older than the legal age of consent. Prostitution of children is often the outcome of trafficking; they are frequently kidnapped or deceived into working in the sex trade. Very few are able to maintain any kind of contact with their families, and relatively few are forced to prostitute themselves for parents or legal carers. After their 'usefulness', they are often left with no choice but to turn to 'survival sex' in order to obtain basic essentials such as food and shelter. Prostitution of children is also often associated with child pornography, and there are evident overlaps between the two. Some people travel abroad to seek out 'exotic' children for sex since young boys and girls are often more easily available for paedophiles who would be at higher risk in their home countries. Estimates suggest that there could be up to ten million children involved in prostitution worldwide (Willis and Levy 2002). The problem is most serious in parts of South America and Southeast Asia, but it exists globally (Lim 1998: 170–71), thus in developed as well as developing countries.

Children who were taken to serve in armed forces have been given less but nevertheless close scrutiny particularly since there was more to it than children as combatants. With the 'arrival' of the CRC in 1989 there was a considerable surge in concern about children in situations of armed conflict, particularly those who became fugitives and refugees thus displaced persons who had often lost homes and families but also their district, region or country of birth. As already seen in Chap. 3, children had gained kudos as participants and victims in South Africa, the West Bank *intifada* and wars in Sierra Leone, Lebanon and elsewhere. When positive action began to be examined, the whole issue (i.e. Boyden) was considered; gradually, it began to focus on child soldiers. In terms of presentation, a swaggering 10-year-old Sierra Leonean with a heavy machine gun over his shoulder, rifle in his hand and a handgun in a holster bearing the rank colonel or general had a certain appeal. Victims were those who were either dead, invalids or in some way or another physically or mentally disfigured, therefore unattractive to the public eye. Until the late twentieth century, it had been easiest to focus narrowly on 'heroic' child soldiers for their part in conflict for them to have full public approval. Then attitudes changed within a very short span of time so that children were then considered only to be victims of those conflicts. The image of the young hero was displaced by a more negative view. Within a short time, concerns were also being expressed by adults living and working in war zones and post-conflict societies. One of the major concerns was whether children's moral development is gravely disturbed by their participation in armed conflict. The accepted view was that young ex-combatants suffered a moral degeneration as a consequence of what they had seen and done (Boyden 2003).

However, new insights into child participants in civil and international wars began to show other aspects of forced service particularly. There were girls and some boys who have been used for sex by fighting men and non-combatant auxiliaries, sometimes referred to as 'sex slaves'. There were widespread physical and mental abuse and rape, others were doing backbreaking work as porters carrying arms, munitions and supplies, whereas others were forced to work as cooks, messengers or spies. Some children were compelled to hurt or kill family members since that would break ties with communities who would no longer wish to have dishonoured people return, children displaced by the conflict and young ex-combatants who were trying to find some kind of normality after the war had ended. It was not only because wars lead to massive numbers of deaths but also widespread dislocation, destruction, devastating fear and trauma along with economic, cultural and social desolation. Social ties are damaged and irretrievably broken, household survival is put at risk and families lose the ability to care for their most defenceless and vulnerable members. Each year, war kills, physically and mentally hurts and harms numerous young people, demoralises many thousands of others and leaves many more without economic, educational, health and social opportunities that are deemed indispensable for children's successful development and well-being. Nonetheless, notwithstanding abundant evidence of a great deal of suffering and pain, there is a view that children are not simply the passive victims of conflict but 'play the game'. They can connect, sometimes enthusiastically, with the circumstances war creates, thereby challenging the conventional viewpoint that has come to rely far more significantly on medically constructed notions of 'victims' and 'traumatisation' (for instance, see Boyden and de Berry 2005) than on the actual testimony of child participants in conflicts, some of whom are indeed physically, mentally or morally damaged. Others show great resilience and are neither victims not traumatised; in fact, some of them have clearly gained from the experience. However, adults defining what happens to children have consigned the child heroes of the First World War and earlier to history along with young political activists and other situations in which many children are indeed damaged but others do come out stronger.

Exceptions are always inevitably going to be found, particularly among children and youth who are orphaned and separated from all contact with family and community and were kidnapped, bought or simply given away by carers to serve in military forces. They have thus become and remain to all intents and purposes the property of those who took or bought them and most certainly those who have been forced to injure or kill their own family members or friends in order to have their ties with their homes and communities broken once and for all often fall outside the remit of the CRC. For those children, the objectives of Article 20 are virtually impossible to fulfil unless fostering or adoption is an option they can accept. To compel or misleadingly entice them into any kind of alternative care would neither be in the spirit of the CRC nor in the interests of children who are highly likely to have little or no remaining faith in adults. To be inclusive, simply listening to their 'voices' or allowing them to 'participate' in order to reach decisions on how they can be helped means not rhetorical inclusion but actively examining their situation with them and allowing them to make ultimate decisions. To choose for them is to forget the aims and intentions of the CRC and other instruments that are for children and not only for those who believe they are working in the best interests of children because they know best. Trafficked children who are offered for adoption where receiving nations sanction their placement and allow statutory processes to make them legitimate are at high risk of traumatisation and negative long-term consequences brought about by those countries naively assuming they are acting in their best interests.

War-affected and street children on the whole are shown to the world in a particular way that portrays them as victims, almost without a will of their own that would allow them any means of choosing and reaching their own destiny in life. In fact what is far too often ignored is that those children have often had no choice other than take control of their lives in order to survive and based on their experience may be more than able to find their own way in life. However, conventional wisdom is that they all need aid and that will come exclusively from adults who intercede in their lives. International organisations working with those children may be quite correct in many cases, but the distinction between those who are and remain vulnerable who would benefit from intervention and others who have gained a great deal of strength and experience from hardship is not found in their fundraising advertisements, reports or other public information. Thus, rather than allowing leeway for resilient children and youth, they draw no distinctions. There is no benefit in having heroes, real-life Huckleberry Finns and Artful Dodgers obstruct rather than promote their work.

It is again an agenda hijacked in order to achieve maximum effect rather than appear to work for only those who genuinely need them.

References

Aptekar, L. (1994). Street children in the developing world: A review of their condition. *Cross-Cultural Research, 28*(3), 195–224.

Bartholet, E. (1996). What's wrong with adoption law? *The International Journal of Children's Rights, 4*, 263–272.

Berger, S. (2012). No end in sight: Why the 'End Demand' movement is the wrong focus for efforts to eliminate human trafficking. *Harvard Journal of Law and Gender, 35*, 523–70.

Boyden, J. (2003). The moral development of child soldiers: What do adults have to fear? *Peace and Conflict: Journal of Peace Psychology, 9*(4), 343–62.

Boyden, J., & de Berry, J. (Eds.). (2005). *Children and youth on the front line: Ethnography, armed conflict and displacement*. New York/Oxford: Berghahn.

Colby, I. (2011). Runaway and throwaway youth: Time for policy changes and public responsibility. *Journal of Applied Research on Children: Informing Policy for Children at Risk* 2/1/4.

Custer, C. (2011, October 10). China's missing children. *Foreign Policy Magazine*. http://www.foreignpolicy.com/articles/2011/10/06/china_missing_children

Dickens, C. (1985). *Bleak house* (1853). New York: Bantam Classics.

Dickens, C. (2003). *Oliver Twist, or, The Parish Boy's progress* (1838). London: Penguin Classics.

Ennew, J. (1986). Children of the streets. *New Internationalist., 164*, 10–11.

Ennew, J., & Milne, B. (1989). *The next generation: Lives of third world children*. London/Philadelphia: Zed Books/New Society Publishers.

FEANTSA. (2007). *European research study into homelessness and employment. Final report for Off the Streets and Into Work prepared by the Centre for Economic & Social Inclusion.* Fédération Européenne des Associations Nationales Travaillant avec les Sans-Abri.

Franklin, S., & McKinnon, S. (Eds.). (2001). *Relative values: Reconfiguring kinship studies.* Durham/London: Duke University Press.

Hecht, T. (1998). *At home in the street: Street children of Northeast Brazil.* Cambridge: Cambridge University Press.

Inciardi, J. A, & Hilary, L. S. (1997). *Children in the streets of Brazil: Drug use, crime, violence, and HIV risks.* Seminar paper. Newark, DE: University of Delaware. http://www.udel.edu/butzin/articles/child.html

ILO. (2002). *Every child counts: New global estimates on child labour.* Geneva: International Programme on the Elimination of Child Labour and Statistical Information and Monitoring Programme on Child Labour.

ILO. (2012). *ILO global estimate of forced labour: Results and methodology.* Geneva: International Labour Organisation.

Lim, L. L. (1998). *The sex sector: The economic and social bases of prostitution in Southeast Asia.* Geneva: ILO.

Louzeiro, J. (1977). *A infância dos mortos.* Rio de Janeiro: Editora Record.

McQueen, J. (1998). *The Candelária Massacre.* Melbourne: Addison Wesley Longman.

Mickelson, R. (Ed.). (2000). *Children on the streets of the Americas: Globalization, homelessness and education in the United States, Brazil and Cuba.* New York: Routledge.

Ortiz, S., & Poertner, J. (1992). Latin American street children: Problem programmes and critique. *International Social Work, 35*, 405–13.

Pumin, Y. (2011). Saving child panhandlers. *Beijing Review, 54*(9), 18–19.

Raymond, B. B. (2007). *The baby thief: The untold story of Georgia Tann, the baby seller who corrupted adoption.* New York: Union Square Press.

Sanders, T. (1987). Brazilian street children: Who they are. *United Field Service International Report 17: Latin America.* Indianapolis, IN: United Field Service.

Scheper-Hughes, N., & Sargent, C. F. (Eds.). (1998). *Small wars: The cultural politics of childhood.* Berkeley: University of California Press.

Scheper-Hughes, N., & Hoffman, D. (1998). Brazilian Apartheid: Street kids and the struggle for urban space. In N. Scheper-Hughes & C. F. Sargent (Eds.), *Small wars: The cultural politics of childhood* (pp. 352–388). Berkeley: University of California Press.

Smith-Gary, L. (2009). International adoptions fuel 'Family Planning' kidnappings. *Equal Writes.* Princeton: Princeton University.

Smolin, D. (2005). *Child laundering: How the intercountry adoption system legitimizes and incentivizes the practices of buying, trafficking, kidnapping, and stealing children* (Working Paper 749). Berkeley Electronic Press Legal Series.

Thomas de Benítez, S. (2007). *State of the world's street children: Violence.* London: Consortium for Street Children.

Twain, M. (2011). *The adventures of Tom Sawyer (1876).* Glasgow: Collins Classics.

UNICEF. (2002). *State of the world's children 2003.* New York: United Nations Children's Fund.

UNICEF. (2005). *State of the world's children 2006: Excluded and invisible.* New York: United Nations Children's Fund.

UNICEF. (2012). *As strikes grip Nepal, children demonstrate against efforts to close schools.* New York: United Nations Children's Fund. http://www.unicef.org/infobycountry/nepal_62513.html.

UNODC. (2009). *Global report on trafficking in persons.* Vienna: United Nations Office on Drugs and Crime.

UNODC. (2012). *Global report on trafficking in persons.* Vienna: United Nations Office on Drugs and Crime.

United States Department of State. (2007). *Trafficking in persons report* (7th ed.). Washington, DC: U.S. Department of State.

United States Department of State. (2010). *Trafficking in persons report* (10th ed.). Washington, DC: U.S. Department of State.
Walker, N. E., Brooks, C. M., & Wrightsman, L. S. (1998). *Children's rights in the United States: In search of a national policy*. Thousand Oaks: Sage.
Weitzer, R. (2007). The social construction of sex trafficking: Ideology and institutionalization of a moral crusade. *Politics and Society, 35*, 447–75.
Williams, C. (1981). *'Street children' and education: a comparative study of European and third world approaches*. Birmingham: University of Birmingham (unpublished PhD thesis).
Willis, B. M., & Levy, B. S. (2002). *Child prostitution: Global health burden, research needs, and interventions*. Bethesda: National Institutes of Health.

Meaningless Phrases

6

When the CRC was adopted, a new language of children's rights appears to have emerged. It is generally a global phenomenon although occasionally one sees jargon from the Anglo-Saxon world implanted into other languages. What is often extraordinary is that in what is ostensibly Oxford English, more than a few Americanisms appear which is surprising given that the USA, whilst a signatory, has not ratified the CRC; thus not being a state party really does not, perhaps should not, have much influence. In fact, the US language of children's rights is often anything but what it is elsewhere in the English speaking world. In the USA it appears to be more often applied to issues related to adoption and fostering without the direct input of children than to the language of the framework of rights the CRC uses.

Whatever the case, there is a new language, at least a number of set and already well-established words and phrases that are spoken and written without forethought any longer. Of course, here they are examined in their English form, but because most of them are so well established, they have naturally been adopted more or less worldwide, sometimes using the English versions but more commonly translations. Although contextually it is the language of children's rights in this case, it is doubtful whether children would have chosen or used the phrases themselves or indeed ever considered any of the concepts attached to them. Some examples have been used already, for instance, 'eliminations' describing those who are favour of the eradication of child labour here. A little more complicated is 'developmentalism' which is either an economic theory stating a view that the best way for poorer nations to develop is through promoting a strong, mixed internal market with high tariffs on imports or developmental psychologist Lev Vygotsky's theory of development of higher cognitive functions in children, whereby reasoning emerges through participation in a social environment. Many such words were originally used by academics or appear in their work and have become mainstream, accepted language, whilst many dictionaries still omit them. There are other words in this book that are part of everyday children's issues language, which to some extent

B. Milne, *Rights of the Child*, Children's Well-Being: Indicators and Research 11,
DOI 10.1007/978-3-319-18784-6_6

have become irreplaceable. They are nonetheless jargon that confuses some people and certainly does not make the language accessible for children.

Moreover, children are an easy target for the use of sentimentality and bathos as a means of drawing sympathy to all that goes wrong for them in our world. It is therefore a magnet for slogans, key phrases and useful political rhetoric that very often tend to gloss over unsuccessful or unnecessary actions or lack of any efforts at all. This chapter examines some of them in the specific context of children's rights, although some of them do possibly apply in other situations, particularly education, health and welfare.

With the CRC and Article 12 in particular, a multitude of organisations, slogans and campaigns have used one variant or another of 'the voice of the children'. The common claim is that every child has the right to a 'voice' on issues that affect them and to therefore have their views taken seriously, although the rider is that that is according to their age and development that determine whether that voice will be heard or not. The argument for this inclusion and freedom of expression when they are heard is in the face of issues where decisions are made by adults but children have to live with the consequences of them. Thus, issues such as climate change, poverty or HIV and AIDS include their views that must then be considered by the decision-makers. It does not ensure that those views will count for very much or say that children have any share in reaching decisions. It is simply the right to have opinions. IGOs and NGOs maintain that they recognise that if they listen to young people, they can then generate more efficient, relevant and sustainable programmes and policies. It has become 'fashionable' to involve young people in programme and policy development as researchers, negotiators and trainers to help other young people make informed decisions about how to participate in issues that matter to them.

Malala Yousafzai, a 16-year-old Pakistani girl, addressed the UN on her birthday in 2013. She is an activist for education and women's rights in the Swat Valley region of her home country. In 2012 a gunman boarded the school bus she was travelling on, asked for her by name and then shot her. A bullet passed through the side of her head and lodged in her shoulder. She was in a coma for some time, eventually being sent to the UK for treatment. Despite a permanent threat to her father and her own life, she continued to campaign for girls and women's right to education (for instance, see Lederer 2013). Hence, she was invited to deliver her speech at the UN. However, it remains to be seen what the outcome of her pleas will be. However, in October 2014 she became the youngest ever winner of the Nobel Peace Prize for her work. Similarly, in the UK, Fahma Mohamed, a 17-year-old girl of Islamic Somali origin, campaigned against female genital mutilation (FGM). She had first heard about FGM when she was 13. Her campaign was directed at stopping FGM in the UK with the 'cutting season' then about to begin (for instance, see Topping 2014).

These two girls particularly but also others are having their voices heard quite rightly; however, the issues they are addressing are worthy of worldwide support. Other children with lesser causes, all or any of which may be important for children, do not share these opportunities. It would appear that an issue must be big before children's voices can be amplified enough to be listened to by people with the capacity to bring about change. Those, of course, are adults who will then pursue change which may be without further discussion with young people.

This of course leads into another catchphrase, children's *participation*. This was the main concern of Chapter 1. Participation is however also a buzzword that is vague enough to mean both everything and nothing. None of the 'participation' articles, 12 to 15, exactly say what children may or should participate in, even Article 15 when it says in Part 1 that:

> States Parties recognize the rights of the child to freedom of association and to freedom of peaceful assembly.

There is no clue to what association might be or likewise the purpose or structure of a peaceful assembly. However Part 2 provides a let-out that could very easily contain the parameters of what either is:

> No restrictions may be placed on the exercise of these rights other than those imposed in conformity with the law and which are necessary in a democratic society in the interests of national security or public safety, public order (ordre public), the protection of public health or morals or the protection of the rights and freedoms of others.

Naturally, 'conformity with the law and which are necessary in a democratic society' depend very much on what the law of the land where either is taking place allows and on whether or not that nation is democratic, theocratic, a dictatorship or any other kind of government and the cultural setting in which they may occur. Similarly, 'public health', 'morals' and 'freedoms' are entirely subjective concepts that are relative to the nation and culture within which they are defined. Thus said, whilst nations may have ratified the CRC without reservations against the participation articles, there is no way of saying what they actually promise. Article 15 simply gives an example of where some possibilities are touched on without doing any more than suggesting they are possibilities.

An almost excessive number of publications have appeared on the topic 'participation'. For the most part they rely heavily on Article 12 CRC to support what are often prescriptive, narrow interpretations of the article. Some are repetitive of the author's previous work, and some also appear not to have advanced very far over quarter of a century. The use of 'Hart's ladder' (1992:9) has been almost incessant, at times giving the impression that authors have not looked beyond the simplest, commonest denominators (see van Beers et al. 2006). Other people have written in terms of their expectations without saying how participation should be handled, taught, trained, researched or practised. They are optimistic but seldom visionary. Where there is great vision, for instance, people who have worked with working children's movements for many years, their work is often shunned, partly because of the association with child labour that the majority of other authors and those who would gain from the experience of those on the ground believe should be eliminated.

There are articles, books, reports and manuals that describe participation including the theory of what it is and how it is done (for instance, Flekkøy and Kaufman 1997; Hart 1992 and 1997; Lansdown 1995 and 2001; Percy-Smith and Thomas

2009; Shier 2001; Treseder 1997), some that look specifically at developing nations (for instance, Johnson et al. 1998) and others written in or for a large number of countries worldwide (for instance, Cussianovich and Marquez 2002 (Peru); Gordon 2009 (USA); Francisco 1999 (Philippines); Petren and Himes 2000, (Nepal); Rajani 2000 and 2001 (Tanzania); Reddy and Ratna 2002 (India); Tanaka et al. 2009 (Japan); Theis 2005 (Thailand); Zhu et al. 2004 (China)). Very little of this extensive generation of work about participation is either the work of children or takes account of what their vision of participation is. It is also sometimes very 'rule bound'. Save the Children (2003) describe their version of *good practice* when consulting with children. Consultation is taken to be a key component of participation; however, it does not ensure children will be entirely involved in programme development thereafter. So the question sometimes arises: above all else it is participation in what? What and when this participation is achieved is the outcome and obvious benefits? There are most certainly as many open questions as there are answers. Thus, there appears to be a stalemate. There is no consensual version of what it is and how children can obtain, keep and use it. This is an area of concern Judith Ennew raised in her keynote address at an international conference in Beijing in 2002.

The idea has been expressed that children should be able to participate in civil society, thus contributing to the greater good of the entire society in which that happens. Vučković-Šahović (2010: iv) looked at the role of civil society in implementation of the general measures of the CRC. She says that: 'An examination of the variety of definitions provided of 'civil society' reveals that it includes, *inter alia*, non-governmental organizations (NGOs), community groups, women's groups, environmental movements, faith-based organizations, professional associations, trade unions, self-help groups, social movements, business associations and advocacy groups'. That, however, does not include children's groups of any kind, for instance, working children's movements or any particular type of organisation that is equipped to include children within its structure. Roche (1999) outlined how it is necessary to reconsider the value of the language of rights and what the social value of that language is. In his view, rights are not just about the state and citizens' association but about how civil society visualises itself. That is to say, to look again at how social exchange and participation occupies the centre of society and how that is essential in examining how we reassess citizenship. The idiomatic way we discuss citizenship, rights and moreover participation is patchy but nonetheless the debate contiguous to these concepts is growing and revealing new potential for social organisation and further discourse.

However, there are barriers between a symbolic and absolute participation as a citizen:

> Children and youth are thus almost entirely without genuine political and economic influence. Therewith they lack the key components of what allows effective participation in civil society. Their citizenship is thus, unless withheld for one of the kind of reasons already described, limited to nationality and some of the ethical and moral duties, even then often under the supervision of adults. Thus children, along with the stateless, nationality-less, criminal and mentally ill, disprove the assumption that it is intrinsically egalitarian. (Milne 2013: 27)

It is the confusion between what nationality and citizenship that makes participation and unlevel playing field. Nationality simply describes the belonging to a nation in which an individual is born and in which he or she is entitled to becoming a national. Citizenship, on the other hand, in its literal fullness describes how an individual who has nationality is given full rights that citizens are entitled to. Heater looks at the origins of citizenship as nationality:

> For two hundred years citizenship and nationality have been political Siamese twins. Before the late eighteenth century the relationship was much looser than we have been accustomed to assume, and the connection is loosening again in our own age as multiple and world citizenships become increasingly evident. (Heater 1999: 95)

The word 'nation' was not normally used until the mid-eighteenth century. Its origins and initial development were in France during the period immediately preceding the 1789 revolution when Abbé Sieyes first used the modern French definition of nation by bestowing on it a precise political meaning that is inseparable from the concept of citizenship (Ibid.:97). Thus, a degree of misunderstanding that has led to confusion between the words has grown almost universally. The exclusion of children has thus become 'hidden' behind the wrong use of the word citizen. However, for participation to be fully realised, this needs to be unravelled. The question then arises whether or not this is possible. As James (2011) asks, is it possible 'children's citizenship' to ever be completely achieved for children? Could it be attained by them even? To be able to argue for it, the proposition that children are given citizenship rather than a more token 'children's citizenship' has to be considered in terms of how 'childhood' is culturally, socially, economically and politically constructed, understood and valued in a multitude of very diverse societies.

Moosa-Mitha (2005) examining this question concludes that in spite of the large number of theories of what children's rights are, especially since the advent of the CRC, children's rights as against full citizenship rights remain generally little looked at theoretically. She approached the question with a view that children's citizenship rights are part of essentially conventional, liberal models of citizenship in which theories of children's rights have been examined and definitions proposed. The difference between the adult 'norms' associated with citizenship in modern liberal democracies overlooks the possibility of full citizenship that in turn allows for fail to consider children's citizenship rights as even 'not yet citizens'. Thus, approaches to citizenship that take into account 'differences' such as social identities that include gender, race, culture, class, sexuality and so on might offer possibilities of defining children's citizenship in ways that take their rights and status as equal participants in civil society seriously, rather than their exclusion, based on their identity as children. Needless to say, that still allows limited participation rather than full as child citizens. This follows from Qvortrup's analysis of the social status of children:

> Children are reduced to *human becomings*, they are a 'project' to be moulded, whilst shielded from the public issues and major social events... (Qvortrup 1991: 7)

Moreover, he considered this part of a dilemma in which neither their agency nor the possibility of their having social capital was accepted:

> The anticipatory point of view reiterates a common sense view of children, as socially and economically, relatively unimportant when compared with adulthood . . . A corollary of this appears to be that children are not credited with human agency . . . (Ibid.:7–8)

> . . . children belong to society – not in the trivial sense of simply being there, nor as a reduced form of raw material to be moulded, nor as the possession of the society or the state. Childhood is part of society in the sense that children do participate in organised activities, and it constitutes a part of the social structure interacting in many ways with other parts. (Ibid.:10)

It is as though by allowing a modicum of loosely defined participation that is easy to both advocate and yet contain within certain parameters that children are given sufficient rights. Participation, for all of the concern with defining it, showing how it works, what children can do but omitting what they are excluded from and extensive training of adults in the application of participation, at best it remains notional. In that sense it is a mean-all-and-mean-nothing buzzword that is part of the partial rights given to children. It also does not achieve anything significant in terms of the ambiguous use of participation and usually nothing whatsoever where any form of citizenship, or in many cases nationality, would later lead to full citizenship rights for those excluded of whom the larger proportion are children:

> The balance of included and excluded embraces an estimated 36 % of the world population below age 19 years, 32.9 million refugees, asylum seekers, IDPs and other stateless persons (2.6 %), many of the approximated nine million adult prisoners (0.7 %) and other people such as those with mental health and legal reasons for exclusion. (Milne 2013: 26)

Exclusion is the opposite of participation as well as of inclusion. There is no easy remedy to exclusion, but to associate ‘participation’ with the excluded is an almost too bizarre way of expressing what should be ‘participation within limits’ at best. This is what also applies almost universally to children who as *human becomings* are still to be, as Qvortrup put it, ‘moulded’ into citizenship and therewith full inclusion. Despite a quarter of a century of the CRC, a longer history of children’s rights and also of contributions and experience as activists, fighters, workers and in and from which a great deal has yet to be learned, the reality is that participation has become an overused word that is more a contradiction in terms because of what it does not mean rather than what it attempts to convey.

What participation has achieved is to a great extent is breaking the bond of indivisibility that is one of the fundaments of human rights by creating a largely sectioned off part of the children’s rights agenda, predicated largely on the basis of Article 12 CRC. Whilst that article is at the core of many examples of ‘participatory’ projects, programmes, actions and more, they also reveal the extent to which those behind them do not really know or understand the CRC, indeed that one article itself. What is often initiated and organised far too often bears no resemblance to Article 12’s content. Participation has also created career opportunities and reputations for a considerable number of people. Some of them now have the same over-interpretation as a repeated message to which they adhere for almost the 25 years life of the Convention; some have become such dominant 'experts' that it can only be practised as proscribed by them. In some respects it is not only divorced from the rest of the CRC but can be rather more an autocratic domain that is 'rule bound' by participation professionals than one in which the incentives or free will to be a participant is a negotiation with children as described in the CRC. To that extent one can very easily point it out as both a distinctly hijacked agenda and what has become a meaningless buzzword.

The word 'agenda' has also been subject of frequent but sometimes vague use. It has been used often in previous chapters and will almost certainly be used again later. However, it is often a shortcut used instead of saying what is meant in full. It is literally the plural of *agendum* but more often than not it is treated as a singular noun with a plural that is usually agendas. It is used to describe a list, an outline, a plan or anything similar regarding things that are to be done or matters to be acted or voted on. Thus, *A World Fit for Children* (UN General Assembly 2002), a document prepared and approved of by the UN General Assembly, is a good example to begin with. It was described as a new agenda for and with the world's children[1] that included 21 specific goals and targets for the then coming decade. The document committed world political leaderships to implementation of the unfinished agenda of the 1990 *World Summit for Children*, then to set out to achieve other aims and objectives, above all those set out in the UN *Millennium Declaration*. It is indeed an agenda, but one that has neither completely achieved its 21-goal plan nor actually going thoroughly down the list. On the other hand it never actually called itself an agenda. It is also neither part of any subtitle or appears in the text. That was left to those who cited it, used it, simply referred or spoke out in its praise.

Otherwise, agenda has tended to be misappropriated for other purposes, many of them only rhetorical. One organisation in Louisiana[2] sets out to make the state one in which all children are able to thrive. Their mission is to make certain that the basic needs of children and families are met, so that children are taken care of and well educated. That begins during early years and continues on throughout youth. It is intended that they will be protected from harm and counteracting racism and other forms of prejudice. The *Ministry of Social Development in New Zealand* (2002) published an *Agenda for Children*[3] described as a 'government strategy aimed at improving the lives of children'. It sets out a set of principles intended to guide government policies and services affecting children with a new 'whole-child' approach to designing child policy and service development. They outline a programme of government policy and research initiatives to help achieve that. It begins with developing a more positive school culture that takes bullying seriously and improves relationships within schools. The focus is thus on violence in children's lives identifying principles for change and action schools had already

---

[1]This will come up again later in this chapter when examining the notion of 'global childhood'.

[2]*Agenda for Children*, Louisiana, USA: http://www.agendaforchildren.org/

[3]*Agenda for Children*, Ministry of Social Development, New Zealand, 2002: http://www.msd.govt.nz/about-msd-and-our-work/publications-resources/planning-strategy/agenda-children/

taken. It focusses on the bigger picture that takes in children's whole lives and circumstances but not just one-off issues or problems. Then it looks at what children require for healthy development instead of only reacting to problems as they arise whilst making the sectors of government concerned work together to support healthy development. They then take account of the CRC and the needs and rights of children. They acknowledge that children's lives are formed partially by the settings they live in and they also structure their lives through their own thoughts and actions. They are seen as citizens in their own right. Again, this has all of the constituent parts of an agenda but should be more appropriately called an 'Agenda *about* Children' since it strictly speaking looks at how government policy was to be developed rather than directly at children or taking them into developing their national programme.

Another dimension of the use of the word agenda is that of paediatrics in the USA. The American Academy of Pediatrics (AAP) has an *Agenda for Children*.[4] The AAP's mission sets out to achieve optimal physical, mental and social health and well-being for all babies through childhood to adolescence and until early adulthood. They emphasise their belief in the innate value of all children who they say are our most enduring and exposed legacy. Furthermore, they say that children ought to have the best possible health and highest quality health care. Their claim is that paediatricians are the best qualified people to provide that health care and call on all paediatricians to support their agenda. It is more a professional declaration of intent *about* children that is not for in the sense of them having active input or any form of consultation.

Lister (2006) uses it interestingly in a chapter under the title *An agenda for children: investing in the future or promoting well-being in the present*? in Lewis (2006). She looks at the nature of the relationship between children, parents and the state and how it has been central to the growth of the modern welfare state and constantly a problem for western liberal democracies. Whereby welfare states have undergone a great deal of restructuring over recent decades, families have also changed. That is to say, their form has changed by the nature of contributions that men and women make to them. Consequently greater attention is now being paid to children by policymakers. This is most frequently of importance as future citizen workers. She examined the implications of social policy for children in the broad context of family and welfare state changes rather than as something coming directly from and aimed at children themselves. It is hardly what one might call a list or plan and certainly does not project forward but draws mainly on evidence accumulated up until the time the piece was written. Whilst extremely interesting in terms of seeing how the state actually perceives children, it actually projects nothing specifically *for* them.

Almost naturally following on from children's voices, participation and agenda, there is the 'children focussed' or 'children centred' anything. Both tend to be used in the singular generically, thus 'child focussed' and 'child centred' but implying the plural. Both are actually much used but almost indefinable because they mean so

[4]*AAP Agenda for Children - Strategic Plan*, 2013: http://www.aap.org/en-us/Pages/Default.aspx

many things but far too often say nothing or used evasively to not say what is really meant. There is also the phrase 'child friendly', which is said to mean something different entirely although it is not particularly easy to tell them apart.

A child-focussed or child-centred approach demands that an attitude towards children that puts them at the centre of their principles is adopted by the entire society or organisation. In practice the idea is to offer a greater degree of meaning to the notion that children need to be protected, cared for, nurtured and protected from the principally adult-controlled world whilst being offered love and understanding. It should also promote the rights of children to be able to form associations and communicate without restraint. Thus, it should allow the freedom of children to experience, believe, discover, query and search for answers. It therefore acknowledges children's contribution to whichever sphere actions and events involving their presence happen to be in. The areas in which great importance is attached are in education and both protection and welfare services. Their inclusion, consultation as is often said, is also considered part of the focussing or centrality of children in activities related to the CRC, often wearing the mantle participation.

In education a child-centred approach is that with a creative curriculum based on the philosophy that children are at the centre of all educational processes. Therefore, they have the freedom to think and enquire as part of learning. Thus, they are able to cultivate their talents and make the most of their potential. When using it teachers should be required to challenge children to develop, either collectively or individually, solutions to questions raised in a safe and considerate manner. This is intended to encourage cooperation and the development of life skills and at the same time the ability to analyse their situation and ultimately their capability of organising themselves. The belief behind this is that if children feel safe, happy and both encouraged and empowered in school, thus greater enjoyment in learning, their performance will increase appreciably and such dilemmas as dropoutism reduce significantly (Doddington and Hilton 2007).

There are apparently some misunderstandings about differences between child-*friendly* and child-*centred* approaches in education. It appears that education professionals have tended to believe that child friendly is essentially the same as child centred. The differences are described as in a child-friendly approach, teachers behave in an ensuring and considerate manner towards the children, irrespective of race, gender, belief or cultural background, and do so without any form of abuse, excessive use of power or physical punishment. The generally held opinion of 'experts' is that children feel safe and are thus encouraged and happy at school so that in turn achievement and performance become measurably better and both failure and dropping out reduced (Wright et al. 2006).

In the welfare and protection sphere, a child-centred approach works on the basis of the safety, welfare and well-being of a child or young person being the principal concern in any child welfare or protection action. Assessment, planning and delivery of services have to be based on the needs of young people, whereby their best interests are paramount in decision-making. They must make certain that there is a positive and trusting relationship between children and those who work with them and encourage participation decision making and issues that concern them when that is considered appropriate. They must also give emphasis to the aims of services which are to improve the safety, welfare and well-being of children which includes ensuring that their needs and wishes are not disregarded when taking into account the concerns of the parents or carers and other family members.

Child-centred or child-focussed and *family*-focussed approaches do not mean they are one and the same thing. The former refers to putting the needs of children at the centre of decisions, whereas the latter puts emphasis on problems and needs of parents or carers that have some kind of impact on children. It assumes that the constant for most children is family and that the majority of them are better off when with that family. The principle is that this approach offers an opportunity to boost families' ability to feel empowered and thus able to take positive steps as necessary or required. It also works on the basis of the notion that families are essential for the welfare of children. In welfare service it is coordinated around assumed family needs. Certainly when looking at it in terms of UK service delivery, the theory is that it can reduce the probability of families being mired in a recurrent series of assessments and referrals (for instance, see Munro 2012). The importance of such approaches was at the centre of the *Department for Education and Skills* (2004) publication *Every Child Matters: Change for Children* that attracted a lot of attention and a positive reception in the UK at that time but has been largely forgotten since.

However, those phrases are all perfectly suited to countries with modern and well-trained education practitioners and highly sophisticated welfare systems that are able to deliver them. The question would remain open whether in the present political and economic climate of many countries in the North alone any of them can be more than patchily achieved, if indeed at all. To this extent the concepts are an ideal rather than a reality that has a basis in an essentially Eurocentric view of the world that are not actually modifiable to suit every cultural and belief setting, let alone where there are no financial or social resources available to make them happen. For a very large part of the world, therefore, they are and may always remain little more than ideals that belong somewhere else but that are generally meaningless.

Children first is another phrase, broadly speaking very close to the child-focussed, child-centred and child-friendly phrases. It describes the duty to protect children. Putting children first means that the safety and welfare of children is everyone's responsibility. The principle is that children have safer lives where everyone is conscientiously and dutifully protecting their well-being. People working with children especially, and across a wide variety of areas, recognise their accountability for providing and ensuring safe practice and reporting any concerns that arise. This is supposed to provide greater transparency and direction for individuals and organisations responsible for recognising and responding properly to abuse and neglect. Thereby, all children and families are supported in order to help them reach full potential, whilst children are supported in a manner that affords them a sense of inclusion in the community. The basic problem with the language of this phrase is that whilst making children the focus of the work, in fact they have relatively little input. That comes notionally in the commitment to making them feel part of their community. It does not stipulate any actual participation. The notion of families being supported to reach full potential is also a 'blank cheque' since potential is an entirely subjective term that has too many meanings and possible targets and outcomes to be meaningful. It put children first without making them the object of what is being done is therefore a statement that is entirely welfare orientated with services directed at children without being essentially inclusive in how it works. In children's rights terms, it neither delivers any nor seems to be rights inclusive. Furthermore, it is an expression that only has meaning in countries with sophisticated welfare provision where the potential for reaching every child who needs intervention can be helped. It does not mean very much for countries with little or no welfare resources. In that sense it is quite meaningless for the majority of children.

The notion of an alliance for children is one that does not very often actually appear to bring children or their organisation together but seems only to commit those who set up an 'alliance' to deliver the message of children's rights, particularly the CRC. The basic principle is that everybody under age 18 years has rights, irrespective of who they are, where or how they live or what their culture and beliefs. Their rights are founded on the principles of what they need to survive and thrive, be that education, health care, protection from abuse and the provision of adequate nutrition and even such key issues as clean drinking water. A normal alliance works on the basis of a belief that takes account of the specific needs of children that recognise the special characteristics in the development, nurture and protection of children that set them apart from adults.

Another basic principle is that all children's rights bear the notion that children are entitled to expect adults to give adequate care, provisions and protection. The state has the duty to provide laws and services to guarantee those rights. Children's rights, as an integral part of human rights, therefore have a universal value. Ultimately, it is the international community who carry the burden of responsibility for children's rights to be protected against abuse or neglect by any individual state party to the CRC. Thus, the best interests of children should be the first consideration for actions that affect them; all children have the right to life, survival and development; all children have a right to participate and all rights belong to all children without discrimination or exception.

Thus, alliances have been set up to work within the children's rights genre and should be working towards some kind of mutual basis for their efforts and shared objectives with common objectives. However, the alliances appear to be very different to each other rather than with shared strategies[5] although there is a network[6] in Europe that coordinates the alliances. There appears to be quite minimal input from children in many cases.

[5]The three examples here show the very different aims and objectives of organisations that call themselves alliances: Scottish Alliance for Children's Rights, http://www.togetherscotland.org.uk/; Edinburgh, Children's Rights Alliance for England, http://www.crae.org.uk/, London, and Aliança pela Infância, alianca@aliancapelainfancia.org.br, São Paulo.

[6]Alliance for Childhood European Network, http://www.allianceforchildhood.eu/, Brussels

As briefly touched on at the beginning of this chapter, the USA has developed its own children's rights language. Their alliances[7] appear to be more child welfare orientated, usually more a family-based activity, and several seem to be far more concerned with adoption and fostering than children's rights as much of the rest of the world understands it. They have little if only occasionally any direct input from children. There is also little to suggest that any of these alliances are in fact allied with each other.

Where there is any kind of common direct message related to children in any of the world's alliances, they appear to share some basic principles. Those include the right to have a 'voice' in matters affecting them, the right to special protection, the right to education and care, the right to play and rest and the right to health services. The first principle is the one that touches on any form of child participation but, although some of the alliances do have children involved, is often only a guiding principle to be applied to the children they represent.

The next hollow phrases are several variations of each 'children are the future' and 'the child cannot wait'. The first is redolent of many quotes by philosophers, poets, politicians and other 'thinkers'. It is an impressive list that includes Aristotle, Khalil Gibran, Albert Einstein, Nelson Mandela, Martin Luther King, Mahatma Ghandi, William Shakespeare, Oscar Wilde, Mark Twain and John F. Kennedy. Very close to the much used expression in the children's rights world, Kennedy said 'Children are the world's most valuable resource and its best hope for the future' in 1963, just a few months before his assassination. Using another variation, Whitney Huston sang 'I believe the children are our future',[8] just giving another example of the popularity of the expression. The Bernard van Leer Foundation used *Children are our future* as the heading of a submission to the *Committee on the Rights of the Child Day of Discussion*: *Implementing Child Rights in Early Childhood* in 2004. *Our Children, our Future: A Report on the Status of Children's Rights in Kenya, 2013* was the title used by the Kenyan government for an executive report. *Our children cannot wait* has been a popular campaign slogan for drives by NGOs and parents' groups to get early childcare, kindergartens, education and similar resources in place. There is also the inclusion of the word 'our' in many versions, thus 'children are OUR future' or 'OUR children cannot wait' type of usage that in the former case refers more to the present generation's future than that of the children themselves and in the latter the children are made into a collective asset or possession with implications for the exclusion of 'their' children.

[7] The four examples here are selected from what appears to be a considerable number throughout the USA: Alliance for Children's Rights, http://kids-alliance.org/, Los Angeles; Alliance for Children and Families, http://www.alliance1.org/, Milwaukee; Alliance for Childhood, http://www.allianceforchildhood.org/, New York, and Alliance for Children, http://www.alliance4children.org/, Charleston.

[8] This is the first line of 'Greatest Love of All' written by Michael Masser and Linda Creed in 1984, released in 1986, originally recorded by George Benson for the 1977 Muhammad Ali biopic *The Greatest*.

Both of these phrases are used as titles of headlines to good effect but seldom followed up at all by whatever follows. The intentions are clearly altruistic, but the way they are used without precise consideration of how and where and they lead towards their absence thereafter shows a strong tendency towards rhetorical rather than literal use. It is sometimes quite ironic that several organisations using either sentiment have quoted part of Chilean poet Gabriela Mistral's *Su Nombre es Hoy* (*His Name is Today*) (Castleman 1982):

> We are guilty of many errors and many faults,
> But our worst crime is abandoning the children,
> Neglecting the fountain of life
> Many things we need can wait
> But the child cannot. Right now is the time;
> His bones are being formed,
> His senses are being developed
> His blood is being made
> To him, we cannot answer, "Tomorrow",
> His name is "Today".

This poem that has been chosen as a *leitmotiv* for an image of some kind of projection forward that overlooks the closing line as well as rarely looking closely at the penultimate line. Although written approaching a century ago, the message it carries includes the notion of children's rights that is lost beyond the dramatic effect of the header. This sadly makes it a disingenuous choice of words by the organisations citing it since they are not pursuing what should be a perfectly clear interpretation.

Thus, to describe children as being the 'future' or that they 'cannot wait' has been used more for dramatic effect than to present any kind of meaningful projection of what will or might be at some stage in the future. That point in time is an unknown factor; it apparently includes the present adult generation when the word 'our' is used and is not actually generation specific. Either expression is thus more of an abstract than a realisable statement.

Then there is the idea of a charter for children. It is, in fact, a notion of very distinguished pedigree. It is the idea that began the journey towards contemporary children's rights. After the First World War finished, Eglantyne Jebb began working with children in Germany and Austria in 1919 where relief was needed in the wake of the war. In 1921, as that was being brought under control, there was a new, greater emergency that came about partly as a consequence of the war, then revolution and civil war, and partly because of the devastating economic policies of the Bolshevik government. In 1923, she consequently turned to the issue of children's rights which she took with her to Geneva for a meeting of the *International Union* with a plan for a Children's Charter. It became, as described in earlier chapters, the Declaration of the Rights of the Child, or the Declaration of Geneva, that was adopted in 1924 by the League of Nations. It was the seed sown that became the CRC.

There is a more recent charter that follows on in the same vein. The *African Charter on the Rights and Welfare of the Child* (ACRWC) (appendix 6) was adopted by the *Organisation of African Unity* (OAU), now the *African Union* (AU), in 1990.

The ACRWC came about because the member states of the OAU believed that the CRC missed important sociocultural and economic realities particular to Africa. It puts emphasis on the need to include African cultural values and experiences when dealing with the rights of the child. It is the only charter for Africa and therefore has the problem of containing many different cultures, economies and belief systems in a single document. Despite that, it is possibly a model for all other parts of the world. Where it is felt that in terms of cultural relativity, because the CRC is configured in a largely northern language and appears to not go into different types of social and economic structures thoroughly, that kind of charter could supplement the CRC.

However, other charters do not tend to be directly for children or even clearly for all of them. One example is *Protecting Children and Young People – The Charter,*[9] from the Scottish government in 2004. It says it is a message to everybody including politicians, communities, parents, families and neighbours. It is also aimed at education authorities, health, social work and the police. It is for people who work directly with children and young people to guide on what is important to them and how to go about helping to protect them. It pledges that those who are at risk of abuse or neglect will get help when they need it as well as have the support of a professional such as a teacher, doctor or social worker who will make sure they are alright and will not be put at further risk. Moreover, they will be listened to so that professionals can use their power to help them, and discussion will be in private when and whenever required. The young people will get help to understand decisions made about their lives. Those working with them must be confident, competent, properly trained and given supported so that services can constantly develop the how and what is done to provide help. That essentially describes services working with children rather than being exactly *for* them.

Then there is the UK's *Crown Prosecution Service* which put up a *Children's Charter, Draft for public consultation* in 2005.[10] It was a document that explained how they deal with cases where children are involved as victims or witnesses. They claimed it was primarily for children, parents, families, guardians and carers and others who work to support children. It went into the many different legal definitions of what a child is showing how some laws use different ages in specific situations and whenever that is the case how they are bound by those laws. For the purposes of that charter they defined children as everyone under the age of 18. It goes on to say that in 1991 the UK adopted the CRC and that Articles 3 and 12 say that adults and organisations must consider the best interests and views of a child. Furthermore, Article 40 says that children have the right of legal aid and to be treated fairly by a justice system that respects their rights. It went on to say they have a duty to safeguard children and do what they can to protect them against harm. Young victims or witnesses need special care and the best interests of children involved

[9] 'Protecting Children and Young People – The Charter', 2004, Edinburgh: The Scottish Government. http://www.scotland.gov.uk/Publications/2004/04/19082/34410

[10] Crown Prosecution Service 'Children's Charter, Draft for public consultation', 2005, York: CPS Policy Directorate. http://www.cps.gov.uk/publications/docs/childrens_charter.pdf

in criminal cases must always be considered, although not the only thing they would consider. In fact it describes legal process and how that should henceforth be practised. That consultation was used to draw up lead to the adoption of the present CPS policy on prosecuting criminal cases involving children and young people as victims and witnesses[11] in 2006. Again, whilst a charter in name, it is much more a statement about legal practice by prosecution service than a charter, and whilst it tries to project a benevolent way of working with young people, it is not exactly for them.

Play England has a *Charter for Children's Play*[12] which sets out a concept about how play should be. Its intention is to be a vehicle for individuals and organisations to examine and improve how they make play and informal recreation available for children and young people and informal recreation. It consists of constant principles on which the play sector is base and states that signing the Charter is a precondition for all Play England members and staff. It states that children have the right to play and need time and space in order to play. Adults should let children play freely near their homes, that children value and gain from staffed play conditions that are enhanced by capable play workers. Children also need time and space to play at school and sometimes also require extra help to be able to enjoy their right to play. It is very much about children's right to play rather than children themselves and sets out an agenda by listing and describing a plan rather than being a charter in place.

The *United States Conference of Catholic Bishops* (USCCB) has a *Charter for the Protection of Children and Young People.*[13] It describes itself as a comprehensive set of procedures for addressing allegations of sexual abuse of minors by Roman Catholic clergy. It also includes guidelines for understanding, remedy, responsibility for and prevention of future abuse. Its intent is to create a safe environment for children and young people that provides healing and reconciliation for victims and survivors. It promises to make immediate and effective response to allegations and thereafter cooperate with civil authorities to discipline offenders and provide for means of accountability for the future to guarantee that the problem continues to be efficiently dealt with. Again it is an example of how a body deals with a problem rather than describing the actual protection of the young people the charter's title appears to address.

The *Government of South Australia* has a *Charter of Rights for Children and Young People in Care*[14] that states the rights of children and young people who are

---

[11]CPS policy on prosecuting criminal cases involving children and young people as victims and witnesses: https://www.cps.gov.uk/victims_witnesses/children_policy.pdf

[12]Play England, 'Charter for Children's Play', 2009: http://www.playengland.org.uk/charter

[13]The United States Conference of Catholic Bishops (USCCB), 'Charter for the Protection of Children and Young People', 2002: http://www.usccb.org/issues-and-action/child-and-youth-protection/charter.cfm

[14]Government of South Australia, Office of the Guardian for Children and Young People, 2006: http://www.gcyp.sa.gov.au/charter-of-rights-2/

under the guardianship or in the custody of the *Minister for Education and Child Development*. Their parliament passed laws saying that any person involved with children in care formally, for instance, social workers or carers, must consider and 'seek to implement to the fullest extent possible, the terms of the Charter'. The charter is used by children and young people to negotiate changes when their rights are not given to them properly and is also used by adults to discuss rights with young people and to represent them. Again it is not so much a charter as an agenda that sets out a set of guidelines for people working with young people.

In general it would appear that the word *charter* is used quite freely as a convenient way of presenting sets of guidelines and rules that govern the working practices and methods of people concerned with the well-being of children. By and large they do not appear to be generally inclusive as they sometimes imply.

Global childhood is another quite meaningless phrase. The modern construction of childhood materialised disconnectedly from the late eighteenth into the twentieth century (Ariès 1965; Zhao 2011). That is to say, at different periods there were different perceptions. At first a child was like most other people, working as soon as possible, uneducated and unsophisticated. There were exceptions, at first among royalty and the aristocracy then as an industrially bourgeoisie appeared their children had a privileged life. Even then it was often a period without a great deal of affection, more often than not a period of sometimes harsh discipline that was thought to shape the future adult. It was also a period when male children were educated and whilst females received tutors who taught them skills necessary for their adulthood, it was usually done in a fashion that shaped a future mistress of a household. The children of the masses were almost unseen. Children in the colonies and other foreign places were largely ignored, except for the occasional example of a 'pickaninny' working as a page or merely the child of a slave. Thus, they were the exception rather than the rule. Those would have been children of mainly African descent although some Asians were becoming gradually more common in the West. The twentieth century saw the emergence of the concept of the standardised global child, a figure eventually enshrined in the CRC. It is a very much Eurocentric view of childhood that even in the North is and never could be an appropriate morphology since differences are always great than the sum of constituent parts that would allow a single typology to exist.

The global child is a variant on the notion of the global citizen who is someone who sees themselves and others as first and principally human beings. He or she does not discriminate against fellow people because of ethnicity, gender, nationality, religion, sexuality, way of life or any other less important characteristics. This global citizen sees differences as interesting rather than strange and treats them as things to be learned about, accepted and respected. Global citizens frequently considered advocates of human rights, who are constantly in touch with global news and affairs. It is therefore considered to be a kind of ethical or political philosophy in which the core proposition is that key social, political, economic and environmental issues in the world should be addressed at all levels. Thus, individuals, civil society, communities and nation states must view the world through a global lens. It refers to an open, culturally, environmentally and socially inclusive ideology that accepts the interconnectedness of all things. From that viewpoint political and geophysical boundaries are an irrelevance so that the solution to challenges is seen to be far more important than solely national interests. Supporters of this philosophy have been described as being influenced by Diogenes of Sinope who is anecdotally said to have declared 'I am a citizen of the world (κοσμοπολίτης)' when asked where he originally came from (Diogenes 1925, Book VI, Chapter 2, line 63[15]). Until quite recently the notion of a global child or childhood did not really exist.

It is a global perception of children's lives throughout the world that follows that precedent of the global citizen. It is critical of how children are represented as being of a particular race, part of a class system and gendered. It also regards the notion that policy on families leads to some of them being labelled normal and others deviant. Depending on which it is has some kind of impact on children. School and work are considered as locations for the control, management and shaping of childhood into preferred adulthoods. Children's involvement in war is linked to globalisation of capital and other negative structures such as organised crime and terrorist groups. However, race, class systems and gender have been described as causing 'multiple insecurities of children in the contemporary world . . . being driven by global capitalism and its constant production of crises in social reproduction' (Wells 2009: 184). Furthermore, 'accounts of North American and European childhoods' (Ibid.: 1) have made light of the importance of global and material structures leading to the neglect of such components as race, class and gender as the social forces that form the character of each different version of childhood. Childhood studies have contributed to the notion of childhood being radically rewritten, partly as an outcome of globalisation that has in turn led to an idealised version of the child who is like the global citizen. As a consequence this notion of the global child is being endorsed by increasingly globalised western views of childhood.

The idea that there could be such a child in a world where not only race, class and gender count but also culture, economics, political influences, nationality, belief, sexuality and whether that child is in a peaceful or war-torn place creates so many permutations that a single model can only be dismissed as wishful thinking. One of the problems is that children's rights seen only through the lens of the CRC and overlooking the entire cultural diversity question appear to use a single human rights language. That is also seen as a quality of the North that wishes to see the global South rebuilt following its standards. The global child, in much the same way as the global citizen, is part of a small minority who is idealised as a model for all that denies the many positives that diversity carries with it. In that sense the notion of either a global child or global childhood are not only meaningless but could also be obstructive in taking children's human rights forward.

[15]Diogenes of Sinope and Diogenes Laërtius are entirely different people. Sinope's words are cited as an anecdote by Laërtius in *The Lives of Eminent Philosophers*. There is no exact evidence whether or not Diogenes of Sinope said anything of the kind or indeed held such a philosophy.

There are, of course, other words and phrases that have become part of the language of children's rights. These served the purpose of examples of some that are most commonly used. On the other hand, this is not a plea for them to be abandoned but instead for more considerations about how they are used. Some careful definition, reconfiguration and less frequent and often insincere use is required.

References

Ariès, P. (1965). *Centuries of childhood: A social history of family life*. New York: Random House.

Castleman, W. J. (1982). *Beauty and the mission of the teacher: the life of Gabriela Mistral of Chile, teacher, poetess, friend of the helpless, Nobel laureate, Smithtown*. New York: Exposition Press.

Cussianovich, A., & Marquez, M. A. (2002). *Towards a protagonist participation of boys, girls and teenagers*. Lima: Save the Children Sweden Regional Office.

Department for Education and Skills. (2004). *Every child matters: Change for children*. Nottingham: DfES.

Diogenes, L. (1925). *The lives of eminent philosophers* (Vol. 1). Harvard: Harvard University Press.

Doddington, C., & Hilton, M. (2007). *Child-centred education: Reviving the creative tradition*. London: Sage.

Flekkøy, M. G., & Kaufman, N. H. (1997). *The participation rights of the child: Rights and responsibilities in family and society* (Children in Charge Series 4). London: Jessica Kingsley Publishers.

Francisco, C. (1999). *Standing up for ourselves! A study on the concepts and practices of young people's rights to participation*. Manila: ECPAT International.

Gordon, H. R. (2009). *We fight to win: Inequality and the politics of youth activism*. New Brunswick: Rutgers University Press.

Hart, R. (1992). *Children's participation: From tokenism to citizenship*. Florence: UNICEF.

Hart, R. (1997). *Children's participation: The theory and practice of involving young citizens in community development and environmental care*. London: Earthscan.

Heater, D. (1999). *What is citizenship?* Cambridge: Polity Press.

James, A. (2011). To be (come) or not to be (come): Understanding children's citizenship. *The Annals of the American Academy of Political and Social Science, 633*(1), 167–179.

Johnson, V., Ivan-Smith, E., Gordon, G., Pridmore, P., & Scott, P. (Eds.). (1998). *Stepping forward – Children and young people's participation in the development process*. London: Intermediate Technology Publications.

Lansdown, G. (1995). *Taking part: Children's participation in decision making*. London: Institute for Public Policy Research.

Lansdown, G. (2001). *Promoting children's participation in democratic decision making*. Florence: UNICEF International Child Development.

Lederer, E. M. (2013, December 7). Malala speech: Pakistani teen speaks out publicly for first time since being shot by Taliban. *The Huffington Post*. http://www.huffingtonpost.com/2013/07/12/malala-speech-pakistani-teen_n_3587906.html

Lewis, J. (Ed.). (2006). *Children, changing families and welfare states*. Cheltenham: Edward Elgar.

Lister, R. (2006). An agenda for children: Investing in the future or promoting well-being in the present? In J. Lewis (Ed.), *Children, changing families and welfare states* (pp. 51–66). Cheltenham: Edward Elgar.

Milne, B. (2013). *The history and theory of children's citizenship in contemporary societies*. Stuttgart: Springer.

Ministry of Social Development of New Zealand. (2002). *Agenda for children*. Wellington: Ministry of Social Development.

Moosa-Mitha, M. (2005). A difference-centred alternative to theorization of children's citizenship rights. *Citizenship Studies, 9*(4), 369–388.
Munro, E. (2012). *Progress report: Moving towards a child centred system* (The Munro review of child protection). Nottingham: DfES.
Percy-Smith, B., & Thomas, N. (Eds.). (2009). *A handbook of children and young people's participation: Perspectives from theory and practice*. London: Routledge.
Petren, A., & Himes, J. (Eds.). (2000). *Children's rights: Turning principles into practice*. Kathmandu: Save the Children Sweden and UNICEF ROSA.
Qvortrup, J. (1991). *Childhood as a social phenomenon* (2nd edn.). Eurosocial Report 36/0. Vienna: European Centre for Social Welfare, Policy and Research.
Rajani, R. (Ed.). (2000). *The political participation of children*. Cambridge, MA: Harvard Center for Population and Development Studies.
Rajani, R. (2001). *The participation rights of adolescents: A strategic approach*. New York: UNICEF.
Reddy, N., & Ratna, K. (2002). *A journey in children's participation*. Bangalore: Concerned for Working Children.
Roche, J. (1999). Children: Rights, participation and citizenship. *Childhood, 6*(4), 475–493.
SCF UK. (2003). *So you want to consult with children? A toolkit of good practice*. London: Save the Children.
Shier, H. (2001). Pathways to participation: Openings, opportunities and obligations. *Children and Society, 15*(2), 107–117.
Tanaka, H., Tanaka, S., & Mori, T. (2009). *Children's participation guidebook*. Tokyo: Japan NGO Network for Education.
Theis, J. (2005). *Defining child and youth participation*. Bangkok: UNICEF EAPRO.
Topping, A. (2014, February 6). Young British-Somali women fight FGM with rhyme and reason. *The Guardian*. http://www.theguardian.com/society/2014/feb/06/british-somali-young-women-fight-fgm-rhyme-reason
Treseder, P. (1997). Empowering children and young people. In *Training manual: Promoting involvement in decision making*. London: Children's Rights Office and Save the Children.
UN General Assembly. (2002). *A world fit for children, resolution S-27/2 adopted by the General Assembly*. New York: United Nations.
van Beers, H., Invernizzi, A., & Milne, B. (2006). *Beyond article 12: Essential readings in children's participation*. Bangkok: Black on White.
Vučković-Šahović, N. (2010). *The role of civil society in implementing the general measures of the convention on the rights of the child* (Innocenti Working Papers 18). Florence: UNICEF.
Wells, K. (2009). *Childhood in global perspective*. Cambridge: Polity Press.
Wright, C., Mannathoko, C., & Pasic, M. (2006). *Child-friendly schools manual*. New York: UNICEF.
Zhao, G. (2011). The modern construction of childhood: What does it do to the paradox of modernity? *Studies in Philosophy and Education, 30*(3), 241–256.
Zhu, Z., Haiyu, Y., & West, A. (Eds.). (2004). *Child participation in action: Concepts and practice from East and West*. Proceedings, papers and plans from the International Seminar on Child Participation in Action. Beijing: Save the Children UK, China Programme and All China Women's Federation Child Work Department.

There Is No Such Thing As Children's Rights 7

This chapter sets out to take the examination of children's rights as part of the entire human rights agenda further by looking at it historically, how it developed, the influence of particular people and the changes of leadership in influential organisations (see also Chap. 1). At present a thorough analysis of children's rights would show that they appear to be a project in progress, epitomised by a movement from concentration on needs, protection and welfare that were the focus of all that was provided for children throughout the twentieth century in particular. Those provisions are now amongst the services moving towards protection through a rights approach. It therefore examines the progress made and ongoing in the development and implementation of those rights.

The questions that arise are whether or not the CRC is recognised universally as part of the human rights agenda and thus whether or not the concept 'children's rights' itself is accepted as part of human rights as distinct from it being an optional extra that is age defined, 0–18 years. It could be ambiguously understood as a welfare instrument that principally uses the word 'rights' rhetorically even though some articles irrefutably set out principles that are unquestionably intended to deliver rights.

Protection of children, in particular young children, is the established and generally accepted objective in most societies. The concepts of children's rights to participation and a greater degree of self-determined opinion are of more recent origin. The 1959 Declaration, as the precursor to the CRC, contains only provision and protection rights. It does not contain or point in the direction of participation. Participation rights for children are more contentious and complicated to implement than protection rights because they are considered as a threat by many adults who believe that they challenge parental authority and family organisation (Lurie 2003). It is also a culturally loaded gun that has every potential for disturbing the long-standing status quo in societies where change is either unwelcomed or does not follow the same kind of path as many countries of the North.

B. Milne, *Rights of the Child*, Children's Well-Being: Indicators and Research 11,
DOI 10.1007/978-3-319-18784-6_7

After the adoption of the CRC in 1989, UNICEF chose to adopt it using four categories: 'survival', 'development', 'protection' and 'participation'. Nigel Cantwell (1993) argued that these choices reflect UNICEF's organisational format whereby emphasis is on survival and development. They are an outcome of UNICEF's history; however, he believed that those categories had the consequence of placing too much stress on survival rights. The reason, he believed, was because it implied survival rights are more important than any other category. He preferred the classification referred to as '3Ps' which are:

The right to provision of basic needs
The right to protection from harmful acts and practices
The right to participation in decisions affecting their lives

His argument was that the 3Ps were seen initially as an instructive tool in which provision, protection and participation rights were both necessary and interdependent elements in the range of human rights to be given to children. Cantwell also warned against construing the 3Ps as distinct and also potentially incompatible types of rights instead of being three separate elements that must be included when preparing policies on any particular issue.

There is also a misconception that children's rights are an autonomous and self-directing 'entity' that is mainly defined by the CRC and to an extent a product of its history and place within the UN system since 1989. It does not however have a life of its own. One of the problems that come with it is the misapprehension that it 'belongs' to a particular UN agency. In order to begin to examine this misconception, the history of the CRC and the UN's work for and with children are briefly described in order to provide a backdrop to some of the reasons why children's rights are misunderstood and not what they are often imagined to be.

The story really begins with the *Declaration of the Rights of the Child* in 1923. At that stage, it was a string of interrelated children's 'rights' proclamations drafted by Eglantyne Jebb, founder of the *Save the Children Movement* and *International Peace Union* that she initially referred to as 'Children's Charter'. The Charter notion was not entirely new. *The Prevention of Cruelty to, and Protection of, Children Act 1889*, in the UK was more commonly known as the Children's Charter. It was not actually a rights charter; it was set out to prevent cruelty against children. It gave the state the power to intercede in relations between parents or carers and children for the first time ever. The police could intervene and arrest anyone found mistreating a child or forcibly enter a dwelling if a child was considered to be at risk. The Act included guidelines on child labour and prohibited begging. Jebb would have known about that so-called charter and may well have taken it into consideration, particularly points 3 and 4 (see Appendix 2).

The Charter was adopted by the League of Nations in 1924 as the Geneva Declaration of the Rights of the Child. It modified Jebb's five-point version slightly; thus, the Declaration is even more clearly a document that describes the protection and welfare of children, although its title refers to 'rights of the child'. Perhaps the original title it bore in 1924, the *World Child Welfare Charter*, is far more appropriate given its content. Whatever the case, it more or less cast the die for later modifications and additions.

In 1946, the International Save the Children Union merged with the *International Association for the Promotion of Child Welfare* to become the *International Union for Child Welfare*. Its first task was to push for the adoption of the Declaration of Geneva, although the title *World Child Welfare Charter* still appeared on some lobbying documents, by the newly formed United Nations. The initial intent was to continue to do practical aid and relief work for children affected by the recently finished Second World War and the harsh period that had immediately followed.

In 1945 there had been no notion of setting up a specialised organisation within the range of new institutions the UN consisted of. There was thus no direct focus on children's rights, and in reality, the Declaration went into a period of being of very little importance. In 1946, the *UN International Children's Emergency Fund* (ICEF) was formed as what is described on their website[1] as an 'accident of early cold war politics'. The situation in Europe was severe, especially with the winter of 1946–1947 being harder than usual. Records show it was the winter with the heaviest snowfalls in the twentieth century and probably not experienced since the winter of 1813–1814. In January there was snow up to 30 cm deep on the ground in places where snow was seldom seen, but in February when in much of Europe winter normally begins to relax its grip, there was freezing rain and frequent snowfalls of which some were blizzards, drifting snow and severe frosts. Temperatures were almost permanently below freezing. Following the destruction of the war and the political standoff between the East and West that was intensifying at that time, many millions of people were still without food, clothes, fuel or adequate shelter. Most people survived on meagre rations that barely covered the most basic needs. The severity of that winter was beyond the capability of many people to cope; thus, large numbers did not survive.

Children were probably the worst affected, with up to half of all babies dying before their first birthday in some parts of Europe. The allies had foreseen the extent of the devastation by the end of the war and had set the *UN Relief and Rehabilitation Administration* (UNRRA) in 1943. The idea was that it would provide general assistance to all people affected by war. However, the relations between the East and West deteriorated, the so-called Iron Curtain was created between the two occupied parts of Europe and the government of the USA refused to use UNRRA as a means of providing relief because it was providing aid to countries in both the East and West.

At the point at which UNRRA's role in the relief effort was to be wrapped up, concerns were raised at its closing meeting in Geneva. The Polish delegate, Ludwik Rajchman, spoke out in protest at the outcome for Europe's war-affected children. The meeting accepted a proposal that UNRRA's remaining funds should be used for children through the establishment of the ICEF. Rajchman has consequently

[1] http://www.unicef.org/sowc96/50years.htm

been thought of as the founder of UNICEF. Maurice Pate, then Executive Director designate (in post 1947–1965), made it conditional that as part of his service, there were no caveats regarding where aid might be used, thus maintaining that the ICEF should give equal support to children in 'ex-enemy countries', irrespective of their race or politics, and, in a number of instances, subsequently defeated and occupied as well as victorious nations. At that time, aid was mainly in the form of mostly dried milk. Children's rights were the last thing they had in mind. Consequently, in December 1946, and just before the harsh winter began, a UN General Assembly resolution prolonged UNICEF's life. The full name the *United Nations International Children's Emergency Fund* became better known by its acronym UNICEF and has remained so ever since. More by chance than design, a temporary children's fund became a full component of international cooperation that has since made up the UN system.

Thus, in essence unintentionally and almost unseen, the international community had therewith also recognised and accepted a new fundamental principle which was that children were above the political divergences and disputes the UN in theory exists for a large part to mediate. However, whilst the protection and welfare of children were recognised as the major part of UNICEF's mandate, they were not seen as a human rights agency.

Their mandate was quickly put under scrutiny. Amongst the most important programmes supported by UNICEF early in their work, a number were in Eastern European countries including Poland, Romania and Yugoslavia and both parts of Germany. At the end of the 1940s, UNICEF supplied aid to both sides of civil wars in both China and Greece. They also gave aid to children in the Middle East displaced by the establishment of Israel when it replaced the British Mandate in Palestine with an independent Arab State, independent Jewish State and 'neutral' Jerusalem in 1948. Much of this was done as neutral, implementing programmes intended to improve maternal and child health using low-cost, preventive health-care measures. Considerable progress was made in developing methods of eradicating diphtheria, malaria, tuberculosis and whooping cough. UNICEF put emphasis on vaccination programmes, breast feeding and rehydration therapy for diarrhoea as means of improving public health. Although UNICEF had been established to provide aid for children affected by war, it remained in existence to assume a much broader role. Whilst its life beyond the postwar emergency had never been intended when the time came in 1950 for the UN to close it down, a successful lobby was mounted to save it. The growing concern about child welfare and survival rates in developing countries from disease or starvation led delegates from the new nations of the 'developing' world to speak out. 'How, asked the delegate from Pakistan, could the task of international action for children be regarded as complete when so many millions of children in Africa, Asia and Latin America languished in sickness and hunger, not because of war, but because of the age-old problem of poverty?' (Black 1996: 8). Once more, an appeal for the continuation of its work did not go unheard, and in 1953, by resolution 802 (VIII) of 6 October, it was unanimously voted to continue the fund for an indefinite period, therewith the General Assembly confirmed UNICEF as a permanent fixture in the UN system.

Thus, initially, UNICEF was definably an aid agency that continued to work impartially by providing relief to both sides in the Nigerian Civil War of 1968 and then to Cambodia in 1979 after the country was invaded by Vietnam under the leadership of the second Executive Director Henry Labouisse (1965–1979). It was the third Executive Director, Jim Grant (1980–1995), who took an active interest in the drafting and implementation of the CRC, so that during his term, UNICEF added children's rights to its mandate.

In UNESCO's *Guide to Archives of International Organizations*[2], UNICEF's mandate is thus described: 'UNICEF was created with this purpose in mind – to work with others to overcome the obstacles that poverty, violence, disease and discrimination place in a child's path. We believe that we can, together, advance the cause of humanity.' Furthermore, 'UNICEF upholds the Convention on the Rights of the Child. We work to assure equality for those who are discriminated against, girls and women in particular. We work for the Millennium Development Goals and for the progress promised in the United Nations Charter. We strive for peace and security. We work to hold everyone accountable to the promises made for children. We are part of the Global Movement for Children – a broad coalition dedicated to improving the life of every child. Through this movement, and events such as the United Nations Special Session on Children, we encourage young people to speak out and participate in the decisions that affect their lives.'

Prior to the CRC, in 1959 the General Assembly had adopted a significantly expanded version as its own *Declaration of the Rights of the Child*. It expanded the Declaration to ten principles in place of the original five. However, lobbying towards the end of the following two decades during which the cause of children was relegated to a lower place, whilst such issues as the environment and world hunger were given priority, brought children back to public attention. As part of that effort, the NGO children's lobby put pressure on the UN to declare 1979 the *International Year of the Child* (IYC).

Instead of presenting development as the rationale for addressing children's needs, the objective of the IYC was to simply focus on 'the child'. This was by no means a return to the earlier welfare because this time it took in numerous difficult issues in uncompromising terms going further than welfarism and philanthropy. It addressed more sensitive topics including child abuse, child labour and sexual exploitation of children. Therewith, the IYC also opened the door to children's rights. During the IYC, 10 years of drafting a new Convention to replace the 1959 Declaration with a more significant instrument began. The plan was to have it ready and approved by the General Assembly in time to celebrate the 30 years of the Declaration. Thus, in 1989, the CRC was adopted by the General Assembly, and on 2 September 1990, it became an international law. The CRC consists of 54 articles (see Appendix 4) that address the basic human rights children everywhere are entitled to. The four core principles of the CRC are non-discrimination; commitment to the best interests of the child; the right to life, survival and development; and

[2] http://www.unesco.org/archives/sio/Eng/presentation_print.php?idOrg=1033

respect for the views of the child. Under the CRC, a child is defined as '... every human being below the age of eighteen years unless, under the law applicable to the child, majority is attained earlier'.

Jim Grant was a visionary leader on a worldwide scale. As Executive Director of UNICEF, he had launched a worldwide child survival and development revolution. Under his direction the outcome was that by 1995, at least 25 million children were still alive who might otherwise have died. Millions of other children enjoyed better health and nutrition. UNICEF had embraced non-discrimination and Grant's vision had also included support for the CRC. In an ideal world today, we would see a world fit for children that was heralded when the CRC fell in place as the final and one of the key building blocks in 1989. However, looking back on the intervening years since 1989, in reality very few steps forward have been made away from welfare to rights approach. Considering also that the delivery of basic services such as health and nutrition should have advanced as a right of all children, the present situation of the world may suggest it is in fact failing.

At present recent advances in new information and communication technologies (ICTs) that have progressed in unparalleled ways over the past decade are having a positive impact on how rights are delivered and monitored in the future. They progressively exert more drive and support change at community level as well as feed into local, national and worldwide economies and support international development efforts. ICTs are being used to support *Communication for Development* (C4D) which stresses the importance of horizontal communication models that are used to make participation, inclusion and empowerment possible. The aim is to transform lives by increasing access to health care, education and information. National and international policy frameworks and guidelines using ICTs are now being developed in the global North but with the intention of rapidly making them as accessible in the South. Here they work for children's rights by testing out whether policy is convincingly based on sound evidence that takes children's experiences and problems into account (Bulger and Livingstone 2013). ICTs are dependent on the viability of well-researched evidence.

Consequently the nature of research is changing to take account of children's rights, participation in particular. Thus, attitudes, beliefs, values, suppositions and practices which ultimately shape the research experience for children rather than simply make them the subject of it are leading to a great deal of consideration of the ethics of working with them. The basic ethical principle is that the human dignity of children and their rights and well-being are respected in all research, regardless of the context. It has been particularly strongly pursued in the social research field and has a long and firmly established pedigree (for instance, see Alderson 1995; Morrow and Richards 1996; Alderson and Morrow 2011). Nevertheless it has been slow in finding a place in children's rights, particularly in the South, and often seen in context with participatory work with children rather than research (for instance, SCF UK 2003). The links between social research and rights that give children the right to be appropriately researched in which rights are the basis has been a more recent development with a working base in the South (for instance, Ennew et al. 2010, Manual 2). UNICEF has now adopted a rights-based research approach further with *Ethical Research Involving Children* (ERIC) (Anderson et al. 2013) that aims to guide researchers and research institutions to understand, plan and conduct ethical research involving children and young people in any cultural, geographical, social or methodological framework or setting. All areas of research that use ethical approaches work on the basis that there is a policy on research that is firmly based in evidence that takes in children in the South increasingly and that the Internet and mobile technologies are increasing the scope of researchers for gathering data in the field (Bulger and Livingstone 2013).

There are still gaps to be filled. One of the biggest is finding a means of research with children in civil and international wars where ethics often have to be sacrificed in order to put protection and basic services first. Ironically it has been warfare that has often led the way the international community has found itself working most directly with children and where they have their longest track record.

The UN and UNICEF particularly were produced as a reaction to war that took the lives of many people and left many more in a desperate situation in its wake. Conceptually the idea of a 'zone of peace' belongs to the work of UNICEF (Evans 1996). Since 1946 they often focussed on children as a means of being able to work on both sides in both civil and international wars. They did that during the 1960s in Biafra, during the Nigerian Civil War in 1968, and later in Cambodia after the 1979 invasion by Vietnam. During the 1980s, the proposal that children be a 'conflict-free zone' in which they were protected from harm and provided with essential services to make sure of their survival and well-being came about. The concept was first proposed by Nils Thedin of *Swedish Save the Children* in a proposal to UNICEF in 1983 (Vittachi 1994). Since Thedin's proposal, numerous agreements to provide relief for children on both sides have been negotiated. For instance, in El Salvador in 1985, negotiations with the government and rebels produced an agreement that the bloodshed should cease for 3 'days of tranquillity'. On 3 days over consecutive months, both sides allowed a campaign that allowed about 20,000 health workers to immunise around 250,000 small children against diphtheria, measles, polio, tetanus and whooping cough. That was repeated each year until the war ended in 1991.

Similar principles were applied in other disputes (Toole 2006). In 1986, the Ugandan government and the National Resistance Army agreed to allow immunisation, personnel and equipment within a corridor of peace. A little later in Lebanon in 1987, conflict was suspended for 3 days to permit all young children to be vaccinated. During 1988–1989 in Afghanistan, immunisation teams were allowed to go to both government and mujahidin-controlled areas and in some raised vaccination levels to over 80 %.

One of the most sustained examples of humanitarian aid working on both sides was in Sudan. The country had been in a state of civil war for several years, and then in 1988, the situation worsened when a catastrophic drought caused around a quarter of a million deaths and displaced almost a million other people. By early 1989, it was apparent that a similar disaster would happen in the coming year. The Secretary General asked UNICEF Executive Director Jim Grant to meet both sides. Operation Lifeline Sudan (OLS) (Taylor-Robinson 2002) was the outcome. OLS enabled relief agencies to negotiate with both the government and rebel Sudan People's Liberation Army (SPLA). They agreed to allow eight 'corridors of tranquillity' to be created. Against all odds OLS achieved considerable success. By that autumn, it had delivered over 100,000 tonnes of food and 4,000 tonnes of medical supplies, and vaccination clinics were set up in all strongholds that accommodated at least 90,000 children in SPLA areas. It also brought about a reduction in the fighting along the corridors. It allowed people to move around the country and began to give them hope. A second period was negotiated in 1990, and in 1995 the SPLA became the first rebel group in dispute with a government to commit itself to the provisions of the CRC.

The Balkans took us through a similar passage in bringing the unknown into our homes throughout the 1990s and into the present century (Glenny 1996). That was particularly so because as Bosnia moved on to be replaced by Kosovo, weaponry diminished as a focus for newsmaking to be replaced by ethnic cleansing. Again children were news of the last resort; for instance, when children were amongst the victims of a bombing by other former Yugoslavians, it was important news, but as victims of 'friendly fire', they tended to be less well presented. The wars had, in fact, begun in 1991 in Slovenia (1991) and Croatia (1991–1995) as Yugoslavia began to break up. The Bosnian War (1992–1995) was followed by Kosovo War (1998–1999). There were insurgencies in the Preševo Valley (1999–2001) in Serbia and Republic of Macedonia (2001) that have their roots in the same conflicts. In 1995 NATO had bombed Bosnia and Herzegovina, and again there were air strikes in Kosovo in the first half of 1999. The latter strikes led to the withdrawal of federal Yugoslav forces from Kosovo, the UN Interim Administration Mission in Kosovo (UNMIK) was set up and the Balkan Wars of the 1990s was brought to an end (Radan 2004). Children were very much overshadowed by political events and news about NATO's role.

Also in the 1990s, the escalation of violence in Indonesia began to attract similar attention. East Timor had been invaded and annexed by Indonesia in 1975 under the pretext of ending the civil war that had broken out that year, preventing it from becoming a communist state (Ramos-Horta 1987). By the late 1990s, the international community that had tolerated the annexation had begun to see the situation otherwise. A report by the Catholic Church had suggested that up to 60,000 Timorese were killed by the end of 1976. This does not appear to include fatalities from the period between the beginning of civil war in August 1975 and the Indonesian invasion of December (Dunn 1995: 66). Other reports gave higher figures. A fierce guerrilla war continued almost until independence in 1999. Where children were part of forced migrations or victims of atrocities, especially when the elderly or Christian priests and nuns were murdered, they made news in order to put an edge on the degree of violence.

From 1990 to 1998, Indonesian military operations in Aceh against the separatist Free Aceh Movement (GAM) had seen the Indonesian army carrying out large-scale and systematic human rights abuses. The war was characterised as the dirtiest of all wars in Indonesia because of the arbitrary executions, torture, kidnappings and disappearances along with torching of villages. Thus, Indonesia also enters the annals of a nation where children died during the life of the CRC; in fact several of these conflicts had taken place during its earliest days.

'Children as a zone of peace' is the phrase that became a common usage in place of 'corridors of tranquillity' after the *Study of the Impact of Armed Conflict on Children* was produced by a high-level commission established by the UN General Assembly and chaired by Graça Machel (1996). In some ways, the phrase might have a place in the previous chapter except that by varying degrees, it has done what was suggested conceptually by Thedin in 1983. A strategy called *Children as a Zone of Peace* (CZOP) was drawn up to provide humanitarian aid during conflict by giving precedence to the rights of children. CZOP was implemented in countries in five regions of the world. The strategy achieved results in terms of its set objectives, including education, immunisation and disease control with further benefits such as respite from violence and developing a sense of national value. Implementing the strategy's objectives is closely linked to the political and logistical realities of each conflict. There are five components necessary for successfully carrying out CZOP: firstly, a preliminary proposal from a trusted third party, followed by high-level negotiations which then need to be followed by creative planning. The next step is a targeted communication and finally a wide range of partnerships amongst various stakeholders. The CZOP has been used at its best as a basis for negotiation and humanitarian intervention.

The Machel report focussed on the more and more damaging impact of conflict on children as victims as well as combatants, thus on the ways in which international conventions have been contravened and on the likelihood of worsening conditions as a growing number of countries begin to see increasing violence.

The Gulf War (2 August 1990–28 February 1991) was the first 'live broadcast' war ever. The CRC entered into force on 2 September 1990, immediately on being ratified by the required number of nations. It was, therefore, contemporaneous with the war. During that war emphasis was very much on the weapons and 'sensational' coverage of actions such as air raids and hits by cruise missiles. There were 'scandals' when civilians were killed or wounded, although those victims were also clearly used as political collateral. It was no longer a distant war but one where we had live television coverage available. During the conflict with Iraq, children were from time to time presented as victims of Iraqi aggression when the best media and political advantage could be achieved. Once the war was over, the increasingly poor state of children in Iraq became news. They became a pawn in the negotiations with the international community. The CZOP strategy appeared not to have worked there. Instead the health (Ascherio et al. 1992; Bierman 1993) and welfare of children became a key reason for Iraq being allowed to trade some of their oil. Thus, in the earliest days of the CRC when it should be assumed enthusiasm for it was at its highest level, children were still used for propagandist purposes to bring into play pity as justification for 'liberating' a country. Part of the justification was the story that the Iraqi invasion of Kuwait was a surprise attack by Saddam Hussein. Iraqi soldiers were reported to be slaughtering newborn babies who were still in incubators in Kuwaiti hospitals. It was eventually exposed as a sensationalist statement made by the daughter of the Kuwaiti ambassador.

Again it was an example of the bathos of the murdered and abused child which, whilst there were clearly child victims of the war, was used to boost public support for that war. This was extended as attention turned to the Kurdish people. Iraqi Kurdistan had been granted autonomous status by the Iraqi government in 1970. A guerrilla war between two Kurdish political factions took place through the 1980s and 1990s that saw over 37,000 people killed and hundreds of thousands forced to leave their homes. Vast swathes of rural Kurdistan were evacuated and thousands of villages destroyed. There were countless extrajudicial summary executions on both sides. Following the Gulf War, attention turned to the plight of Kurdish civilians although by then it had been a long ongoing conflict. Its status was reconfirmed as an autonomous entity within the federal Iraqi Republic in 2005 after the 2003 invasion.

In 2003 a coalition led by the USA invaded Iraq on the grounds where Saddam Hussein's people were developing weapons of mass destruction (WMDs). At the outset the invasion was welcomed by the Shia minority who had been oppressed by the old regime. The invasion also caused violent conflict between sectarian and newly liberated political groups. There was also hostility between the recently liberated Shia minority and Sunni Muslim majority. In 2008, the *UN High Commissioner for Refugees* (UNHCR) reported that around 4.7 million people had been displaced by the conflict and the Red Cross was reporting Iraq's humanitarian being one of the most critical in the world. It took the live broadcast of war a stage further. However, far less attention was paid to the situation of children because of the emphasis on the political and sectarian outcomes of the war.

The war in Somalia (2006–2009) received less attention although it was reported that over 16,000 civilians had been confirmed killed and about 29,000 wounded since the start of the insurgency in December 2006 (Sheikh 2008). One point nine million civilians were reportedly displaced from homes in Mogadishu alone in 2007. Exact figures on how many were children are not known. There are around 16 ongoing, including the Syrian conflict whilst writing this, and 14 other wars that have finished that are generally less well reported up until 2013. Genocide, rape and torture are the key themes that attract attention and media reports, but what do we really know about the children? In stark contrast we are beginning to be informed about places and their regimes in great detail. Where children do become central to these areas is in the aftermath when reconstruction draws in 'child savers' who busy themselves with the renovation of institutions full of neglected orphans, who are often in reality the physically and mentally disadvantaged ones who have been placed in institutions prior to the conflicts. However, they provide a very precise humanitarian face of aid and reconstruction. This is, of course, secondary exploitation that feeds on the sympathy of donors particularly.

Where then do the CRC and children's rights in general fit into this bleak picture? Currently child rights appear to have represented an unfinished movement from needs/welfare/services approaches towards rights approach. Most certainly one can begin to identify that in war situations but without any clear indication of what is being done for the children. That is to say, the NGOs and UN agencies on the ground may be giving them shelter and food along with medical attention and sometimes schooling, but we learn little from what we are told about what happens to them. Whilst we can assume with a degree of accuracy that as many as possible will be resettled where they came from and reunited with families where necessary or possible, we cannot say generally what is being done to re-orientate them to 'normal' life and prepare them for their future. There is a rather vulnerable bare belly under the surface of what we would expect. The CRC is not really suited to all situations, and such conflict situations as those used as examples are perhaps at the cutting edge. One part of the Preamble says that:

> Considering that the child should be fully prepared to live an individual life in society, and brought up in the spirit of the ideals proclaimed in the Charter of the United Nations, and in particular in the spirit of peace, dignity, tolerance, freedom, equality and solidarity,

This is an ideal that sets the goal of preparing each child for the rest of their life that conforms of itself to a set of the noblest and highest ideals. With the experience of war with the many frightening and potentially, if not in actual fact, physically and psychologically injurious events a child may have experienced, the qualities 'dignity, tolerance, freedom, equality and solidarity' may be entirely alien concepts and the 'spirit of peace' a notion so abstract that it may never make any sense to that damaged individual. The 1974 *Declaration on the Protection of Women and Children in Emergency and Armed Conflict* makes the promise of protection but none of the other standards. One of the closing parts of the Preamble of the CRC promises that:

> Recognizing that, in all countries in the world, there are children living in exceptionally difficult conditions, and that such children need special consideration,

which effectively pledges protection as far as it is possible, but no more than that. Further, parts or the whole of the articles of the CRC may apply to these children in conflict situations, including 3, 6, 16, 24.1, 29.1d, 38.1 and 4 and 39. Taking just the latter two:

Article 38

> 1. States Parties undertake to respect and to ensure respect for rules of international humanitarian law applicable to them in armed conflicts which are relevant to the child.
>
> 4. In accordance with their obligations under international humanitarian law to protect the civilian population in armed conflicts, States Parties shall take all feasible measures to ensure protection and care of children who are affected by an armed conflict.

Article 39

> States Parties shall take all appropriate measures to promote physical and psychological recovery and social reintegration of a child victim of: any form of neglect, exploitation, or abuse; torture or any other form of cruel, inhuman or degrading treatment or punishment; or armed conflicts. Such recovery and reintegration shall take place in an environment which fosters the health, self-respect and dignity of the child.

we see again a very high set of standards but also some difficult issues that need to be resolved before any promises can be kept. Those may include, for example, how does any nation ensure respect for the rules of international humanitarian law when two or more parties are engaged in conflict? Which one of two or more groups in a country takes ultimate responsibility for that country's observance of those rules and how can those be monitored and implemented throughout the whole country? Where third parties are involved that are foreign countries, how is responsibility delegated to them and again monitored and implemented? Recent action in Iraq, for instance, has seen foreign powers intervene, and more recent examples of warfare at long distance with the use of drones make these notions almost unachievable. With respect to Article 39 particularly, how is the recovery of a child ensured in a war-torn and possibly very physically damaged nation where medical services, supplies and personnel alone may be scarce resources?

This is not in or of itself a criticism of the CRC or children's rights generally, but is looking realistically at how all the best intentions in the world are sometimes interpreted to mean far more than can ever be delivered in the real world. Here war has been used as an example, but in later chapters, equally important questions will be raised. One of them does sometimes relate to the reasons for national and international conflicts. That is the question of culture and how it shapes different societies. Thus, we might ask of children's rights and cultural relativity, what relevance the CRC has? Since many of the notions of children's and human rights generally have origins in the western sphere where despite diversity there are also many shared cultural characteristics, how do those work in other societies where beliefs, cultures and many other aspects of their social structure do not share them?

In the broadest framework of rights, we still have a common denominator: the human being. Human rights are about the protection of rights irrespective of age or any other classifier and offer protection to individuals although to all intents and purposes, they often appear to be for specific groups by age, gender, ethnicity, belief and so on. Although expressed in the plural form and directed at men, the 1789 *Déclaration des droits de l'homme et du citoyen* of the French Revolution set the agenda for the language that continues to be used in only a slightly different form today to describe each individual's rights. Children are one of the groups that are part of the whole of humanity, and whilst used generically the CRC does use the singular form 'child'. Although some people will insist otherwise, in fact it is entirely correct to say that there is no such thing as children's rights but only human rights of which the CRC is one on many parts.

References

Alderson, P. (1995). *Listening to children: Children, ethics and social research*. London: Barnados.

Alderson, P., & Morrow, V. (2011). *The ethics of research with children and young people: A practical handbook*. London: Sage.

Anderson, D., Fitzgerald, R., Graham, A., Powell, M. A., & Taylor, N. (2013). *Ethical research involving children*. Florence: UNICEF.

Ascherio, A., Chase, R., Coté, T., Dehaes, G., Hoskins, E., Laaouej, J., Passey, M., Qaderi, S., Shuqaidef, S., Smith, M. C., & Zaidi, S. (1992). Effect of the Gulf War on infant and child mortality in Iraq. *New England Journal of Medicine, 328*(13), 931–36.

Bierman, A. (1993). The Gulf War and infant and child mortality in Iraq. *New England Journal of Medicine, 328*(18), 1358 (correspondence with journal).
Black, M. (1996). *Children first: The story of UNICEF, past and present*. Oxford: Oxford University Press.
Bulger, M., & Livingstone, S. (2013). *A global agenda for children's rights in the digital age: Recommendations for developing UNICEF's research strategy*. Florence: UNICEF.
Cantwell, N. (1993). *Monitoring the convention through the idea of the '3Ps'* (pp. 121–130). Eurosocial report 45/1993. Vienna: European Centre for Social Welfare Policy and Research.
Dunn, J. (1995). The Timor affair in international perspective. In P. B. R. Carey & G. Carter Bentley (Eds.), *East Timor at the crossroads: The forging of a nation* (pp. 59–72). Honolulu: University of Hawai'i Press.
Ennew, J., Abebe, T., Bangyai, R., Karapituck, P., Kjørholt, A. T., Noonsup, T., Beazley, H., Bessell, S., Daengchart-Kushanoglu, P., & Waterson, R. (2010). *The right to be properly researched: How to do rights-based, scientific research with children*. Bangkok: Knowing Children.
Evans, J. L. (1996). *Children as zones of peace: Working with young children affected by armed violence*. Early childhood counts: Programming resources for early childhood care and development. Washington, DC: The Consultative Group on ECCD, World Bank.
Glenny, M. (1996). *The fall of Yugoslavia: The third Balkan War*. London: Penguin.
Lurie, J. (2003). The tension between protection and participation – General theory and consequences as related to rights of children, including working children. *Journal of Social Work Theory and Practice, 6*(7), 2003–2004.
Machel, G. (1996). *United Nations Study on the impact of armed conflict on children*. New York: United Nations.
Morrow, V., & Richards, M. (1996). The ethics of social research with children: An overview. *Children and Society, 10*(2), 90–105.
Radan, P. (2004). *The break-up of Yugoslavia and international law*. Abingdon: Taylor & Francis.
Ramos-Horta, J. (1987). *Funu: The unfinished Saga of East Timor*. Trenton: Red Sea Press.
SCF UK. (2003). *So you want to consult with children? A toolkit of good practice*. London: Save the Children.
Sheikh, A. (2008). *Somalia conflict kills more than 2,100 this year*. Reuters. http://www.reuters.com/article/2008/06/26/us-somalia-conflict-idUSL2661036420080626
Taylor-Robinson, S. (2002). Operation Lifeline Sudan. *Journal of Medical Ethics, 28*(1), 49–51.
Toole, D. (2006). *Peace-building strategies: Transition from relief to development: Why children and early intervention matter*. New York: UNICEF.
Vittachi, V. T. (1994). *Between the guns: Children as a zone of peace*. London: Hodder and Stoughton.

Childhoods Past

8

In 1988 when *The Next Generation* was completed, it bore the subtitle *Lives of Third World Children*. It would be difficult to repeat that subtitle exactly as it was then. Firstly, the expression 'third world' is no longer as commonly used with what was often understood to be the so-called 'second world' more or less gone. The countries that it was composed of by and large belong to different spheres of influence and their political systems have mostly entirely changed. Moreover, that definition is also taken to include the last 'discovered' or explored parts of the world. That is so long ago as to be almost irrelevant today.

Secondly, it included 12 case studies. Not all of those countries are classified 'third world' or even developing nations any longer. In fact four of them, Brazil, India, China and South Africa, now come under the acronym BRICS that describes core members of an association of five major emerging national economies. South Africa became part of that group in 2011; the other is Russia, also included after the original 12 nations in this chapter. All are rapidly developing or newly industrialised countries distinguished by large, fast-growing economies, with significant influence on regional and global affairs. All of them are also G20 members, the forum for governments and central bank governors from 20 of the world's major economies. That they may well still suffer enormous economic and social problems and the phenomena affecting childhood described then persist today, they are nonetheless countries that have changed status. In some cases they have moved up international economic ranking to pass once-established leading nations who are now in decline. There are now even countries that were not then listed among the poor nations who now have the status 'poor'. Moreover, there are so many common traits that have ended the rich and poor nation dichotomy as it was at that time. Whatever the case may be, since 1988 political events have reshaped the world extensively, and these have influenced other events which, in turn, have often had impact on children. Thus, rather than only look at the 12 case study nations, the events of 1989 and what has happened since have been added.

B. Milne, *Rights of the Child*, Children's Well-Being: Indicators and Research 11,
DOI 10.1007/978-3-319-18784-6_8

The case studies were Sierra Leone, Somalia, Mozambique, India, Peru, South Africa, Nicaragua, Brazil, Lebanon, Thailand, China and Cuba. It was a carefully considered choice of countries in which events were affecting children's lives every day, usually for the worse but with a few optimistic signs. To use some kind of rough guide, we looked at infant mortality rates (IMR) in those countries as well as events to show the environment in which children entered the world. Ongoing events told the rest of the story.

There are always slightly different sources of IMR; however, we used them to determine the order in which we presented the countries. The IMR we chose to use at the time showed Sierra Leone with the third-worst mortality rates in the world. That remains unchanged. Mozambique has risen to second in our list and fourth globally. Somalia, despite almost constant conflicts and grinding poverty, is now our third, tenth in the world. India, despite being an increasingly successful economic force, is still in fourth place and 39th worldwide. South Africa is up from sixth to fifth and 59th globally. Brazil, now becoming a fast-climbing economic giant, is up from eighth to sixth and 63rd in the world. Peru has gone down from fifth to seventh and 64th worldwide. Nicaragua is also down from seventh to eighth, 65th in the world. China, the raging industrial and financial giant in the present world, is up from eleventh to ninth and 72nd globally. Lebanon has gone from ninth to tenth, eightieth worldwide. Thailand is now eleventh from tenth, 89th overall. Finally, Cuba remains in twelfth position and is 124th in the world.

Looking at those countries at that time, we were attempting to examine whether African wars were on the media 'map'. Sierra Leone (see Bates 2008; Harris 2014; IndexMundi.com 2012; Keen 2005; UNICEF 2014) was one of the poorest countries in the world. It hardly featured on any kind of media map. There had been an alleged attempt to overthrow the president in 1987 which led to a number of government officials including the vice-president. That was where it stood in 1988. By the end of 1989 several of the alleged plotters had been hung. In October 1990 the president set up a constitutional review commission to assess the one-party constitution. A commission recommended re-establishing a multiparty system which became effective in 1991. In 1992 there was a military coup, which sent the president into exile, and a National Provisional Ruling Council (NPRC) was set up. In 1996 there was a further coup that displaced the leaders of the previous one. In 1997 there was yet another military coup which sent the president into exile. After less than a year in control, the junta was overthrown by the Nigerian-led ECOMOG (Economic Community of West African States Ceasefire Monitoring Group) forces.

Between 1991 and 2001 at least 50,000 people had been killed in Sierra Leone's protracted civil war and hundreds of thousands more displaced to become refugees in neighbouring countries. In 2001 UN forces moved into rebel-held parts of the country and began to disarm the rebels, so that at the beginning of 2002 the civil war was declared over. In 2007 Sierra Leone finally held free presidential and parliamentary elections, but no candidate won the 50 %-plus-one-vote majority fixed in the constitution on the first round of voting. A run-off election was held later in 2007, and Ernest Bai Koroma of the All People's Congress (APC) party was elected. He was re-elected president for a second and final term in November 2012.

Sierra Leone was in a constant state of conflict from 1987 until 2002 and from 1991 to 2001 an almost incessant civil war. Even then it took a further 5 years to establish an elected and stable government. Since then there has been slow progress but the country is now showing signs of a successful transition. Sierra Leone has relied on mining, particularly diamonds and some gold, as its economic base, also being among the largest producers of bauxite and titanium worldwide. Despite Sierra Leone's considerable natural wealth, 70 % of the population still live in poverty. Little has ever been widely reported about the country's conflicts, leaving the large numbers of casualties and displaced people almost unknown.

In 2010 a free health-care initiative was launched to provide free health care for children under 5 years and pregnant and lactating women. It particularly targets the poorest. Parents of children from birth to age 5 no longer pay for consultations, vaccination and hospitalisation at health centres and hospitals. A wide-ranging service includes treatment of malaria, diarrheal diseases, pneumonia, severe malnutrition and paediatric HIV. At present Ebola fever is posing a significant new risk. The National Ministry of Health and its partners believe that vulnerable communities are at high risk of contracting it given the amount of cross-border activity to neighbouring countries with a sizeable outbreak in 2014.

Education is compulsory for all children for 6 years of primary and 3 years of secondary education. However, a shortage of schools and teachers has made implementation impossible. The civil war caused destruction of over 1,200 primary schools; in 2001 67 % of school-age children were still without places. The situation has improved with primary school enrolment at least double and the reconstruction of schools since the end of the civil war. The situation of Sierra Leonean children is now gradually improving, but it is not unlikely that a revisit of this work in another quarter of a century may not find the most extensive progress.

Mozambique (see Braathen 2003; Cabrita 2000; IndexMundi.com 2012; UNICEF 2014) has a long history of violence that is now apparently under control, if not absolutely over. After independence in 1974, from 1977 to 1992 there was a protracted and violent civil war (see FitzGerald and Stewart 2001) between the opposition forces of anti-communist Mozambican National Resistance (RENAMO) rebel militias and the Front for the Liberation of Mozambique (FRELIMO) regime. The failure of central government planning and resulting economic and infrastructure collapse, lack of investment in productive resources and nationalisation of privately owned industries and widespread famine undermined any chance the country had of finding peace and stability. During the greater part of the civil war, the FRELIMO government was unable to put into effect real controls outside of urban areas, many of them cut off from the capital. The war saw massive human rights violations on both sides with RENAMO exacerbating chaos by using terror and indiscriminate targeting of the civilian population. The government executed several thousand people whilst trying to extend control throughout the country. In 1986, President Samora Machel died when his plane crashed on the way back from an international meeting in Zambia. His successor, Joaquim Chissano, implemented extensive changes in the country and reforms such as changing from

Marxism to capitalism and began peace talks with RENAMO. The new constitution of 1990 made provision for a multiparty political system, market-based economy and free elections.

The civil war ended in the second half of 1992. The resettlement of refugees has brought great population stability, and successful economic reform led to a high growth rate. The country has enjoyed a remarkable recovery, achieving an average annual rate of economic growth of 8 % between 1996 and 2006 and around 7 % by 2011. Serious floods during early 2000 slowed GDP growth to 2.1 %, but full recovery was achieved in 2001 with growth of 14.8 % since. Growth in the future depended on several major foreign investment projects, continued economic reform and the recovery of agriculture, transport and tourism. In 2013 approximately 80 % of the population was employed in agriculture, the majority in small-scale subsistence farming that still suffers from inadequate infrastructure, commercial networks and sufficient investment. However, in 2012 more than 90 % of arable land was still uncultivated with potential thus open for expansion in that sector.

Nevertheless, Mozambique still has one of the highest child mortality rates in the world. Increases in the level of child and maternal well-being have not been even across the country where large numbers of children and women, especially in remote rural areas, remain at high risk. Every year approaching an average of 86,000 newborn infants die before reaching age 1 and a further average of 38,000 die before reaching 5 years. Gains at first made to reduce child mortality are now seriously threatened by HIV and AIDS. Over 400 people become infected every day on average, of which around 85 are infants infected through mother-to-child transmission. Malaria remains the foremost killer of children, contributing to around 33 % of all child deaths. Poor nutrition continues to affect many children and mothers; around 45 % of children under the age of 5 are physically underdeveloped, and malnutrition is the primary cause of at least half of all child deaths. Over the past two decades, infant mortality rate has at least fallen from 147 to 90 per 1,000 live births and the under-5 mortality rate has decreased from 219 to 138 per 1,000. Progress is being made, but it is slow and it will be many years before improvements are significant.

Somalia was already in a state of chaos in 1988. President Barre had seized power in 1969 and established the Somali Democratic Republic. In 1991 his government collapsed as the Somali Civil War broke out (Bradbury and Healy 2010). Without the authority of a central government, the country's inhabitants slipped backed into local forms of resolving conflicts (Fergusson 2014). A few autonomous regions emerged in the north in the subsequent process of decentralisation. The early 2000s saw the formation of interim federal administrations. One of them, Somaliland, declared independence from the rest of Somalia in 1991 but has thus far only limited international recognition as a republic. A Transitional National Government (TNG) was established in 2000, followed by a Transitional Federal Government (TFG) in 2004 that re-established institutions such as a single army in Somalia. In 2006 the TFG, with the help of Ethiopian troops, took control of most of the nation's southern conflict zones from the Islamic Courts Union (ICU). The ICU then divided into more radical groups such as Al-Shabaab. They fought the TFG and its allies for control of the region but the rebels lost most of the territory that they had taken control of up until 2012. During 2011–2012, a political process that created standards for the establishment of permanent democratic institutions was created. The new administrative framework wrote a provisional constitution that was adopted in 2012 so that Somalia became a federation. Following the end of the TFG's interim mandate that year, the Federal Government of Somalia, the first permanent government in Somalia since the beginning of the civil war, was formed.

The country has undergone a period of intense reconstruction, particularly the capital Mogadishu. Over time, Somalia has maintained a healthy informal economy that is based principally on livestock, remittances and telecommunications (Samatar 2008). Things have improved with the end of civil conflict; however, progress is slow for the youngest citizens. However, Somalia is very drought prone and frequently faces extreme food insecurity. That is aggravated by poor health care and the lack of access to safe drinking water and safe sanitation facilities. Pastoralist groups make up around half the population and are widely recognised as being marginalised in terms of access to health, sanitation and education due to their nomadic life. One out of every ten children still dies before their first birthday. Although no comprehensive information is available, it is believed that the main causes of infant and child mortality are such illnesses as pneumonia (up to 25 %), diarrhoea (around 20 %), measles (more than 10 %) and neonatal disorders (just under 20 %). Education is still poor, girls do not universally enjoy access to schools and the dispersion of the population, especially the nomadic groups, makes a universal model a very difficult proposition.

The 1990s was a historic decade in India. 1989 had changed the face of the country when Rajiv Gandhi resigned as prime minister after his party, the Indian National Congress, lost about half of its seats in the general election. Opposition parties formed a minority government under V. P. Singh. There was a period of turmoil until well into 1991 but since then a relative political stability. Economic growth rates increased rapidly as policies were liberalised, although not as quickly as in China. The rate of growth of population and fertility and infant mortality rates (MR) decreased. Two polarising trends emerged in national politics. The first was the politics of social justice based on caste, following implementation of the 1980 Mandal commission report (Ramaiah 1992: 1203–1207). Then there was the politics of religion based on Hindu nationalism, particularly marked by demolition of the Babri Masjid Mosque in 1992 and ensuing communal riots. Nonetheless, as the government liberalised economic policies, growth surged and the foundation was laid for India becoming one of the fastest-growing economies of the world (Sharma 2011). Prime minister Manmohan Singh was largely instrumental in bringing about change, although India, with its socialist past, did not manage to push economic reforms as aggressively as China which raced ahead from being only just ahead of India to double the GDP (four times higher rate of growth) due to a more vigorous rate of economic reform. The License Raj was brought to an end. GDP per capita nearly doubled from US$1,380 in 1990 to US$2,420 in 2000. The rate of growth was then the eleventh fastest in the world. Foreign direct investment, previously contributing under 0.1 % to GDP, came nearer to contributing 1 %.

Foreign exchange reserves, which had fallen to more or less zero, surged up to 50 billion US dollars. Short-term external debt of 350 % of foreign exchange reserves plunged to 25 %. Foreign direct investment which was mainly from the UK, Germany, Japan and the USA began to be positive. The Indian rupee plunged from an exchange rate of 25:1 to 45:1 against the US$. The contribution of the service sector to GDP increased vastly and rapidly. Economically India was thriving but socially it was generally stagnant.

The CRC was accepted enthusiastically by India. Much was promised; however little was achieved. There has been a proliferation of laws and regulations passed through parliament for the protection of children and their rights.[1] Child labour has been an area seeing a great number of changes. In India the law states that children under the age of 18 should not work; however, there is no unequivocal ban on child labour. It is generally permitted in most industries except those deemed 'hazardous'. The *Child Labour (Prohibition and Regulation) Act, 1986*, is one of the most contentious acts related to children in India. It is supplemented by the *Child Labour (Prohibition and Regulation) Rules, 1988*, describing how the act functions. The act delineates where and how children aged 14 and above can work and where they cannot. The provisions of the act were intended to be implemented immediately after the publication of the act in 1988, except for part III that outlines the conditions under which children may work which came into effect in 1993. Although a further law, the *Child Labour Act Amendment, 2006*, banned child labour in hotels and restaurants and the use of children as domestic servants, there continues to be high demand for children as hired help in the home. More recently, in 2008, other occupations were added, such as those involving excessive heat or extreme cold, food processing and brewing, cut timber handling and loading, logging, work in warehouses, diving, mechanical fishing and processes involving exposure to silicates such as in pencil making, slate mining, quarrying and the agate industry. A further amendment in 2008 added work in a circus and caring for elephants to the list. It is, however, endless and has many further amendments to come.

Most current estimates are coming from either those trying to entirely eliminate it or those working with working children's movements in the country. They are poorly documented but range from the government's conservative estimate of 12 million children aged 13 and under to higher estimates from children's rights activists as high as around 60 million. In reality, numbers are not as important as the fact that little is being done to address the issue because the economy is booming and demand for child workers has increased. *The Juvenile Justice (Care and Protection) of Children Act of 2000* made it a crime, punishable with a prison term, for anyone to procure or employ a child in any hazardous employment or in bondage. Prosecutions are few and far between.

---

[1]See ILO: http://www.ilo.org/dyn/natlex/natlex_browse.details?p_lang=en&p_country=IND&p_classification=04&p_origin=COUNTRY&p_sortby=SORTBY_COUNTRY

The *Commission for the Protection of Child Rights Act, 2005*, provided a constitution of the Commission for the Protection of Child Rights and Children's Courts to try offences against children or violations of their rights. It covers the CRC, in effect since 1992, and the National Charter for Children, 2003. The Charter restated India's constitutional commitment to the cause of the children that set out to stipulate that no child would remain hungry, illiterate or ill and add many of the commitments shown in the acts made before and subsequent to its adoption. Another act passed aimed to contribute on the one hand to ending child labour and on the other increasing the skills potential in India is the *Right of Children to Free and Compulsory Education Act, 2009*. It gives every child from age 6 to 14 years the right to free and compulsory education at local schools up to completion of elementary education. It also makes provision for the obligations it places on government and local authorities to implement it. The *Right of Children to Free and Compulsory Education (Amendment) Act, 2012*, amended the 2009 act to extend application to children with disabilities. The *Prohibition of Child Marriage Act, 2007*, set out to end the marriage of children. It set out in law that a male under age 21 years or female under age 18 is not allowed to marry. All existing child marriages were declared void. There was also the *Protection of Children from Sexual Offences Act, 2012,* and *Rules* in the same year to protect children against sexual abuse and harassment, pornography and other offences plus provide for the establishment of special courts to try those offences and for matters connected with them. It was amended by the *Criminal Law (Amendment) Act, 2013*, adding a new section on children adding that use of alternative punishments would be permitted under condition that the 2013 act does not derogate any other act.

Despite these and other significant laws, the lives of many children have not significantly changed in practice. Street children are a good example. According to some UN sources, there are 11 million street children in India; however, independent estimates show that the number is approximately 20 million and another is that more than 400,000 but nowhere near the higher figures exist (Chatterjee 1992). Another source claims that whilst 18 million children work on the streets in India, only somewhere between 5 and 20 % of them actually live there (Singh and Purohit 2011: 103). Alone child labour legislation should have significantly reduced those numbers; however, there are various problems ranging from the presence of street families whose children are naturally part of the large number through to visibility that makes accurate compilation of numbers virtually impossible. This social phenomenon appears to defy the fact that India has experienced enormous economic growth and success at the same time. Projections are on the other hand at least showing that this new prosperity has seen consistent decline in IMR and U5MR, with the rate of decline higher in the current decade than the previous decade. Nonetheless, the most comprehensive projections are showing that at the current rate of decline, India is still very unlikely to meet the objectives of the Millennium Development Goal (MDG) which set out to reduce U5MR by two-thirds between 1990 and 2015 (NIMS, ICMR and UNICEF, 2012). Much remains to be done.

South Africa underwent the most dramatic changes in 1989. It began when, following a stroke, Piet Botha resigned his party's leadership and presidency leading the way to the end of *apartheid*. Botha had already met Nelson Mandela face to face in prison for the first time ever. He had invited Mandela to a meeting over tea that was probably the turning point. After Botha's resignation, F. W. de Klerk became the last president of apartheid South Africa when the general election returned the National Party to power with a very much reduced majority. President de Klerk subsequently announced the abolition of the *Separate Amenities Act*. Walter Sisulu was released from prison. Mandela was to follow in 1990. Under Mandela's leadership of the ANC, apartheid was dismantled in a series of negotiations from 1990 to 1993 that finally ended when the ANC won the general elections in 1994.

Under apartheid, babies, children and young people had sometimes been targeted during township violence. The police had then also arrested young children who refused to end school boycotts and return to classes. Sometimes parents had to search anxiously for them in jails and beg for their release. Things began to change. Working and street children are as present as ever before although the country is now the richest in Africa, despite vast inequalities in income (see Leibbrandt et al. 2012). Two particular issues have come more to the fore than others, education and HIV/AIDS.

After apartheid, the separate, racially designated departments of education were replaced by provincial departments under the auspices of the national Department of Education. According to the *Bill of Rights* in the Constitution, the state has an obligation to progressively make education available and accessible. Even very recently 27 % of 6th grade students were effectively illiterate (Spaull 2013). Only 4 % of the best-off students are functionally illiterate revealing a serious division in literacy between income groups. Spatial segregation of groups by racial definition thus continues to affect educational opportunities. Black, poor students are confronted with obstacles to access to the best schools which are usually in wealthy neighbourhoods. Although they are entering higher education in growing numbers, there is still a marked difference in the racial distribution of students. Recently, the proportion was almost 60 % of whites and around 50 % of Indians entering any form of higher education, compared to under 15 % of coloureds and 12 % of blacks (for instance, see Branson et al. 2013; Lam et al. 2013). As of 2013, the global competitiveness survey (Schwab 2013) ranked South Africa last out of 148 for the quality of mathematics and science and 146th for the quality of general education, behind almost all other African countries in spite of having one of the biggest budgets for education on that continent. Education thus remains one of the worst areas of performance post-apartheid and one of the greatest causes of unrelenting inequality and poverty.

The other major concern has been HIV/AIDS. There are infected as well as affected children with various estimates averaging 410,000 of ages 0–14 living with HIV and 2,500,000 orphaned due to AIDS aged 0–17 in 2012 (for instance, UNGASS 2012). Recently the battle against HIV/AIDS has apparently been turned round (Maurice 2014); therefore, it is probably too early to say and perhaps a further follow-up in 25 years may answer that.

1989 was the year of the first free Brazilian presidential election for 29 years, following the end of military dictatorship in 1985 that had lasted over 20 years. Fernando Collor de Mello and Luiz Inácio 'Lula' da Silva received enough votes to qualify for the second round a month later. At the second round Collor de Mello won. It appeared that democracy would change the country for the better. However, the transition was slow to develop. One particular event drew attention to the situation of children more than any other until then or since.

Just after midnight, in the early morning of July 23, 1993 (Hecht 1998: 120), an event occurred that caused international protest and brought the situation of Brazilian street children more into focus than ever before (Scheper-Hughes and Hoffman 1998: 352–388). A group of men who would later be identified as off-duty policemen opened fire on a group of street children sleeping rough outside one of Rio de Janeiro's most prominent landmarks, the Church of Our Lady of the Candelária. It became known as the Candelária Massacre. Just before the shootings, the policemen picked up three boys returning to Candelária from the beach to take away to be shot elsewhere. Although left for dead, one of them, Wagner dos Santos, survived, eventually left Brazil in order to save his life and has since contributed to changing the political landscape (Rochester 2008). Outside the church, eight of 70 street children were killed by the men as they slept. They were tried for the killings, but only two were convicted. According to survivors, the morning of the day before the massacre, a group of children had thrown stones at police cars. Some of the policemen had allegedly told them that they would soon get them. The children from Candelária were often given warnings by the police; therefore, they left without being worried about it. At midnight, cars stopped at the Candelária church. Next, shots were heard. The children tried to take cover, but eight were dead and several wounded.

The international community severely condemned the attack as too many in Brazil asked for the prosecution of those who shot the Candelária church children. One of the children, Sandro Rosa do Nascimento, later hijacked a bus but during the long confrontation he shot a passenger and was then killed by police after he left the bus. He was restrained by police after his hostage was shot in the face by an officer then three times in the back by Sandro as she fell to the ground. Bystanders reacted by beating and throwing stones at him. He was arrested by police officers but died of asphyxiation in the police vehicle on the way to the police station. The officers were charged with his death but found not guilty. This face-off between a homeless person and police sparked a debate of the relationship between the homeless and the mainstream in developing countries worldwide. A social worker later tracked the fate of the 62 survivors finding that 44 were already dead and most never made it beyond adolescence. They were either killed by police or on the street in other incidents.

The situation of street children has fluctuated since although living standards and most other indicators for children are improving with the country's economic boom. If anything, Brazil's growing prosperity has received more attention than all else. In 2013–2014 the attention of the world was drawn towards the enduring inequality that is still inherent when inhabitants of *favelas* that were being cleared to build stadiums and other facilities for the 2014 football world cup were exposed. Brazil has come a long way but has far to go.

Since 1988 Peru has moved two places in the ranking of our 12 country studies and is now one of the almost unnoticed 'middle-income' countries. During the first presidency of Alan García until 1990, the country plunged into a severe economic crisis, social unrest and violence. The economy entered a period of hyperinflation with the political system in crisis due to the country's mounting internal conflict (Benson et al. 2007: 37–38). In 1990 Alberto Fujimori won the presidency in a run-off against popular author Mario Vargas Llosa. The country's poor economic performance, which had included inflation as high as 2,800 % per annum, continued to inflict social turmoil. Furthermore, they suffered economic and social disruption caused by *Sendero Luminoso* and other terrorist groups and the government's often ineffective response to them (Manrique 2002; Scott Palmer 1994). *Sendero* was founded by university professor Carlos Abimael Guzmán (*Presidente Gonzalo*) following Maoist principles. In a period of less than 20 years, around 30,000 people were killed in actions against or involving *Sendero*. *Movimiento Revolucionario Túpac Amaru* (MRTA) was also causing a great deal of disruption in Peru's urban areas (Manrique 2002). In 1992 Fujimori responded to the economic and social crises by dissolving congress and the judiciary then consolidating power in a Government of Emergency and National Reconstruction, in an attempt to end institutional corruption and abuse of power, also promising to present a revised constitution for a referendum and hold new elections. His actions were referred to as an *autogolpe*, or self-coup, including suspension of civil liberties and concentrating executive powers on his own office. That was well received, and then his popularity increased when *Sendero* leader Guzmán was captured and their strongholds such as Ayacucho lost (Rochlin 2003: 3–4). By 1994 Fujimori was trying to recover Peru's standing with international creditors, thus attracting foreign investment back to the country (Thorp and Zevallos 2002).

Peru's social and economic crises were behind massive internal migration from rural areas to cities with unemployment rates of over 50 %; in some areas many were without a means to earn the basic needs. Although they have since seen double-digit economic growth, Peru's majority has been left behind. In parts of the Andean highlands, malnutrition affects the lives of more than half of all, and whilst Peru has one of the highest economic growth rates in the world, at least 30 % of people still live well below the poverty line (The Heritage Foundation 2014: 354). Despite the global economic crisis, Peru achieved a GDP growth of 8.7 % by the end of September 2010, therewith consolidating its status as a middle-income country (IMF 2012). By and large, the proportion of the population living below the poverty line continued to decline, going down from 36.2 % in 2009 to 34.8 % in 2010. Poverty was in decline generally but increased by 0.5 % among rural populations reflecting an increasing trend outside of slowly prospering cities since 2008.

The free market and economic liberalisation pursued by Alan García during his second term, 2006–2011, and continued by current president Ollanta Humala has attracted significant foreign investment and begun to draw millions out of poverty. Humala, who once led a failed uprising against Alberto Fujimori, ran for office promising more state intervention to help the poor. Nonetheless, he has respected the rule of law and radical governance anticipated has in fact been moderate governance.

The country's key natural resources, including gold, copper and silver, have been used expediently to contribute to improving living standards. Recently economic growth has been well above the Latin American average. The US–Peru Free Trade Agreement has helped to expand trade and employment, and the country has joined numerous other free trade agreements including being a founding member of the Pacific Alliance (The Heritage Foundation 2014).

Despite economic growth, according to the Ministry of Education, in 2010 66.3 % of children aged 3–5 years were registered in early education, although that was less than 1 % increase since 2008 (PROMEB 2011). The gap between rural and urban areas for that indicator was 20 %, clearly favouring urban children. Primary school enrolment increased by 1.9 % over 5 years to an average above 90 % although school year repetition rates were above 20 %, especially affecting 3 in 10 children in rural areas compared to 1 in 10 in urban areas and 35 % among the poor against 13 % among the better off. Forty-five per cent of indigenous children were in grades below their age profile (Doan 2013; Snyder 2008). Based on the child labour surveys carried out in 2007–2008 (INEI 2009; UNICEF 2010), at least 37 % of children between the ages of 5 and 13 (66 % rural, 21 % urban) participate in the labour market for at least 1 h per week (see also Ensing 2008a, b). All forms of abuse, violence and neglect persist in Peru and children who suffer dispossession within economically deprived communities still have little choice but the street or work (Thomas De Benitez, 2007: 17; INEI 2007, 2009). Thus, the presence of street children is as notable as ever before in the cities (Strehl 2010). Whilst the cities themselves are modernising, little has changed behind the façades since Salazar Bondy (1974) wrote *Lima la horrible*. The Aymara- and Quechua-speaking ethnic groups are markedly neglected, whilst Amazonian groups are almost never mentioned, and it is essentially in the most prosperous urban areas that greatest progress is being made. Whilst much has been achieved in step with economic progress, there is far more than that still to be done.

Nicaragua has also seen considerable change. In 1990 the *Frente Sandinista de Liberación Nacional* (*FSLN*) who had been in government since 1979 lost to the *Unión Nacional Opositora* (*UNO*) which was a broad-based association of opposition parties. In 1990 when Violeta Chamorro took up her almost 7-year presidency, Sandinistas, to all intents and purposes, still controlled the military, trade unions and judiciary. The government set out to strengthen democratic institutions, press forward with national reconciliation, stabilise the economy, denationalise state-owned businesses and begin to put an end to human rights violations (for instance, see Spalding 1994: 156–188; Booth and Walker 1999: 35–38 and 69–100). A new law was passed in 1996 that put more control over the police and law enforcement generally.

The 1996 election put the *Alianza Liberal Nicaragüense* (*ALN*) led by Arnoldo Alemán in office. Alemán continued privatisation of the economy and promotion of new infrastructure projects that were supported by foreign aid received after Hurricane Mitch in 1998. Several senior officials were forced to resign in mid-2000, and Alemán was subsequently convicted of corruption and sentenced to 20 years in prison. Later that year there were municipal elections in which Alemán's alliance again had a sizeable majority; however, FSLN also did well in urban areas with wins in a considerable number of departmental capitals including the capital Managua. The presidential and legislative election at the end of 2001 saw ALN re-elected to the Nicaraguan presidency with FSLN led by Daniel Ortega doing well. The next election in 2006 was won by Daniel Ortega, returning him to power after 16 years in opposition (see Wilm 2011; Morris 2011). The 2011 general election resulted in the re-election of Ortega. In 2014 the National Assembly approved constitution change that allows him to run for a third successive term. Since his election Nicaragua has experienced positive economic growth and political stability without apparent widespread corruption.

Nicaragua ratified the CRC in 1990 with a strong legal framework to adopt it into. The country made plans and policy for the protection of children and delivery of their rights; however, those laws are difficult if not impossible to enforce, and the country lacks funds for implementation. It is still a very poor country that struggles to deliver children's rights to a satisfactory standard of living, health and education or development. An estimated 500,000 children are still without schools and of those who attend, only around 45 % complete education. U5MR is still high because of respiratory diseases, diarrhoea, malnutrition and meningitis, with infant and 0–5-year mortality rates of, respectively, 22 and 26 per 1,000 live births. Considerably over 10,000 young people live and/or work on the streets. According to the ILO, National Institute of Development Information and National Commission for the Eradication of Child Labour in Nicaragua, there are estimates of between 240,000 and 320,000 children working in Nicaragua. These include at least 20,000 children aged between 5 and 9 years, upward of 70,000 between 10 and 13 years with the largest number aged 14–17. CEACR (2014) noted that according to UNICEF statistics for 2000–2010, 15 % of children below 14 years are still working. More than half of working children are in rural areas and only around 60 % of them attend school. There have also been incidences of human trafficking including children recorded.

Thus, it can be said that in real terms Nicaragua whilst having the best intentions is still unable to live up to what is expected of state party to the CRC; however, it is little different to the other countries revisited here.

China had an unexpected year of upheavals in 1989. The death of Communist Party chairman Hu Yaobang marked the beginning of the Tiananmen Square protests by students from Beijing, Nanjing, Shanghai and Xian. Over one million protestors marched through Beijing demanding greater democracy. Uyghur and Hui Muslim protesters also demonstrated in front of the government building in Ürümqi. The General Secretary of the Communist Party, Zhao Ziyang, met demonstrators in Tiananmen Square to call for moderation and open discussion to end the protest, although a little later the government declared martial law. A 10 m tall Goddess of Democracy statue was erected in Tiananmen Square by students. A massacre then occurred when the military intervened. The confrontation was covered live on television and seen worldwide.

However, since 1989 China has undergone dramatic change. In 1990 the Shanghai Stock Exchange opened as economic liberalisation began. In 1992, Chairman

Deng Xiaoping toured the country to set faster economic reforms in motion and quash the influence of party conservatives opposed to market liberalisation, followed in 1996 by the yuan held in current accounts being convertible to enable free flows of money for international trade. 1997 saw Hong Kong reverting to Chinese rule and President Jiang Zemin visiting the USA, the first time by the head of state for over a decade, and ending the diplomatic isolation post-Tiananmen; a year later Bill Clinton returned the visit. Zhu Rongji took over as premier and immediately began to reform state-owned enterprises, contain smuggling and overhaul health care. Not long after, the Communist Party allowed private entrepreneurs to become members. In 2005 China freed the yuan from its dollar peg, thus letting it float. Two years later China passed Germany to become the world's third largest economy. It is now the world's second largest (Naughton 2008; Huang 2008).

Recently China has attempted to move away from its traditional view of children (Behnke Kinney 2004). From the beginning of the 1980s, China had a one-child policy (Greenhalgh 2003; Button 2011) which was relaxed at the end of 2013. In 2014 the first provinces allowed parents a second child. When China ratified the CRC, the Standing Committee of the National People's Congress, the main legislative body, made a reservation to Article 6 of the CRC on the inherent right to life, stating that China would fulfil its obligation under the conditions of planned birth provided by Article 25 of their constitution (UN 1989).

China is very ambitiously developing education. Under the Compulsory Education Law (1986, revised 2006; see Zhang 2011; Kipnis 2011), children go to school at age 6, or 7 in less-developed areas, for 9 years of compulsory, free education. In order to promote the balanced development of all schools, local authorities are forbidden to have schools that differentiate in pupils' abilities, thus prohibited from dividing classes into streams for the more down to less able which was the situation before the law was implemented. Entrance examinations for basic education are also banned. The curriculum in all schools is set by the Ministry of Education. Textbooks are reviewed and some censored by the government but may be used with the approval of the state. The local government implementation of statutory educational requirements varies from the economically well-developed East to less-developed West and between urban and rural areas (Luo et al 2012). In western rural areas compulsory education is not yet fully operational. Local authorities at and above county level are required to set up special schools to provide compulsory education for children with special needs. These schools are equipped with facilities adapted for study and the physical needs of disabled children. Special-needs children who are capable of studying in normal schools must be accepted without any form of discrimination and educational aid for their study provided in accordance with the law (Pang and Richey 2006).

The minimum age for work in China is 16. Before the Labour Law was passed in 1994 (People's Republic of China 1994), the State Council issued the Provisions on the Prohibition of Using Child Labor in 1991 (Ministry of Commerce 1991); they were amended in 2002. Despite legal requirements, child labour is accepted as a persistent problem whereby they normally work in low-skill service sectors or small workshops and businesses such as shoe, textile or toy manufacturing (Jing

2008; Lieten and Hindman 2009). There are also estimated to be around 1.5 million street children in China. Most of them appear to have left home to escape either domestic violence or poverty. When they are on the streets, they lack access to health care, education and social support. They are also vulnerable to abuse, disease and exploitation (Lam and Cheng 2008).

Despite such flaws in the system, China appears to be improving the situation of children. The *Law on the Protection of Minors* (People's Republic of China 2007) is one of a number of laws and regulations protecting children and their rights. The law places responsibility for the protection of children on families, schools and the government in respect of the protection of their rights and also protection in all other legal areas that affect them. The increased focus on children is part of the programme of modernisation that has been part of China's rapid climb as an economic success and promises to continue and improve. The intent is that a well-educated workforce will be part of the means by which China will come to occupy the place as the world's leading economy and maintain that position but not in and of itself a pro-child effort. However, the lives of children appear to be improving nonetheless.

In Lebanon in 1989, in West Beirut, a bomb exploded near the motorcade of President Moawad killing him, and in the same year the Taif Agreement (National Reconciliation Accord) was reached in Taif in Saudi Arabia as the basis for the end of the civil war and the return to political normality. The principle was to end the long-enduring war and make political steps to include the demographic shift to a Muslim majority. It also set out to reinstate Lebanese authority over southern Lebanon which was then occupied by Israel and set a time frame for Syrian withdrawal over 2 years. The accepted agreement between Israel and Syria ended in 2000 when peace negotiations broke down and Israel pulled out of Lebanon. The more forceful Middle East policy of the USA and the assassination of former prime minister Rafiq Hariri in 2005 brought about a period of joint European and US pressure to end Syrian interference in its neighbour's politics. Damascus subsequently withdrew its troops from the country. In 2006 the July War between Hezbollah and Israel took place with Israel launching a major military attack. They bombed the southern suburbs of Beirut, the airport and parts of southern Lebanon in retaliation to the capture of two Israeli soldiers by Hezbollah. The conflict ended with acceptance of a Security Council Resolution by Israel and Lebanon. Israeli forces withdrew across the border. Although the resolution calls for disarmament of Hezbollah, neither the Lebanese government nor UNIFIL has set out to disarm Hezbollah (Picard and Ramsbotham 2012; Hudson 1997).

Lebanon had endured almost 15 years of civil conflict, coming very close to total chaos so that the harm to the civil population, especially children, was complex to assess and even more difficult to restore. Lebanon became a state party to the CRC in 1991 and to the *Optional Protocol on the Sale of Children, Child Prostitution and Child Pornography* in 2004. On February 11, 2002, Lebanon signed but still has to ratify the *Optional Protocol on the Involvement of Children in Armed Conflict*.

One of the legacies of the 15 years of civil war in Lebanon has continued the sectarian structure of the Lebanese political and social environment which undermines the authority of the state. It has led to disparities in the quality of and access to basic services in education, health and so on and left the considerable number of refugees, mainly Palestinians and Iraqis, vulnerable and the judiciary and legal system weak. The ability to offer protection to children along with persistent political instability and human rights violations makes it difficult to see the entire picture. It most markedly affects the well-being of vulnerable children, for instance, those, from low-income families, who are abused; refugees, of migrant workers, in conflict with the law; disabled and working children; and others with particular need of protection. The state's failings limit its capacity to adequately monitor the situation of children within families, low-income areas, schools, institutions, refugee camps and detention centres (Ressler 2008). Thus, whilst there has been peace since 2006 internally, the country still has far to go. However, with conflicts on its borders and with terrorist groups based in the country, there is no certainty of enduring peace. The situation for children therefore remains uncertain.

In Thailand Hurricane Gay was probably the best known event of 1989, killing and displacing many people. Two years later there was a military coup that began almost incessant political change and instability. A junta that called itself the National Peace Keeping Council replaced what they said was a corrupt regime. The NPKC put a civilian prime minister in office, Anand Panyarachun, who answered to the military. His anti-corruption and simple measures were popular. The next election was in 1992 when a coalition appointed coup leader Suchinda Kraprayoon prime minister, thus breaking a pledge made to the king and raising suspicion that the new government was a military regime in disguise. That brought about the biggest demonstrations ever seen in Bangkok. Suchinda brought military units into the city to contain the demonstrations by force which led to a massacre and then riots in which hundreds died. After intervention by the king, Anand was appointed interim prime minister until elections. Those put Chuan Leekpai in office until 1995. He was defeated by a coalition of conservative and provincial parties led by Banharn Silpa-Archa. Corruption charges brought about early elections in 1996. General Chavalit Yongchaiyudh's New Aspiration Party won a narrow victory. His deputy PM, Thaksin Shinawatra, stood for election with his new party, Thai Rak Thai, in 2001. Thaksin's government was accused of corruption, despotism, treason, massive conflicts of interest, non-diplomatic actions and gagging the press. Thaksin was personally accused of tax evasion, selling off the assets of Thai companies to international investors and insulting the king. His human rights record was also heavily censured. In 2006 he was removed from office by a coup d'état whilst in New York for a UN meeting. The forthcoming election was cancelled, the constitution was suspended, some ministers were arrested and the parliament was dissolved. Thaksin went into exile in the UK. A general election took place in 2007 and Samak Sundaravej, a Thaksin loyalist, won the majority and democracy rule was restored (see MacGregor Marshall 2014).

In 2014, the military, led by General Prayuth Chan-ocha, launched a coup d'état against a caretaker government following a 6 month-long political crisis. A junta called the National Council for Peace and Order (NCPO) took control of the country. The constitution was annulled, martial law and a national curfew were imposed, political gatherings were prohibited, politicians and anti-coup activists were arrested and detained, the Internet was censored and the media was taken under military control. The NCPO began to deal with illegal foreign workers, who were seen as a threat. A large number of foreign migrants, many of them women and children, left the country immediately.

Behind the political upheavals attention particularly turned to the sexual exploitation of children in Thailand. The *World Congress Against Commercial Sexual Exploitation of Children* held in Stockholm in 1996 had shown particular interest in the situation in Thailand (ECPAT International 2001). Many of the children in the sex industry appeared to have been trafficked to Thailand from Cambodia, Myanmar and Laos and a few others from elsewhere and as far away as Eastern Europe. Various cross-border trafficking measures have been put in place with provision for trafficked individuals to be treated as victims and not illegal migrants and to be repatriated safely through diplomatic channels, prosecution of traffickers and establishment of a joint task force on bilateral cooperation between at least Cambodia and Thailand and other countries eventually. Programmes to prevent child prostitution and trafficking of children have been introduced throughout the country. In the field of law enforcement, training courses for police officers, social workers and other professionals have been put in place. Despite those measures, there has been an increase in the number of young people illegally migrating from neighbouring Mekong countries that are susceptible to the offers of employment and are often trafficked who are then forced to go into the commercial sex industry (UNIAP 2010).

Besides the sex industry, children have been exploited for their labour, particularly in the fishing industry, and there are considerable numbers of street children. Estimates have reported as many as 40 % of street children in Bangkok being Cambodian Khmer, Burmese and Vietnamese (Friends-International 2010; Sricharatchanya 2011).

Cuba remains in the twelfth position of the case study countries despite changes that might easily have seriously affected children. An extended period of economic crisis known as the ‘Special Period’ began in 1991, essentially due to the dissolution of the Soviet Union and, thus in chain, the Comecon of which it was a member. The economic depression was at its most severe until the mid-1990s and then to some extent declined in severity towards the end of that decade (for instance, see Kapcia 2008; Mesa-Lago and Vidal-Alejandro 2010). Fidel Castro delegated powers to his brother Raúl in 2006 and then stepped down as president in 2008 to be entirely replaced by his brother. Raúl is himself now in his 80s, thus signposting the inevitability of the end of the original regime that has governed the country since 1959.

Cuba has been undergoing gradual change and liberalisation. There are nonetheless still tensions within the system. The foremost is between economic growth policy and the social welfare of the population. That extends to tensions between centralisation and decentralisation of governance, which includes between the country’s socialist identity and the influence of globalisation and consumerism which have grown with increased tourism and the Internet and between both the public and private labour market sectors. The question arises whether the state will be able to maintain the reliability of health and education policies without very exacting government control and guidance. By extension, the question arises as to whether the state can attract and encourage the necessary committed professionals when other sectors will inevitably offer better opportunities and salaries. Under those circumstances, can the state then continue its weighty public investment in child development? Furthermore, would the state also be able to sustain high levels of participation of advocates, facilitators and people's organisations that support the effort afforded to children in their agenda?

Whilst political controls are still strict, Cuba is still the top-ranking developing country when it comes to protecting children's rights, according to the 2012 Child Development Index (CDI) (SCF UK 2012). The index is constructed from three indicators: health (an estimated probability of U5MR), nutrition by percentage of children aged less than 5 years who are moderately or severely underweight and education by percentage of primary school-age children who are not enrolled in schools. Cuba's recent progress raised it from second place in Latin America, behind Argentina, during the 1990s to the top position in the period between 2000 and 2006 (SCF UK 2008). This reflects Cuba's progress since the 1990s in child health, nutrition and education, despite considerable difficulties caused by and during the Special Period. Whilst there are still controls on political participation and freedom of expression that have implications for those areas in the CRC, delivery is nonetheless impressive in the protection and provision areas.

Finishing writing 'The Next Generation' in the third quarter of 1988, we could never have foreseen how much would happen in the coming year that began to shape the geopolitical world we now live in. A timeline tells how it happened briefly. 1989 was not only the year in which the CRC was adopted but was also a historically key turning point that started with Poland moving towards private enterprise instead of central control, coming to a head with the fall of the Berlin Wall that November. It ended in with the splitting up of the Union of Soviet Socialist Republics at the end of 1991. The so-called Cold War period was over. It was also the year the World Wide Web was first considered by Tim Berners-Lee in Switzerland and that would be free for all to use in 1993. The first text message was also sent in 1989 using the Short Message Service (SMS). In 1991, 2G digital platform was first used in Finland on the GSM standard. That set off massive competition as new operators challenged 1G network operators. Finland had the first network offering commercial person-to-person SMS in 1994.

In 1989 George Bush succeeded Ronald Reagan as president of the USA. The Polish government held formal talks with *Solidarity* for the first time since 1981. The Soviet Union announced all troops had left Afghanistan ending the war. Poland officially began to liberalise currency exchange and take steps towards capitalism. The Estonian flag was raised at the Pikk Hermann castle tower in the capital Tallinn after 44 years in the USSR. The Socialist Republic of Serbia passed constitutional changes revoking the autonomy of the Socialist Autonomous Province of Kosovo. That set off 6 days of rioting by the Albanian majority during which several people died. The first contested elections for the Soviet parliament saw losses for the

Communist Party. In Poland, Solidarity was legalised and allowed to take part in semi-free elections. Hungary dismantled 240 km of barbed wire along its border with Austria. President Bush sent almost 2,000 troops to Panama to protect US citizens. Conflict between ethnic Uzbeks and the Turkish minority began in the Uzbek Soviet Socialist Republic with over 100 people killed. After Solidarity's victory in the Polish elections, President Jaruzelski nominated Tadeusz Mazowiecki as prime minister, the first non-communist minister in 42 years. Presidents of five Central American countries agreed that US-backed 'contras' fighting the government of Nicaragua should be disbanded and expelled from bases in Honduras by the end of that year. Two million people in Estonia, Latvia and Lithuania joined hands to demand independence by forming an unbroken 600 km human chain they called the 'Baltic Way'. Hungary removed all remaining border restrictions with Austria then opened its western borders to refugees from the German Democratic Republic. Vietnam announced the withdrawal of its troops from Cambodia, ending the 11-year-long occupation.

Around 7,000 East Germans who had travelled to Prague were allowed to leave for the west. The East German government closed the border with Czechoslovakia to attempt to prevent further emigration to the west. The Dalai Lama was awarded the Nobel Peace Prize. In Leipzig protesters demanded legalisation of opposition groups and democratic reforms. The East German leader, Erich Honecker, stepped down after a series of health problems to be succeeded by Egon Krenz. The Hungarian National Assembly voted to restore multiparty democracy. The border between East Germany and Czechoslovakia was reopened; East German refugees arrived in Hof in West Germany after travelling through Czechoslovakia. The government of East Germany resigned although Egon Krenz remained in office. Günter Schabowski of the SED unintentionally announced that new regulations for travelling from East to West Germany would be put in effect immediately during a press conference. East Germany consequently opened checkpoints in the Berlin Wall, thus allowing its citizens to travel freely for the first time in decades. A peaceful student demonstration in Prague was broken up violently by riot police. It started a revolution that brought down the government by the end of that year. The number of peaceful protesters in Prague grew from around 200,000 the first day before to an estimated 500,000 the next. After 1 week of demonstrations demanding free elections and other reforms, General Secretary Miloš Jakeš and other leaders of the Communist Party resigned and Karel Urbánek replaced him and the Communist Party announced they had given up monopoly on political power. Later elections voted in the first non-communist government in more than 40 years. East Germany's parliament abolished constitutional provisions that had given the communist-dominated SED monopoly on power; Egon Krenz, the entire politburo and the Central Committee resigned 2 days after. Lithuania became the first Soviet republic to abolish Communist Party monopoly on power.

At the end of 1989, Romanian Revolution began in Timişoara when rioters broke into the Committee Building and did extensive damage, although attempts to set the building on fire were prevented by the military. Nicolae Ceauşescu addressed about 110,000 people outside the Communist Party HQ in Bucharest.

The crowd began to protest, so he ordered the army to attack them. After a week of bloody demonstrations, Ion Iliescu took over as president. Ceauşescu fled his palace in a helicopter to escape execution when it was attacked by rioters. Romanian troops, who the previous day had carried out Ceausescu's orders to attack demonstrators, changed sides and joined the revolution. Nicolae and Elena Ceauşescu were captured in Târgovişte and executed after being found guilty of crimes against humanity. Poland's president signs the Balcerowicz Plan on the last day of 1989, ending the state socialist system in Poland. In 1990 Tsakhiagiyn Elbegdorj announced the establishment of Mongolia's democratic movement, which then peacefully changed the second oldest communist country into a democracy. The political division between East and West was over; therewith the Cold War ended. Bangladesh, Benin and Sudan all ratified the CRC on the same day; thus, more than 20 state parties came into effect later that year.

The world should have settled down and become far more peaceful with itself. However, that was not to be. The relationship between the West and Islam had changed radically in 1979 when the Iranian Revolution began and had seen ever greater tension mount. In 1993 a truck bomb was set off below the North Tower of the World Trade Centre in New York City. The over 600 kilo device was intended to bring down the North Tower to topple into the South Tower bringing both towers down thus killing tens of thousands of people. The attack failed but six people were killed and over a thousand injured. There were several other similar attacks and a few hijacks, but the 1998 US embassy bombings in Dar es Salaam and Nairobi were part of a series of attacks that occurred in which hundreds of people were killed and injured simultaneously. The events drew the names of Osama bin Laden and Ayman al-Zawahiri and their terrorist organisation al-Qaeda to public attention for the first time. From then on there was a 'war on terrorism' mainly focussing on al-Qaeda.

On the morning of September 11, 2001, 19 hijackers took control of four aircraft after they had taken off from Boston, Newark, and Washington, DC. They were large planes carefully chosen to be hijacked because they were heavily fuelled for long flights and carried a large passenger and luggage load. At 08:46 five hijackers crashed the first plane into the northern side of the World Trade Centre's North Tower, and just after 09:00 another five hijackers crashed the second plane into the southern side of the South Tower. Another five hijackers flew a third aircraft into the Pentagon after 09:30. A fourth plane under the control of four hijackers crashed near Shanksville, Pennsylvania, southeast of Pittsburgh just after 10:00 when passengers fought the hijackers. The target was believed to have been either the Capitol or White House. The flight deck voice recorder revealed how crew and passengers had tried to regain control of the plane once phone calls told them that other flights had been crashed into buildings that morning. To avoid being defeated and detained, the hijackers rolled the plane and intentionally crashed it. Three of the buildings in the World Trade Centre complex collapsed as a result of structural damage. The South Tower collapsed at 09:59 after burning for 56 min in a fire caused by the impact of the plane with its fuel exploding. The North Tower collapsed at 10:28 a.m. after burning for over one and a half hours. When it collapsed, debris fell on 7 World Trade Centre building causing severe damage and fires. They burned for many hours, damaging the building's structure so that it collapsed early that evening. The Pentagon was seriously damaged. Two thousand nine hundred ninety-six people including the 19 hijackers died. There were no survivors on the flights; over 2,600 died in the towers and on the ground nearby, with a further 125 deaths at the Pentagon. That event changed the relationship between the West and Islam for the worse. It continues to be a very serious problem at present.

The invasion of Iraq in 2003 led by the USA and backed by the UK on the basis of Iraq's alleged weapons of mass destruction (WMDs) that were considered a threat to their security and that of their allies did not help the relationship between the West and Islam improve. Investigations following the occupation revealed that Iraq had ended its nuclear, chemical and biological weapon programmes in 1991 and that none had been active at the time of the invasion although they allegedly intended to resume production. Iraqi insurgencies, the conflict between Sunni and Shia groups and the emergence of a new faction of al-Qaeda exacerbated the situation. Child malnutrition rates rose approaching 30 %, and the knock-on effects saw reports that 60–70 % of Iraqi children were reported to still be suffering from psychological problems in 2007 (IRIN 2007).

In 2008 there was a global financial crisis. The exact start and end of the recession that caused it at the national level varied between countries with some countries not experiencing it at all. Australia, China, India, Indonesia and South Korea, for example, did not have a recession, but several countries in Europe had a second recession about 3 years after the first. It affected the entire world economy with greater damage to some countries than others. To a point it was the worst global recession since the Second World War. Those who were already hit by poverty and accompanying pressure that economic crashes cause naturally suffered more than most.

This chapter's title is 'Childhood's Past'. The chapter itself only mentions children fleetingly here and there, but since it is a résumé of what happened since the end of the 1980s, children are naturally included, indeed very profoundly so. Political and economic changes are also their history; therefore, it is also their past that has contributed to shaping the lives of others, the majority of course, who survive to become adults, and thus it continues to contribute to all others born since and yet to be born. In that sense it describes a significant part of those childhoods. Children as part of the entire human race are always simply included without being singled out as one of its distinct groups.

Since 1989 there have been continuing and new wars, new crises and generally little progress made in the delivery of rights to children. This has been examined very briefly in the context of 12 countries and a very selective and short scrutiny of global events. It does not allow for other changes, often for the worse such as the now less sensationally presented but still growing HIV and AIDS phenomenon, changes in societal values as materialism pushes the richest and poorest further apart and other perhaps less global issues such as the plight of Roma people in Europe and perhaps most recently the growing Ebola crisis in Africa and potentially on other continents. Each of these and many more affect children as well as adults. They can also contribute to children not enjoying their rights. Much of the hope that came in

1989 with the CRC remains largely unfulfilled. Some positive steps have been made in several of the 12 case study countries but there is no absolute certainty that they can be sustained, let alone taken further. The mainly political changes that began at more or less the same time as the adoption of the CRC have naturally overshadowed it. In reality, such a convention is indeed a small thing compared to world-changing events which have also borne pressure on the newly emergent countries that signed and ratified only a very short time after renewed independence or coming into being with all of the social and economic issues inherent to their circumstances. That progress has been made at all since 1989 is astonishing given how high the odds were stacked against it.

References

Bates, R. (2008). *When things fell apart: State failure in late-century Africa*. New York: Cambridge University Press.

Behnke Kinney, A. (Ed.). (2004). *Representations of childhood and youth in early China*. Stanford: Stanford University Press.

Benson, S., Hellander, P., & Wlodarski, R. (2007). *Peru*. London: Lonely Planet.

Booth, J. A., & Walker, T. W. (1999). *Understanding Central America*. Boulder: Westview Press.

Braathen, E. (2003). Democratic decentralisation in Mozambique? In M. Newitt, Malyn with C. Patrick and N. Macqueen (Eds.) *Community and the state in Lusophone Africa* (pp. 99–126). London: King's College.

Bradbury, M., & Healy, S. (2010). Endless war: A brief history of the Somali conflict. *Accord: African Journal on Conflict Resolution*, (21), 10–14.

Branson, N., Ardington, C., Lam, D., & Leibbrandt, M. (2013). *Changes in education, employment and earnings in South Africa – A cohort analysis* (SALDRU Working Papers 105). Cape Town: Southern Africa Labour and Development Research Unit, University of Cape Town.

Button, G. (2011). China's one-child policy and the population explosion. *Indian Journal of Economics & Business, 10*(4), 467–480.

Cabrita, J. (2000). *Mozambique: The tortuous road to democracy*. New York: Palgrave.

CEACR. (2014). *Observation 2013, 103rd International Labour Conference session (2014), Convention concerning Minimum Age for Admission to Employment, 1973 (No. 138)*. Geneva: Committee of Experts on the Application of Conventions and Recommendations, International Labour Organisation.

Chatterjee, A. (1992). *India: The forgotten children of the cities*. Florence: UNICEF.

Doan, B. (2013). *Introduction to education in Peru*. Monterey: Monterey Institute of International Studies.

ECPAT International. (2001). *Five years after Stockholm, The fifth report on the implementation of the Agenda for Action adopted at the World Congress against Commercial Sexual Exploitation of Children* (p. 112). Bangkok: End Child Prostitution, Child Pornography and Trafficking of Children for Sexual Purposes.

Ensing, A. (2008a). *Child labour in the urban sectors of Peru*. Amsterdam: Foundation for International Research on Working Children (IREWOC).

Ensing, A. (2008b). *Hazardous forms of child labour in Peru: Lessons from research*. Amsterdam: Foundation for International Research on Working Children (IREWOC).

Fergusson, J. (2014). *The world's most dangerous place: Inside the outlaw state of Somalia*. London: Black Swan.

FitzGerald, V., & Stewart, F. (Eds.). (2001). *War and underdevelopment: Volume 1: The economic and social consequences of conflict: Economic and social consequences of conflict*. Oxford: Oxford University Press.

Friends-International. (2010). *Bangkok street children profile*. Bangkok: Friends-International with UNIAP.

Greenhalgh, S. (2003). Science, modernity, and the making of China's one-child policy. *Population and Development Review, 29*(2), 163–196.

Harris, D. (2014). *Sierra Leone: A political history*. Oxford: Oxford University Press.

Hecht, T. (1998). *At home in the street: Street children of Northeast Brazil*. Cambridge: Cambridge University Press.

Huang, Y. (2008). *Capitalism with Chinese characteristics: Entrepreneurship and the state*. New York: Cambridge University Press.

Hudson, M. C. (1997). Trying again: Power-sharing in post-civil war Lebanon. *International Negotiation, 2*(1), 103–122.

IMF. (2012). *Peru: 2012 Article IV consultation*. Washington: International Monetary Fund.

IndexMundi.com. (2012). *Sierra Leone Population below poverty line – Economy*. Charlotte: Indexmundi.com.

INEI. (2007). *Encuesta de Trabajo Infantil (ETI)*. Lima: Instituto Nacional de Estadística e Informática.

INEI. (2009). *El trabajo infantil en el Perú: Magnitud y perfiles vulnerables – Informe nacional 2007–2008*. Lima: Instituto Nacional de Estadística e Informática.

IRIN. (2007). *Iraq: Traumatised Iraqi children suffer psychological damage*. New York: UN Office for the Coordination of Humanitarian Affairs. http://www.irinnews.org/report/73258/iraq-traumatised-iraqi-children-suffer-psychological-damage

Jing, L. (2008). China's new labor contract law and protection of workers. *Fordham International Law Journal, 32*(3), 1083–1131.

Kapcia, A. (2008). Cuba after Fidel: Continuity and change. *Global Dialogue, 10*(1-2), 120–129.

Keen, D. (2005). *Conflict and collusion in Sierra Leone*. Oxford: Palgrave Macmillan.

Kipnis, A. (2011). *Governing educational desire. Culture, politics and schooling in China*. Chicago: The University of Chicago Press.

Lam, D., & Cheng, F. (2008). Chinese policy reaction to the problem of street children: An analysis from the perspective of street children. *Children and Youth Services Review, 30*(5), 575–584.

Lam, D., Ardington, C., Branson, N., & Leibbrandt, M. (2013). *Credit constraints and the racial gap in post-secondary education in South Africa* (NBER Working Papers 19607). Cambridge, MA: National Bureau of Economic Research.

Leibbrandt, M., Finn, A., & Woolard, I. (2012). Describing and decomposing post-apartheid income inequality in South Africa. *Development Southern Africa, 29*(1), 19–34.

Lieten, G. K., & Hindman, H. D. (2009). Child labor in China: An overview. In H. D. Hindman (Ed.), *The world of child labor: An historical and regional survey* (pp. 860–866). New York: M.E. Sharpe.

Luo, R., Zhang, L., Liu, C., Zhao, Q., Shi, Y., Rozelle, S., & Sharbono, B. (2012). Behind before they begin: The challenge of early childhood education in rural China. *Australasian Journal of Early Childhood, 37*(1), 55–64.

MacGregor Marshall, A. (2014). *A kingdom in crisis: Thailand's struggle for democracy in the twenty-first century*. London: Zed.

Manrique, N. (2002). *El tiempo del miedo : La violencia política en el Perú, 1980–1996*. Lima: Fondo Editorial del Congreso del Perú.

Maurice, J. (2014). South Africa's battle against HIV/AIDS gains momentum. *The Lancet, 383*(9928), 1535–1536.

Mesa-Lago, C., & Vidal-Alejandro, P. (2010). The impact of the global crisis on Cuba's economy and social welfare. *Journal of Latin American Studies, 42*(4), 689–717.

Ministry of Commerce, People's Republic of China. (1991). *Provisions on the prohibition of using child labour*. Beijing: People's Republic of China.

Morris, K. (2011). *Unfinished revolution: Daniel Ortega and Nicaragua's struggle for liberation*. Chicago: Lawrence Hill Books.

Naughton, B. (2008). A political economy of China's economic transition. In L. Brandt & T. Rawski (Eds.), *China's great economic transformation* (pp. 91–135). New York: Cambridge University Press.

Pang, Y., & Richey, D. (2006). The development of special education in China. *International Journal of Special Education, 21*(1), 77–86.
People's Republic of China. (1994). *Labour Law of the People's Republic of China*. Beijing: Standing Committee of the Eighth National People's Congress.
People's Republic of China. (2007). *Law on the protection of minors, 2007* (p. 5). Beijing: Gazette of the Standing Committee of the National People's Congress.
Picard, E., & Ramsbotham, A. (Eds.). (2012). Reconciliation, reform and resilience: Positive peace for Lebanon. *Accord: An International Review of Peace Initiatives*, (24).
PROMEB. (2011). *Acta del Comité para el Proceso de Selección para Evaluación Final*. Lima: Proyecto de Mejoramiento de la Educación Básica.
Ramaiah, A. (1992). Identifying other backward classes. *Economic and Political Weekly, 27*(23), 1203–1207.
Ressler, A. E. (2008). *Child rights situation analysis for Lebanon*. Beirut: Save the Children Sweden.
Rochester, J. (2008). *The Candelária Massacre: How Wagner dos Santos Survived the Street Children's Killing That Shook Brazil*. London: Vision Paperbacks.
Rochlin, J. F. (2003). *Vanguard revolutionaries in Latin America: Peru, Colombia, Mexico*. London: Lynne Rienner Publishers.
Salazar Bondy, S. (1974). *Lima la horrible*. Lima: Biblioteca Peruana.
Samatar, A. I. (2008). Somalia's post-conflict economy: A political economy approach. *Bildhaan: An International Journal of Somali Studies, 7*, 126–168.
SCF UK. (2008). *The Child Development Index 2008*. London: Save the Children UK.
SCF UK. (2012). *The Child Development Index 2012: Progress, challenges and inequality*. London: Save the Children UK.
Scheper-Hughes, N., & Hoffman, D. (1998). Brazilian apartheid: Street kids and the struggle for urban space. In N. Scheper-Hughes & C. Fishel Sargent (Eds.), *Small wars: The cultural politics of childhood* (pp. 352–388). Berkeley: University of California Press.
Schwab, K. (2013). *The global competitiveness report 2013–2014*. Geneva: World Economic Forum.
Scott Palmer, D. (Ed.). (1994). *Shining path of Peru*. New York: St. Martin's Press.
Sharma, C. K. (2011). A discursive dominance theory of economic reforms sustainability. *India Review, 2*(10), 126–184.
Singh, A., & Purohit, B. (2011). Street children as a public health fiasco. *Peace Review: A Journal of Social Justice, 23*(1), 102–109.
Snyder, S. (2008). The roots and repercussions of educational inequality on the indigenous populations of Peru. *Stanford Journal of International Relations, 10*(1), 52–59.
Spalding, R. J. (1994). *Capitalists and revolution in Nicaragua: Opposition and accommodation, 1979–1993*. Chapel Hill: University of North Carolina Press.
Spaull, N. (2013). Poverty and privilege: Primary school inequality in South Africa. *International Journal of Educational Development, 33*(5), 436–447.
Sricharatchanya, H. (2011). *The road home for trafficked children in Thailand*. Bangkok: UNICEF Regional Office for East Asia and the Pacific.
Strehl, T. (2010). *Street-working and street-living children in Peru: Conditions and current interventions*. Leiden: Foundation for International Research on Working Children (IREWOC).
The Heritage Foundation. (2014). *Index of economic freedom 2014*. Washington, DC: The Heritage Foundation.
Thomas de Benítez, S. (2007). *State of the world's street children: Violence*. London: Consortium for Street Children.
Thorp, R., & Zevallos, G. (2002). *The economic policies of the Fujimori years: A return to the past?* (QEH Working Paper Series, Working Paper Number 83). Oxford: Queen Elizabeth House.
UN. (1989). *General Assembly Resolution 44/25, annex, 44 UN General Assembly Official Records Supplement (No. 49) at 167, U.N. Doc. A/44/49 (1989); 28 International Legal Materials 1448 (1989)*. New York: United Nations.

UNGASS. (2012). *Global aids response progress report 2012: Republic of South Africa*. Pretoria: South African National AIDS Council for the United Nations General Assembly Special Session.

UNIAP. (2010). *The Mekong region human country datasheets on human trafficking 2010* (pp. 24–29). Bangkok: United Nations Inter-Agency Project on Human Trafficking.

UNICEF. (2010). *UNICEF annual report for Peru 2010*. New York: United Nations Children's Fund.

UNICEF. (2014). *State of the world's children 2014: Every child counts*. New York: United Nations Children's Fund.

Wilm, J. (2011). *Nicaragua, back from the dead! An anthropological view of the Sandinista movement in the early 21st century*. New York: New Left Notes.

Zhang, X. (Ed.). (2011). *China's education development and policy, 1978–2008*. Leiden/Boston: Brill.

Are Children's Rights Worth Pursuing? 9

Are children's rights worth pursuing? The obvious answer is 'Yes'. Perhaps one might begin to draw comparisons with the progress of women's rights over roughly the last century. Some very clear clues may also be drawn from the rights of minorities. The reality is that children belong to all genders, races, religions, cultures, and socioeconomic status, and whatever other categories people can possibly fall into. Therefore, knowing that they cross all sections of humanity except age, can we really justify their classification as an identifiable group from birth to the age of 18 years? If so, then naturally they should have a distinct framework of rights as with all other 'protected' groups. They then become a 'minority', which is ironic given that demographically, using birth until the age of 18 years, they are the largest single definable group of human beings and are a very large part of the whole human race.

It is very difficult to work with the definition 'child' when their ages are used to demark distinctions anyway (infants, pre-school, school age, pubertal, youth, etc.). Although there is a slow but inexorable merging of cultures as examined in earlier chapters, there are still good grounds for making a number of imperative cultural distinctions. Although a great deal of the world is at some stage of development as a modern industrial society, there is a minority, albeit a significant number when added together globally, of people who still live in pre-literate, pre-industrial societies. Is it not cultural imperialism to impose 'a, b, c' and '1, 2, 3' on non-literate societies who are perhaps still traditional hunter–gatherers? The door should always be open for those who choose to enter the modern world. However, attempts to give indigenous peoples rights and protections is contradicted by then imposing the CRC on their children to the letter, thus (for instance) obliging them to go to school. What is imposed is no longer a right but an imposition: removed choices become diktat and rights are abused when interpreted too literally and forced uncompromisingly upon people.

There is a view that this state of affairs, in which it is an imposition, allows children themselves insufficient control over their lives and makes them susceptible

B. Milne, *Rights of the Child*, Children's Well-Being: Indicators and Research 11,
DOI 10.1007/978-3-319-18784-6_9

to being controlled by over-interpretation. Jenks (1996: 43) in his chapter 'The conceptual limitations on a sociological approach to childhood' (*op.cit.*: 32–51) follows the *repressive state apparatuses* thesis proposed by Althusser (1971: 127–188), which in turn has been analysed in a 'post-Marxist' context by Stuart Hall (1985: 98–103) in a manner that would describe this legal instrument, as it applies to children, as within the definition of Althusserian repressive state apparatuses. This is an analysis within the framework of the sociology of childhood as it stood in the mid-1990s, which is expressed through Jenks' proposition that the repressive state apparatuses thesis can be applied to children's rights conceptually. It is perhaps a product of its time. Sociology itself was at a 'crossroads', whereby Marxist cultural theorists such as Hall were generally moving closer to a pro-human rights point of view. That was a move away from Marx's very strict methodological commitment to the historical method, wherein he consistently sought the social construction and influence of human institutions and conventions that probably best describe his brief encounters with, and indifference toward, human rights. In his early work, Marx formulated the notion of human rights serving *homo economicus,* thus individuals who were only concerned with their individual, essentially unsocial, self-interest (for instance, see Bottomore 1964).

Article 2 of the CRC sets out the following non-discrimination principles:

1. Parties shall respect and ensure the rights set forth in the present Convention to each child within their jurisdiction without discrimination of any kind, irrespective of the child's or his or her parent's or legal guardian's race, colour, sex, language, religion, political or other opinion, national, ethnic or social origin, property, disability, birth or other status.

This appears to say that each state party as a modern political unity has the duty to impose and enforce the CRC, conditional on ratification without reservations, because they are agreeing to 'respect and ensure the rights set forth in the present Convention to each child within their jurisdiction without discrimination of any kind', which could be interpreted in two ways. The first is that 'no discrimination' might mean that no distinction be allowed between ethnic groups with their own cultures and beliefs, language, and traditions so that *all* children be treated as a homogenous group. On the other hand, the non-discrimination principle could very well mean that no intervention be allowed since that would then discriminate against children who do not conform to the national model of childhood adopted by state institutions. In this latter case, the possibility exists that non-discrimination could exclude the vast majority of children in some states on the basis of the differences between various indigenous groups and the standard applied to define childhood by the national government. Such states, having signed and ratified the CRC on the basis of its governmental definitions, would not be able to ensure the rights of each child within their jurisdiction without discrimination.

In that sense, a repressive state apparatus view may be justifiably identified by use of an absolute non-discrimination principle that would *impose* rights on children, thus by default the rest of their group, namely all adults, whose duty it would become to enforce and maintain them in any given state. That may give rise to resistance to imposition, at which point the obligations proposed by the CRC could justifiably be described as being ethnocentric or discriminatory, possibly even on the basis of class or gender. Those who are behind the enforcement and encourage it could be accused of cultural imperialism, which is precisely the kind of accusation the UN does not want levelled at it.

At first there was no ethical philosophy attached to children's rights; the moral status of children was by and large based on such notions as justice within families, particularly as attention turned to abuse and the extent to which all forms of that phenomenon were more likely to be situated within the family than within society at large. At that stage, child protection was still held to be far more important than their rights, since it was the duty of the adults in a position to intervene to 'rescue' children and 'penalise' abusive parents and carers. The right to be protected was a necessary imposition that did not require the informed consent of the child victim. Participation in any form came after children were saved and then usually in a very restricted form that allowed them little contribution, if any, to their placement in institutional care, foster homes, and alternatives that would ensure their safety. It was, of course, their right to be protected, but that was based on the decisions of adults empowered with a duty to protect, including those at a higher level for whom the individual child was usually little more than a case file on which they ordered action.

We should also not be lured into exclusively attaching children's rights to the CRC. Well before drafting was completed, the topic was already under scrutiny. In his 1986 edited book *The Rights of Children*, Bob Franklin was looking at children's rights toward a future in which they would be citizens rather than objects:

> Participation stands for the right to do things, express oneself and have an effective voice as an individual child and be part of a larger group. The rights to freedom are considered so vital to adults. They offer self-determination, access to particular freedoms and choice and protection. What happens when minors have access to them too? Children's rights to protection and welfare do not touch upon the power relationship between adults and children, but the rights to freedom do (Franklin 1986: 24).

His question was looking at a time when such rights and the freedom they offer become a normal part of life. He was questioning whether, when young people are given the opportunities that come with participation and a share in decision making, they would be social subjects instead of objects of the politics of childhood who stand alongside adults. A real transformation can only take place between generations when everybody shares the status of being a subject, an individual with agency. He took into account the views held by John Holt who, in 1974, argued for electoral rights for people of any age, irrespective of whether they be child or adult, to be exercised entirely on the basis of 'the individual chooses to take part in public affairs' (Holt 1974). His position was that the rights, privileges, and duties of adult citizens be made available to any young person who wishes to use them, thus accepting the political responsibilities of citizenship. This questions the assumption that adults have responsibility for children in the political sphere. In turn, this reminds us that classical theorists of democracy such as John Locke (Dunn 1982) and Jean-Jacques Rousseau (for instance, Rousseau 1991 and 1998) considered that responsibility is limited to within the private sphere of dependent relations as against the public domain, where rights represent autonomy. Indeed, democracy was considered only to be possible where there is a pronounced public–private divide. Thus, the dichotomy of political and familial dependency as separable realms is a fallacy. It does not support but instead undermines democracy. Since politics and family life are interdependent, both demand awareness of individual members' different experiences, irrespective of age. This excludes the omission of children as individuals with experiences that cannot be denied or taken from them. They are an inherent quality, which it is their natural right to have. Thus, not allowing them any participation in the political sphere is social control and thus deprivation of their rights. This, in turn, bears the hallmarks of what Qvortrup described as the reduction of children to *human becomings* (Qvortrup 1991: 7).

With the intellectual search for a new sociological explanation for human rights, the study of citizenship rights, which has been an important development in contemporary sociology, has been, broadly speaking, ignored, supposedly on the basis of the assumption that it does not apply to children. Analysis of human rights had been hitherto problematic for sociologists, since cultural relativism and distinction between fact and value had essentially undermined the established tradition of the natural law basis for any rights discourse. Recent developments in the reorganization of old nation states and the circumstances of newly emergent nation states, along with political changes, the globalization of politics, and the way in which family life and very closely related matters—such as human reproduction—brought the question of human rights to the fore of social and political discourse and research (for instance: Turner 1993) have dominated. This was concurrent with growing interest in the field of children's rights following the adoption of the CRC in 1989 and the rapidly increasing number of signatories and states party.

Within human rights-focused sociology, children as bearers of rights were becoming a new subject for theoretical examination. James and Prout (1990) edited what has since been considered the first significant contribution to the sociology of childhood. In the introduction to that work, they acknowledge the opportunity to discuss and exchange ideas at the first 'Ethnography of Childhood Workshop' in Cambridge, 1986, created and organised by Judith Ennew.[1] Ironically, Ennew, although a social anthropologist, had a firm grounding in theoretical sociology and was, as she remained for the rest of her life, resolutely Marxist. One of the attributes of Marxist theory was dialectical analysis and method, thus using different concepts that exist together or affect each other to try to discover their legitimacy by considering those ideas together with opposing ideas. She questioned what the ideas and values being presented were? Then she looked at problems and limitations of those ideas, the basis on which they were constructed and maintained, and their implications. This was, for her, an incentive to look at the 'new' idea of children's rights as opposed to the conventional welfarist approach that was child protection. That, she believed, fitted perfectly in a sociological framework where the necessary epistemological method was already in place. Empirical research now had the

[1] I was also involved in the organization of and a participant at the workshop.

task of engaging in research procedures that led to new findings on the situation of children given the set of assured rights the CRC gave them. The empirical knowledge generated would be based on demonstrable objective facts that would be determined through data gathered through observation and testing the application and outcome of rights as a force for change.

Subsequently, as the then 'new' sociology of childhood developed, it was very different in that it involved children as contributors and negotiators, demonstrating a shift in power from parent and society to child, thus giving them a 'voice' of their own and contextual agency. This was assumed to influence research with children: first, it included them in the research rather than have research only conducted *about* them, which was often very statistical, depended on limited numbers of 'case studies' but mainly used secondary data drawn from existing work from which the basis of arguments could be extrapolated and against which a new discourse would develop. Participatory methods, despite some flaws described earlier, included children as participants in the sense of being not only active subjects but also, in an increasing number of cases, being researchers alongside professional social scientists, particularly social anthropologists. Thus, beginning slightly earlier but essentially parallel to sociology, the anthropology and ethnography of childhood came about.

Despite this new wave of research, sociology (in fact, the social sciences in general) and human rights, by and large, remained distant and displayed little comfort with each other when they met. James and Prout's (1990) now seminal work included only one contributor (Boyden 1990: 191–198) who went into any kind of detail about rights, in fact only fleetingly mentioning the CRC and its effect at all. Disappointingly, the sociology of childhood and children's rights remain uncomfortable 'bedfellows'.

So, clearly there were, and indeed remain, limitations. According to Brennan and Noggle (1997:1), at that point in time the discourse on ethical philosophy, justice within families, and the moral status of children continued to be only partial. At the time they were looking at children's rights with a view to finding feasible means of constructing and building on a philosophical basis for thinking about the moral rights of children and employment of the theory. Their view promoted a notion of children as individuals with identities, histories, and personal attachments. They stated a view that even young children have a moral status. This added to the argument that hitherto children had been reduced to 'human becomings' and thus were an undertaking whereby they would be shaped into the 'human beings' they would become (Qvortrup 1991: 7).

Brennan and Noggle (1997) proposed and argued that there were three sound assertions about the moral status of children: first, the *equal consideration thesis*, where children would be entitled to the same moral standards as adults; second, the *unequal treatment thesis*, where children from particular age groups are legitimately allowed to be barred from doing particular things adults are permitted to do; third, the *limited parental rights thesis* allows parents to legitimately employ discretion in the manner in which they raise their children. These three concepts described a balanced view that contrasted with extreme views that rebuffed one or more of those notions, for instance the 'children as property' view or radical child libertarian positions of the kind described by Archard (1993: 45–46) who considered their position to be the 'most passionate and radical defence of the most extensive rights for children'. In the intervening period, the three positions described by Brennan and Noggle have, broadly speaking, been passed by. Depending on global location, the dominant culture, and the position occupied by parents and other adults generally, the end of the *unequal treatment thesis* remains an ambition of many children's rights campaigners. However, with age as well as all other human interrelationships, equal moral consideration does not mean that all individuals will ever possess the same bundle of rights and duties. Various role-dependant rights do not apply to children anyway (Brennan and Noggle 1997: 6). Thus, we saw an attempt to put rights into a framework that was removed from the often legal theory-based view of how rights are achieved and held and the setting in which they are legitimised and upheld. Brennan and Noggle, in looking at children as individuals with identities, histories, and personal attachments, were already seeing them as social actors rather than simply potential bearers of rights. These ideas go full circle back to what Locke and Rousseau were implying without explicitly mentioning children.

Similarly, Judith adopted a similar view in which she saw children as individuals who often shared common traits. They also shared common causes, problems, and all else. They also normally shared most things with adults. They were, in her view, individuals with agency who could not simply be cast in a single mould as an 'ideal' child. She also revised her earlier inclination to use the word 'childhood'. That is, the period of time during which a person is a child that is not at all related to what individuals are as sentient beings. Therefore, she preferred to refer to the sociology of 'children', likewise applying the same to all other disciplines and domains so that her brainchild the *Ethnography of Childhood Workshops* would need to be called Ethnography of *Children* Workshops if ever future meetings were held.

However, the CRC is a human rights instrument; there it exists on the basis of the principle that human rights are standards that recognise and protect the dignity of all human beings. They govern how individual human beings live in society, with and beside each other, also describing their relationship with governments and the obligations those governing have toward them. Thus, human rights law obliges governments to do particular things and sets out to prevent them doing others. Individuals also bear responsibilities in the manner in which they use those rights and in that they must respect the rights of others. No government, group, or individual person has the right to do anything that violates another's rights when it has signed and ratified a human rights instrument. Unfortunately, no arrangements exist to deal with countries that are not party to specific instruments who violate their citizens' rights; and little more can be done than censure those countries that are party to these instruments yet violate them. Other countries also try but fail to uphold such standards. Likewise, countries exist that may well wish to espouse them but have no real means of doing so. This allows such statements as the chapter heading used by Jody Heymann and Amy Raub in UNICEF's report on 25 years of the CRC: 'The

Convention on the Rights of the Child: What it Would Mean to Fulfil its Potential' and their explanation that follows a carefully chosen subtitle (UNICEF 2014: 105–116).

The base principle is that human rights are inherent, that is to say we are born with them and they are ours to enjoy as an expression of our common humanity. They are neither owned by specific people nor can they be given as a reward or gift. They are said to be inalienable, which means that individuals cannot give them up and they cannot be taken away, including when governments or other bodies neither recognise nor protect them. They are said to be universal in that they belong to all people, in all places irrespective of age, sex, race, religion, nationality, or economic or other status or condition in life. They belong to each and every one of us equally and no right is superior to any other, thus there are no 'small' rights. They are indivisible and interconnected so that they focus on individuals and communities together. Although human rights are divisible into two typologies—civil and political rights and economic, social, and cultural rights—they cannot be applied separately or as separable categories because the enjoyment of one right usually depends on fulfilment of all other rights. When people are denied civil and political rights, such as their political participation, they are also without means to protect economic, social, and cultural rights that cover basic needs such as education and healthcare.

Likewise, where basic survival needs are not met, civil and political rights may be of no value as people become first and foremost concerned with getting sufficient food and shelter. Different rights cannot be considered in isolation. Understanding of this structure is essential for the promotion, protection, and fulfillment of children's rights because the CRC is part of that structure. In light of the proposition that children are individuals with identities, histories, and personal attachments who are social actors rather than merely bearers of rights, we must respect that, whilst rights are inherent, the choice of whether children want the rights the CRC offers, in part, whole, or not at all, as individuals must rest with them. Now that they have been prepared, passed, adopted, and adopted into law, they are more or less irrevocable, thus can be pursued. Thus far, they say very little about individual rights but are distinctly for all children, so that for them to be genuine human rights this element of choice must eventually be recognised. This is a major reason for the elimination of the primacy of children's advocates, who are far too frequently unaware of what children really want or need.

This demands that children become far more participant in all processes, eventually being their own advocates. At such point in time as children's rights cease to be of interest, only then will children have achieved what is due to them and then the CRC can be regarded as redundant since the principles on which it is built will be superseded by the acceptance that all rights extend to all people irrespective of age, sex, race, religion, nationality, or economic or other status or condition in life and thus an aged-based instrument is not required. This follows the principle that, although women's rights have not yet been universally accepted and put into practice so that the separation according to gender that was far more prevalent a century ago is ended, most parts of the world recognise them as full citizens with economic and political franchise. That is to say, in law if not in practice, women now enjoy the same rights as men, which in time will make the need for a distinct category of women's rights redundant. However, at the same time, the slow progress of women in a roughly comparable context is the most illustrative expression of the fact that considerably more time than the first 25 years of life of the CRC is required to accomplish what it sets out to do, but what has been achieved is not insignificant when examined comparatively.

Nonetheless, there seems to be a shroud of ignorance surrounding children's issues in general. Protection and welfare as they are devised and managed by adults often appear to cancel out many of their rights. There are obvious exceptions, such as including the often talked and written about 'children's voice'. This has come to mean that a child or group of children must say something, no matter how tokenistic their words might be. However, that they say something does not ensure that those words will be taken into account or acted upon. Whereas children's participation was for a time the 'buzz word' and tokenism was the main thing to avoid above all else, that has had its day. Now the emphasis appears to be again on protecting children. It appears to be an environment in which adults know best and thus will 'guide' children, therefore not needing to take too many (if at all any) of the rights described by the CRC into account. The underlying dilemma is that the world, and the rush of enthusiasm felt in 1989 and for a few years immediately thereafter a quarter of a century ago, has moved on, and now we see the world through different eyes. It is a world that has seen many changes, some for the better but far too many for the worse, which has changed the priorities of many people working in the human rights and closely related areas. In other words, the CRC is no longer as in vogue as it was, and perhaps to some extent has been forgotten. It is time to remind the world. Part of the task is to get governments and the bodies who bear responsibility to revisit children's rights, to find out more, and regain the previous momentum.

That also requires the support of all possible resources. Whether it is NGOs, government departments, academic institutions, or any other bodies that can offer this support, is less important than that they are well informed. This would be helped a great deal by research that provided the information required to enable all-comers to work with children's rights. Whilst the small children's rights 'world' is pursuing research in its own area, albeit very much less than perhaps 20 years ago, the wide range of research areas covered by social scientists, medicine, and other disciplines is not making adequate allowance for human rights as a force for change that has a considerable amount of influence on children's lives.

What is almost certainly absent is any real knowledge that relates to adults and children's rights. For instance, it would be useful to know how adults who have been accustomed to absolute authority react to the notion of children as participants in decision making. For them, their world was probably one in which children were totally deferential, they did as instructed by adults, had no opinions or real choices and that was how all generations preceding them had maintained the *status quo*. Without knowing which countries those people are in, and what rights these countries have given children, working with those adults is unrealistic. More important is knowing what their reactions may be. This and all other issues arising are largely 'unknowns' that are neglected by the focus on researching children and similarly producing a considerable amount of 'child-friendly' information.

Consequently, changes need to be made to the nature of a range of disciplines carrying out child research to take into account human rights and particularly those we consider children's rights. They also need to research adults as participants with children and overseers of the delivery of those rights *vis-à-vis* handed down assumptions about the ability of children to possess these rights. Furthermore, it would be invaluable to know how that might affect the intergenerational relationship that comes with them. Once these and all other questions have been examined, then it will be possible to inform adults appropriately and also to create a necessary dialogue between adults and children to build the necessary bridges. Some people may consider this an unwelcome imposition. It is potentially a difficult battle that is yet to commence and is likely to last a very long time; however, it is one that cannot be disregarded because the subject is *children's* rights.

Thus, attitudes, beliefs, values, suppositions, and practices that ultimately shape the research experience for children rather than simply make them the subject of such research, are leading to serious consideration of the ethics of working with children. The basic ethical principle is that the human dignity of children and their rights and wellbeing are respected in all research, regardless of context. It has been particularly strongly pursued in the social research field and has a long and firmly established pedigree (for instance, see: Alderson 1995; Morrow and Richards 1996; Alderson and Morrow 2011). Nevertheless, this has been slow to find its place in children's rights, particularly in the global South and is often seen in context with participatory work with children rather than research (for instance: Save the Children 2003). The links between social research and rights that give children the right to be appropriately researched in which rights are the basis has been a more recent development with a working base in the South (for instance: Ennew et al. 2010, Manual 2). UNICEF have now further adopted a rights-based research approach with *Ethical Research Involving Children* (ERIC) (Anderson et al. 2013), which aims to guide researchers and research institutions to understand, plan, and conduct ethical research with and involving children and young people in any cultural, geographical, social, or methodological framework or setting. All areas of research using ethical approaches work on the basis that there is a policy on research that is firmly evidence based, increasingly taking in children in the South and that the internet and mobile technologies are increasing the scope of researchers to gain data in the field (Bulger and Livingstone 2013).

The last years of Judith Ennew's life included working on how children should be properly researched. The better the research, the better the information available to those rights will eventually be delivered. However, it is an approach that does not simply make the assumption that a few children trained in fairly straightforward research methods, usually participatory methods, is sufficient. It is intended that children are involved at all levels and in all stages of research, thus deciding on what the research will focus, its targets, aims, and intents, and all else. However, it does not mean that children must carry out the research in the field at all, they may work with adult researchers but that work may be entirely conducted by adults. There are good reasons why adults may be the better option, including cultural and risk-based reasons. It is not the case that only *child-to-child methods* can be used for a participatory approach, as people often slavishly insist.

However, children should always be involved in the analysis of data and presentation of findings. Reporting can be carried out not simply in a language specifically for children or for adults but in a manner that is mutually intelligible. It is research that will inform not only children but is equally aimed at adults. By not being bound by the virtual straightjacket of a narrow range of participatory methods it also has the flexibility to develop, change, and improve indefinitely to reach a point at which one could say children are being properly researched. However, great differences between places, people, and circumstances exist; thus, proper research is only definable at a micro level, in contrast with participatory research, which tends to be replicated at a macro level. It also works on another simple premise, which is that, strictly speaking, the term 'children's rights' is wrong. They are a part of 'human rights', within which some rights are specifically designed for young people. Thus, the information generated by this proper research in which children are involved is completely located within the broader human rights topic in such a way that it can not only cross-refer with other specialist areas, such as disability and women's rights, but also simply be part of the entire rights agenda. This approach to the proper research of children is required as a means not only of examining their rights but also informing universally.

Recent advances in information and communication technologies (ICTs), which have undergone unparalleled progression over the past decade, are positively impacting what we know about how rights are delivered (or not, as the case may be) and might be monitored in the future. They progressively drive and support change at the community level, feed into local, national, and worldwide economies, and support international development efforts. ICTs are being used to support *Communication for Development* (C4D), which stresses the importance of horizontal communication models used to enable participation, inclusion, and empowerment. The aim is to transform lives by increasing access to healthcare, education, and information. National and international policy frameworks and guidelines using ICTs are now being developed in the global North but with the intention of rapidly making them as accessible in the South. Here, they work for children's rights by testing out whether policy is convincingly based on sound evidence that takes children's experiences and problems into account (Bulger and Livingstone 2013). ICTs are dependent on the viability of well researched evidence. Urs Gasser, Director of the Berkman Center for Internet and Society at Harvard University, laid out a Web-based vision in UNICEF's report on the first quarter century (UNICEF 2014: 117–121) when he referred to the 'the interplay between children's rights and information and communication technology' (*ibid*: 118). It is, of course, dependent on finance and resources, but the Web is gradually becoming increasingly accessible and one must hope it will play an increasingly significant and beneficial role in children attaining their full human rights by knowing what they are, how to demand they be applied, and how to use them themselves.

The dilemma beyond taking children's experiences into account is how to transmit that knowledge to not just those officially and professionally responsible or engaged, but to the grassroots of all societies, which includes taking the message out to adults and children together, not separately, as has previously so often been the case. The predicament that comes with informing adults and children together is that rights are typically explained in a way that is meant for either adults or children but not both, thus making dialogue between the two difficult if not sometimes impossible. This is where, if what Judith Ennew started is to succeed, the ICTs and all other means of informing about rights need to become far more inclusive by allowing children's input at each and every stage of the process. It is undoubtedly a proverbial mountain yet to be climbed, but, in a very literal interpretation of the CRC, it is actually a requirement, thus something we are actually obliged to do rather than simply think about doing or perhaps trying out.

One of the necessities is that the 'pick and choose' approach to the application of the CRC must end. Some years ago, there was an explosion of activity around Article 12 and to a lesser extent the other 'participation' articles. Specialisation is probably inevitable when and wherever people with specific professional skills and interests are involved. However, whilst participation was in vogue, the wrong impression was being given to those whose interests were elsewhere and it appeared as though they were not equal to the children's rights faction grouped around that one article. It is a broad-ranging convention that is very easily apportioned into sectors, but the need for it to remain generic is greater than portions of the cake being shared out, never to fit back together as it was when first made.

Along with this tendency to be selective is the predisposition of some individuals and bodies to interpret, modify, or even concoct what is said. A recent example was the inclusion of a box placed by the French NGO *Secours Populaire Français* in a small book of games produced by *SNCF* (*Société Nationale des Chemins de fer Français*) for children travelling on their TGV trains (SNCF 2014: 12).[2] The extract is as follows: 'Le sais-tu? Un enfant sur trois ne part pas en vacances. Pourtant les vacances sont essentielles au bien-être de tous, c'est même un droit inscrit dans l'article 31 de la Convention international des droits de l'enfant'. (*Did you know? One child in three does not go away for holidays. Yet holidays are essential for everybody's wellbeing, it is even a right included in article 31 of the international Convention on the rights of the child.*)

The *Secours Populaire Français* website (www.secourspopulaire.fr) carries no actual link to the CRC, this particular Article of the convention, or further explanation of how the NGO arrived at this conclusion, although links do open a page on holidays for children. Neither the French and nor the English versions of the Article refer to a right to holidays:

[2]*Joue avec le petit Nicolas et TGV, direction les vacances* is a 16-page booklet of games given to young passengers on the high-speed TGV trains. It is based on the Laurence Tirard film *Les Vacances du petit Nicolas* released in July 2014 in France.

Article 31

1. Les Etats parties reconnaissent à l'enfant le droit au repos et aux loisirs, de se livrer au jeu et à des activités récréatives propres à son âge et de participer librement à la vie culturelle et artistique.
2. Les Etats parties respectent et favorisent le droit de l'enfant de participer pleinement à la vie culturelle et artistique et encouragent l'organisation à son intention de moyens appropriés de loisirs et d'activités récréatives, artistiques et culturelles, dans des conditions d'égalité.

Article 31

1. States that Parties recognize the right of the child to rest and leisure, to engage in play and recreational activities appropriate to the age of the child and to participate freely in cultural life and the arts.
2. States that Parties shall respect and promote the right of the child to participate fully in cultural and artistic life and shall encourage the provision of appropriate and equal opportunities for cultural, artistic, recreational and leisure activity.

One might assume it to be an interpretation of 'rest and leisure'; however, that would be a version that applies by implication in the affluent North but is largely a meaningless aspiration in the poor countries of the South and least affluent of the North. The drafting of the CRC has clearly very skillfully not included holidays for very sensible reasons. However, this NGO has seen fit to put words into the CRC that were not there. It is a single recent example, and many others can be found with relatively little effort.

Article 28 states in Part 1 that 'Parties recognize the right of the child to education, and with a view to achieving this right progressively and on the basis of equal opportunity, ...'. Then 1a through 1e emphasize the importance of formal structures, which is to say school through to higher education, although 1d is perhaps more open if one wishes it to be. Points 2 and 3 follow in the same vein. There is no accommodation for informal and unstructured education such as learning by example and experience, which is the case, for instance, in the few remaining pre-literate societies and where formal education is not available. It simply imposes a moral duty to formally educate and thus overlooks the preparation of children for a life within their society and its culture. Thus, civil and social education has been omitted as a right even though they are generally, or at least should be, more important than literacy and numeracy. It may be an oversight; however, that does not mean it should be ignored or passed over and consistently allowed to be used as a trump card for the education professions to justify their arguments to the exclusion of those who, for instance, may be defending indigenous rights by arguing that imposition of structured formal education is very likely to have a negative influence on entire groups, indeed to the end of the culture as it has been for many hundreds or perhaps thousands of years. It is also vulnerable to contradictions, whereby within civil education in formal education the respect for and preservation of identity and culture often feature in curricula. However, this blind spot is not challenged. Occasionally, naively and with the best of intentions, the narrow view of education it projects is far more destructive than all else, as it thus removes rather than bestows or upholds the rights of those who have schooling in formal, curriculum-led education.

A problem also exists with the 'best interests' principle in Article 3, Part 1. It promises that 'In all actions concerning children ... the best interests of the child shall be a primary consideration.' This is a right that is imposed via a judgment of what is meant by the principle 'best interest'. The entire way in which Article 3 is phrased is out of the hands of children to begin with, and is then highly subjective. The unprejudiced delivery of rights needs to be objective. It is a right that clearly needs to have an open dialogue with each individual so that no child is 'possessed' by those whose best interests are judged by others. In real terms, can the imposed rescue of children from wars and natural disasters be justified when this means they are separated from family and home, the environments in which they may wish to remain, irrespective of how dire or even life-threatening the incoming outsiders judge it to be. It often raises the question of children's competence, since imposed best interests such as being rescued without actually knowing how well they might cope, indeed even learn a great deal and thrive on, the basis of the experience, may be denied. Even the removal of children from abusive or exploitative situations, very much a northern hemisphere issue, tends to be an enforced rather than a consulted action. A subjective best interest principle is applied that, more often than not, leaves no space or time for a dialogue with the child to be rescued so that he or she approves and is able to go freely. This has always been the problem for people engaged in actions with working children who see the elimination of child labour as a blunt tool that simply strikes but excludes dialogue or any accounting for circumstances. The 'forcible' removal of children from the streets, rescuing child sex workers, child soldiers, and so on is similar. That is by no means an argument that what they are doing is in any sense right, but simply an illustration of how the 'best interests' principle renders those who assess what that means and then act on it almost godlike in their application. The principle should long before now have been closely scrutinized and its application extended to clearly spell out the importance of it being a negotiated status that absolutely needs to be used on a person-by-person basis. It is not a 'fits all' notion that neither differentiates between individual and collective needs nor is acknowledged as being subjective. Thus, the principle needs to be reassessed and perhaps entirely rephrased and expanded to spell out what it should mean.

Similarly, there is the problem that lack of information has allowed even seemingly well informed professionals to misuse the CRC in content, concept, and name. People working in the children's rights environment have found it vexing to get together with professionals whose work is with or related to children and be told that such-and-such can be found in what they refer to as the 'UNICEF Charter of Children's Rights' or similar instead of its correct name. These are situations in the presence of people who are using random statements that are apparently never, or at least almost undetectably, reproduced in written form. It is very frustrating to be firmly told that something that is not in the CRC as it is being described is not only being made up, but also shows ignorance in terms of the correct title of the convention and that it is a UN convention and not a treaty of one of its agencies. Once these details are discussed and the person corrected, although there are those who will not accept that, it becomes apparent that it is simply a lack of information and 'education' that generates such damaging errors.

Although all of these errors and defects are trivial compared with the task of universally applying the CRC so that all children enjoy the rights it describes, they contribute little to the work that must be carried out for many years to come. Clearly the intent is not evil; however, they expose the vulnerability of the CRC to interpretation on the one hand and the fact that information is clearly not sufficiently accessible to avoid such errors. The fact there are such defects exposes exactly the kind of susceptibility that gives critics and opponents of the notion of children's rights the basis for generating arguments that stand in the way of delivering them. However, as much as anything else, that organizations and individuals who should be precisely informed clearly are not, shows the failure of the UN system, the NGOs, and all others to inform and provide some kind of leadership. The report of the Secretary-General on the status of the CRC, August 2014 (UN General Assembly 2014) reviews the positive outcomes the CRC has brought with it; however, pages 9–14 examine what has not worked and pages 14–18 examine how to leverage resources and bring about innovations that will advance children's rights. It is just over half of the entire report.

Ultimately, this lets children down because the commitments made with each ratification still need to be fulfilled up to a quarter of a century after accession to the convention. Many more countries that are striving to achieve this are not delivering children their rights as adequately as they should. In fact, there would appear to be no state party that is absolutely fulfilling the stated goals of the CRC, and very few are even close to doing so. For those who invested great hope in the CRC, in some ways the UN now has the appearance of a toothless tiger that also has neither remaining claws nor the ability to pounce and that growls rather than roars fearsomely. Using that simile, the Committee is merely a tiger cub that depends very much on the adult; it still only growls and has no power to do much more. Even given that some countries have been affected by war and other conflicts, have undergone changes of regime for the worse, have experienced natural disasters, and that the economic crisis will have played a significant role, the majority of countries should still have been able to work toward full implementation of the CRC. However, those of us with a wider human rights perspective are aware that it is far from only the CRC that suffers this neglect.

This draws us toward a point, one at which an increasing number of people working in the children's rights arena are arriving. Judith Ennew particularly believed it, as do I, as the author of this work that attempts to account for both of our points of view and those of others we have known. In practice and rationally, Judith did not in fact believe in 'children's rights'. She believed, and therefore always tried to practice, an approach in which she accepted that children, like all other people, were bearers of *human rights*. That is, that human rights are indivisible. What she and an increasing number of others accepted was that rights were divided into specialized areas so that children, as with women, the disabled, ethnic minorities, and all other people, could be delivered specific rights suited to their immediate needs and situation. Her view was that, over the fullness of time, this temporary measure was only an antecedent to all people sharing precisely the same rights without any form of compartmentalization, segregation, or discrimination.

Eventually, once the CRC was firmly established, the process could begin to move toward its obsolescence. The ultimate aim was to see a time when a single treaty described all human rights without this kind of compartmentalisation. In a more idealised world, even that treaty should become obsolete once humanity had reached a state in which social and economic justice ended the need for goals driven by treaties, and all people could share the world as equals. It is an ideal only and as realists no doubt the people who have seen the need to move the CRC on toward integration in human rights also know that problems exist within the human rights world alone. Children's rights and human rights are very often treated very separately; the former is very clearly not comfortably placed alongside the latter, yet there is no doubt that the right of children to have rights is, by its very nature, a human rights issue. Thus, an increasing number of us prefer to use the term the *human rights of children* rather than *children's rights* in order to show that it is not a concept contained in some kind of 'straitjacket' and thus something that limits the freedom of action or initiative to use those rights given to children inclusively within the entire rights environment.

That 'conflict', along with compartmentalization of the CRC into specific areas, frequent discord in research, poor and lacking information, and misuse of the concept of children's rights and the CRC, does not help progress. In this respect, since the vast wave of enthusiasm that swept around the world in and immediately after 1989 has not maintained its momentum, the convention itself may appear to some to need to be revisited as were the two preceding declarations were in their time. Whilst the CRC is a binding convention in all but a small number of countries, actualizing many of its precepts are beyond the economic capability of many countries. That is without looking at geophysical, geopolitical, cultural, political, social, religious, and all other implications that impede application. It is a very high ideal to aspire to but an even higher one to achieve. That does not mean it is not time to take a breath, think again, and look for ways and means as to how it can be improved. Thus, the answer to the question asked by the title of this chapter can only be that children's rights are worth pursuing, but no actual solutions are offered.

In the 2014 report on 25 years of the CRC by UNICEF, Kevin Watkins very appropriately says and asks (UNICEF 2014: 69)

> The strength of the Convention cannot be measured in ratifications, national laws or government declarations. Ultimately, the real test is whether or not its provisions make a difference in the lives of children. How does the Convention help a young Bangladeshi girl denied education because she is forced into marriage? This, after all, is a country in which over one quarter of girls is married by the age of 15. What hope and opportunity does the Convention provide to a child in Haiti or Kenya forced by poverty into hazardous and exploitative child labour? How does it help children in the Syrian Arab Republic or in Gaza where fundamental rights are violated with apparent impunity by indiscriminate violence? In our increasingly prosperous but obscenely unequal world, how is the Convention helping

> children left behind because of poverty, gender, ethnicity, racial origin, geographical location and other markers for disadvantage? What is it doing to expand opportunity for the world's most marginalized and disadvantaged children?

The question remains as to how we go about dealing with that and more from the point we have arrived at after a quarter of a century? This is, after all, a book written to follow on from a work completed in 1988 and published a few months later during the year of the CRC's adoption 1989. Its main title, *The Next Generation*, was looking at young people who were moving toward adulthood who would then be the progenitors of a generation, many of whom are now adults themselves; indeed some of the older ones may already be grandparents. That assumes they are still alive and are able to be parents themselves, which many may well not be. We do not know how many have died, or how, when, or where they died. We do not know how many have been displaced and have been refugees, asylum seekers, or have simply constantly moved on. Similarly, we do not know how long that was for or whether they have ever been able to return 'home'. There is no way of knowing which of them have been successful in their endeavors and how many have been and remain in dire poverty and misery.

Equations and possible numbers are unknowns. We cannot speculate but simply imagine what might have happened. Whatever the case, new generations are being born and will be for as long as humanity exists. For their sakes, rights very much need to be pursued on the basis of the spirit of the vast amount of engagement and commitment shown by those who gave us each layer of children's rights during the twentieth century. None of those people would appear to have fought for this cause for their own vanity or ego but for children. It is in the hands of future generations to carry that work forward for each following generation.

References

Alderson, P. (1995). *Listening to children: Children, ethics and social research.* London: Barnados.

Alderson, P., & Morrow, V. (2011). *The ethics of research with children and young people: A practical handbook.* London: Sage.

Althusser, L. (1971). Ideology and ideological state apparatuses. In *Lenin and philosophy, and other essays* (pp. 127–188). London: New Left Books.

Anderson, D., Fitzgerald, R., Graham, A., Powell, M. A., & Taylor, N. (2013). *Ethical research involving children.* Florence: UNICEF.

Archard, D. (1993). *Children. Rights and childhood.* London/New York: Routledge.

Bottomore, T. (Ed.). (1964). *Karl Marx: Early writings.* New York: McGraw-Hill.

Boyden, J. (1990). Childhood and the policymakers. In A. James & J. Prout (Eds.), *Constructing and reconstructing childhood* (pp. 184–215). London/New York/Philadelphia: Falmer Press.

Brennan, S., & Noggle, R. (1997). The moral status of children: Children's rights, parent's rights and family justice. *Social Theory and Practice, 23*(1), 1–26.

Bulger, M., & Livingstone, S. (2013). *A global agenda for children's rights in the digital age: Recommendations for developing UNICEF's research strategy.* Florence: UNICEF.

Dunn, J. (1982). *The political thought of John Locke: An historical account of the argument of the 'two treatises of government'.* Cambridge: Cambridge University Press.

Ennew, J., Abebe, T., Bangyai, R., Karapituck, P., Kjørholt, A. T., Noonsup, T., Beazley, H., Bessell, S., Daengchart-Kushanoglu, P., & Waterson, R. (2010). *The right to be properly researched: How to do rights-based, scientific research with children*. Bangkok: Knowing Children.

Franklin, B. (Ed.). (1986). Introduction and children's political rights. In *The rights of children* (pp. 1–23 and 24–53). Oxford: Basil Blackwell.

Hall, S. (1985). Signification, representation, ideology: Althusser and the post-structuralist debates. *Critical Studies in Mass Communication, 2*(2), 91–114.

Holt, J. (1974). *Escape from childhood*. Boston: E. P. Dutton.

James, A., & Prout, A. (Eds.). (1990). *Constructing and reconstructing childhood: Contemporary issues in the sociological study of childhood*. London: Falmer Press.

Jenks, C. (1996). *Childhood*. London: Routledge.

Morrow, V., & Richards, M. (1996). The ethics of social research with children: An overview. *Children and Society, 10*(2), 90–105.

Qvortrup, J. (1991). *Childhood as a social phenomenon* (2nd ed.). Eurosocial Report 36/0. Vienna: European Centre for Social Welfare, Policy and Research.

Rousseau, J.-J. (1991). *Emile; Or on education*. Harmondsworth: Penguin Classics.

Rousseau, J.-J. (1998). *The social contract, or principles of political right*. Ware: Wordsworth Classics.

SCF, U. K. (2003). *So you want to consult with children? A toolkit of good practice*. London: Save the Children.

Société Nationale des Chemins de fer Français (SNCF). (2014). *Joue avec le petit Nicolas et TGV, direction les vacances*. Paris: SNCF.

Turner, B. (1993). Outline of a theory of human rights. *Sociology, 27*(3), 489–512.

UN General Assembly. (2014). *Status of the convention on the rights of the child: Report of the secretary-general*. New York: United Nations.

UNICEF. (2014). *25 Years of the convention on the rights of the child: Is the world a better place for children?* New York: United Nations Children's Fund.

Appendices

Appendix 1

Janusz Korczak (Dr Henryk Goldszmit) never actually wrote a Declaration of Children's Rights but over time a number of authors have compiled some of the rights he described from early in his works such as How to Love a Child, *1919, and* The Child's Right to Respect, *1929, and through to his response to the 1924 Declaration of the Rights of the Child in the 1929 work in which he wrote: 'The authors of the Declaration of Geneva have mistaken duties for rights. Instead of making demands they try to persuade. The Declaration is only an appeal for goodwill, a request for more understanding'. He had not completed what has been listed as 'his' declaration by adding other rights at the time of his death in 1942.*

Declaration of Children's Rights

The child has the right to love.
The child has the right to respect.
The child has the right to optimal conditions in which to grow and develop.
The child has the right to live in the present.
The child has the right to be himself or herself.
The child has the right to make mistakes.
The child has the right to fail.
The child has the right to be taken seriously.
The child has the right to be appreciated for what he is.
The child has the right to desire, to claim, to ask.
The child has the right to have secrets.
The child has the right to 'a lie, a deception, a theft'.
The child has the right to respect for his possessions and budget.
The child has the right to education.
The child has the right to resist educational influence that conflicts with his or her own beliefs.
The child has the right to protest an injustice.

B. Milne, *Rights of the Child*, Children's Well-Being: Indicators and Research 11,
DOI 10.1007/978-3-319-18784-6

The child has the right to a Children's Court where he can judge and be judged by his peers.
The child has the right to be defended in the juvenile-justice court system.
The child has the right to respect for his grief.
The child has the right to commune with God. The child has the right to die prematurely.

Appendix 2

This is the initial version of the Declaration of the Rights of the Child very slightly amending the version drafted by Eglantyne Jebb in 1923 and adopted by the League of Nations in 1924.

Geneva Declaration of the Rights of the Child

By the present Declaration of the Rights of the Child, commonly known as 'Declaration of Geneva', men and women of all nations, recognising that mankind owes to the Child the best that it has to give, declare and accept it as their duty that, beyond and above all considerations of race, nationality or creed:

1. The child must be given the means requisite for its normal development, both materially and spiritually;
2. The child that is hungry must be fed; the child that is sick must be nursed; the child that is backward must be helped; the delinquent child must be reclaimed; and the orphan and the waif must be sheltered and succoured;
3. The child must be the first to receive relief in times of distress;
4. The child must be put in a position to earn a livelihood, and must be protected against every form of exploitation;
5. The child must be brought up in the consciousness that its talents must be devoted to the service of fellow men.

Appendix 3

Declaration of the Rights of the Child

Adopted by UN General Assembly Resolution 1386 (XIV) of 10 December 1959

WHEREAS the peoples of the United Nations have, in the Charter, reaffirmed their faith in fundamental human rights and in the dignity and worth of the human person, and have determined to promote social progress and better standards of life in larger freedom,

WHEREAS the United Nations has, in the Universal Declaration of Human Rights, proclaimed that everyone is entitled to all the rights and freedoms set forth therein, without distinction of any kind, such as race, colour, sex, language, religion, political or other opinion, national or social origin, property, birth or other status,

WHEREAS the child, by reason of his physical and mental immaturity, needs special safeguards and care, including appropriate legal protection, before as well as after birth,

WHEREAS the need for such special safeguards has been stated in the Geneva Declaration of the Rights of the Child of 1924, and recognized in the Universal Declaration of Human Rights and in the statutes of specialized agencies and international organizations concerned with the welfare of children,

WHEREAS mankind owes to the child the best it has to give,

The General Assembly
Now, therefore,
Proclaims

This Declaration Of The Rights Of The Child to the end that he may have a happy childhood and enjoy for his own good and for the good of society the rights and freedoms herein set forth, and calls upon parents, upon men and women as individuals, and upon voluntary organizations, local authorities and national Governments to recognize these rights and strive for their observance by legislative and other measures progressively taken in accordance with the following principles:

1. The child shall enjoy all the rights set forth in this Declaration. Every child, without any exception whatsoever, shall be entitled to these rights, without distinction or discrimination on account of race, colour, sex, language, religion, political or other opinion, national or social origin, property, birth or other status, whether of himself or of his family.
2. The child shall enjoy special protection, and shall be given opportunities and facilities, by law and by other means, to enable him to develop physically, mentally, morally, spiritually and socially in a healthy and normal manner and in conditions of freedom and dignity. In the enactment of laws for this purpose, the best interests of the child shall be the paramount consideration.
3. The child shall be entitled from his birth to a name and a nationality.
4. The child shall enjoy the benefits of social security. He shall be entitled to grow and develop in health; to this end, special care and protection shall be provided both to him and to his mother, including adequate pre-natal and post-natal care. The child shall have the right to adequate nutrition, housing, recreation and medical services.
5. The child who is physically, mentally or socially handicapped shall be given the special treatment, education and care required by his particular condition.
6. The child, for the full and harmonious development of his personality, needs love and understanding. He shall, wherever possible, grow up in the care and under the responsibility of his parents, and, in any case, in an atmosphere of affection and of moral and material security; a child of tender years shall not, save in exceptional circumstances, be separated from his mother. Society and the public authorities shall have the duty to extend particular care to children

without a family and to those without adequate means of support. Payment of State and other assistance towards the maintenance of children of large families is desirable.

7. The child is entitled to receive education, which shall be free and compulsory, at least in the elementary stages. He shall be given an education which will promote his general culture and enable him, on a basis of equal opportunity, to develop his abilities, his individual judgement, and his sense of moral and social responsibility, and to become a useful member of society.

   The best interests of the child shall be the guiding principle of those responsible for his education and guidance; that responsibility lies in the first place with his parents.

   The child shall have full opportunity for play and recreation, which should be directed to the same purposes as education; society and the public authorities shall endeavour to promote the enjoyment of this right.
8. The child shall in all circumstances be among the first to receive protection and relief.
9. The child shall be protected against all forms of neglect, cruelty and exploitation. He shall not be the subject of traffic, in any form.

   The child shall not be admitted to employment before an appropriate minimum age; he shall in no case be caused or permitted to engage in any occupation or employment which would prejudice his health or education, or interfere with his physical, mental or moral development.
10. The child shall be protected from practices which may foster racial, religious and any other form of discrimination. He shall be brought up in a spirit of understanding, tolerance, friendship among peoples, peace and universal brotherhood, and in full consciousness that his energy and talents should be devoted to the service of his fellow men.

Appendix 4

Convention on the Rights of the Child

Adopted and opened for signature, ratification and accession by General Assembly resolution 44/25 of 20 November 1989
entry into force 2 September 1990, in accordance with article 49

Preamble

The States Parties to the present Convention,

Considering that, in accordance with the principles proclaimed in the Charter of the United Nations, recognition of the inherent dignity and of the equal and inalienable rights of all members of the human family is the foundation of freedom, justice and peace in the world,

Bearing in mind that the peoples of the United Nations have, in the Charter, reaffirmed their faith in fundamental human rights and in the dignity and worth of the human person, and have determined to promote social progress and better standards of life in larger freedom,

Recognizing that the United Nations has, in the Universal Declaration of Human Rights and in the International Covenants on Human Rights, proclaimed and agreed that everyone is entitled to all the rights and freedoms set forth therein, without distinction of any kind, such as race, colour, sex, language, religion, political or other opinion, national or social origin, property, birth or other status,

Recalling that, in the Universal Declaration of Human Rights, the United Nations has proclaimed that childhood is entitled to special care and assistance,

Convinced that the family, as the fundamental group of society and the natural environment for the growth and well-being of all its members and particularly children, should be afforded the necessary protection and assistance so that it can fully assume its responsibilities within the community,

Recognizing that the child, for the full and harmonious development of his or her personality, should grow up in a family environment, in an atmosphere of happiness, love and understanding,

Considering that the child should be fully prepared to live an individual life in society, and brought up in the spirit of the ideals proclaimed in the Charter of the United Nations, and in particular in the spirit of peace, dignity, tolerance, freedom, equality and solidarity,

Bearing in mind that the need to extend particular care to the child has been stated in the Geneva Declaration of the Rights of the Child of 1924 and in the Declaration of the Rights of the Child adopted by the General Assembly on 20 November 1959 and recognized in the Universal Declaration of Human Rights, in the International Covenant on Civil and Political Rights (in particular in articles 23 and 24), in the International Covenant on Economic, Social and Cultural Rights (in particular in article 10) and in the statutes and relevant instruments of specialized agencies and international organizations concerned with the welfare of children,

Bearing in mind that, as indicated in the Declaration of the Rights of the Child, "the child, by reason of his physical and mental immaturity, needs special safeguards and care, including appropriate legal protection, before as well as after birth",

Recalling the provisions of the Declaration on Social and Legal Principles relating to the Protection and Welfare of Children, with Special Reference to Foster Placement and Adoption Nationally and Internationally; the United Nations Standard Minimum Rules for the Administration of Juvenile Justice (The Beijing Rules); and the Declaration on the Protection of Women and Children in Emergency and Armed Conflict, Recognizing that, in all countries in the world, there are children living in exceptionally difficult conditions, and that such children need special consideration,

Taking due account of the importance of the traditions and cultural values of each people for the protection and harmonious development of the child, Recognizing the importance of international co-operation for improving the living conditions of children in every country, in particular in the developing countries,

Have agreed as follows:

PART I

Article 1

For the purposes of the present Convention, a child means every human being below the age of 18 years unless under the law applicable to the child, majority is attained earlier.

Article 2

1. States Parties shall respect and ensure the rights set forth in the present Convention to each child within their jurisdiction without discrimination of any kind, irrespective of the child's or his or her parent's or legal guardian's race, colour, sex, language, religion, political or other opinion, national, ethnic or social origin, property, disability, birth or other status.
2. States Parties shall take all appropriate measures to ensure that the child is protected against all forms of discrimination or punishment on the basis of the status, activities, expressed opinions, or beliefs of the child's parents, legal guardians, or family members.

Article 3

1. In all actions concerning children, whether undertaken by public or private social welfare institutions, courts of law, administrative authorities or legislative bodies, the best interests of the child shall be a primary consideration.
2. States Parties undertake to ensure the child such protection and care as is necessary for his or her well-being, taking into account the rights and duties of his or her parents, legal guardians, or other individuals legally responsible for him or her, and, to this end, shall take all appropriate legislative and administrative measures.
3. States Parties shall ensure that the institutions, services and facilities responsible for the care or protection of children shall conform with the standards established by competent authorities, particularly in the areas of safety, health, in the number and suitability of their staff, as well as competent supervision.

Article 4

States Parties shall undertake all appropriate legislative, administrative, and other measures for the implementation of the rights recognized in the present Convention. With regard to economic, social and cultural rights, States Parties shall undertake such measures to the maximum extent of their available resources and, where needed, within the framework of international co-operation.

Article 5

States Parties shall respect the responsibilities, rights and duties of parents or, where applicable, the members of the extended family or community as provided for by local custom, legal guardians or other persons legally responsible for the child, to provide, in a manner consistent with the evolving capacities of the child, appropriate direction and guidance in the exercise by the child of the rights recognized in the present Convention.

Article 6

1. States Parties recognize that every child has the inherent right to life.
2. States Parties shall ensure to the maximum extent possible the survival and development of the child.

Article 7

1. The child shall be registered immediately after birth and shall have the right from birth to a name, the right to acquire a nationality and. as far as possible, the right to know and be cared for by his or her parents.
2. States Parties shall ensure the implementation of these rights in accordance with their national law and their obligations under the relevant international instruments in this field, in particular where the child would otherwise be stateless.

Article 8

1. States Parties undertake to respect the right of the child to preserve his or her identity, including nationality, name and family relations as recognized by law without unlawful interference.
2. Where a child is illegally deprived of some or all of the elements of his or her identity, States Parties shall provide appropriate assistance and protection, with a view to re-establishing speedily his or her identity.

Article 9

1. States Parties shall ensure that a child shall not be separated from his or her parents against their will, except when competent authorities subject to judicial review determine, in accordance with applicable law and procedures, that such separation is necessary for the best interests of the child. Such determination may be necessary in a particular case such as one involving abuse or neglect of the child by the parents, or one where the parents are living separately and a decision must be made as to the child's place of residence.
2. In any proceedings pursuant to paragraph 1 of the present article, all interested parties shall be given an opportunity to participate in the proceedings and make their views known.
3. States Parties shall respect the right of the child who is separated from one or both parents to maintain personal relations and direct contact with both parents on a regular basis, except if it is contrary to the child's best interests.
4. Where such separation results from any action initiated by a State Party, such as the detention, imprisonment, exile, deportation or death (including death arising from any cause while the person is in the custody of the State) of one or both parents or of the child, that State Party shall, upon request, provide the parents, the child or, if appropriate, another member of the family with the essential information concerning the whereabouts of the absent member(s) of the family unless the provision of the information would be detrimental to the well-being of the child. States Parties shall further ensure that the submission of such a request shall of itself entail no adverse consequences for the person(s) concerned.

Article 10

1. In accordance with the obligation of States Parties under article 9, paragraph 1, applications by a child or his or her parents to enter or leave a State Party for the purpose of family reunification shall be dealt with by States Parties in a positive, humane and expeditious manner. States Parties shall further ensure that the submission of such a request shall entail no adverse consequences for the applicants and for the members of their family.
2. A child whose parents reside in different States shall have the right to maintain on a regular basis, save in exceptional circumstances personal relations and direct contacts with both parents. Towards that end and in accordance with the obligation of States Parties under article 9, paragraph 1, States Parties shall respect the right of the child and his or her parents to leave any country, including their own, and to enter their own country. The right to leave any country shall be subject only to such restrictions as are prescribed by law and which are necessary to protect the national security, public order (ordre public), public health or morals or the rights and freedoms of others and are consistent with the other rights recognized in the present Convention.

Article 11

1. States Parties shall take measures to combat the illicit transfer and non-return of children abroad.
2. To this end, States Parties shall promote the conclusion of bilateral or multilateral agreements or accession to existing agreements.

Article 12

1. States Parties shall assure to the child who is capable of forming his or her own views the right to express those views freely in all matters affecting the child, the views of the child being given due weight in accordance with the age and maturity of the child.
2. For this purpose, the child shall in particular be provided the opportunity to be heard in any judicial and administrative proceedings affecting the child, either directly, or through a representative or an appropriate body, in a manner consistent with the procedural rules of national law.

Article 13

1. The child shall have the right to freedom of expression; this right shall include freedom to seek, receive and impart information and ideas of all kinds, regardless of frontiers, either orally, in writing or in print, in the form of art, or through any other media of the child's choice.
2. The exercise of this right may be subject to certain restrictions, but these shall only be such as are provided by law and are necessary:
   (a) For respect of the rights or reputations of others; or
   (b) For the protection of national security or of public order (ordre public), or of public health or morals.

Article 14

1. States Parties shall respect the right of the child to freedom of thought, conscience and religion.
2. States Parties shall respect the rights and duties of the parents and, when applicable, legal guardians, to provide direction to the child in the exercise of his or her right in a manner consistent with the evolving capacities of the child.
3. Freedom to manifest one's religion or beliefs may be subject only to such limitations as are prescribed by law and are necessary to protect public safety, order, health or morals, or the fundamental rights and freedoms of others.

Article 15

1. States Parties recognize the rights of the child to freedom of association and to freedom of peaceful assembly.
2. No restrictions may be placed on the exercise of these rights other than those imposed in conformity with the law and which are necessary in a democratic society in the interests of national security or public safety, public order (ordre public), the protection of public health or morals or the protection of the rights and freedoms of others.

Article 16

1. No child shall be subjected to arbitrary or unlawful interference with his or her privacy, family, or correspondence, nor to unlawful attacks on his or her honour and reputation.
2. The child has the right to the protection of the law against such interference or attacks.

Article 17

States Parties recognize the important function performed by the mass media and shall ensure that the child has access to information and material from a diversity of national and international sources, especially those aimed at the promotion of his or her social, spiritual and moral well-being and physical and mental health.

To this end, States Parties shall:

(a) Encourage the mass media to disseminate information and material of social and cultural benefit to the child and in accordance with the spirit of article 29;
(b) Encourage international co-operation in the production, exchange and dissemination of such information and material from a diversity of cultural, national and international sources;
(c) Encourage the production and dissemination of children's books;
(d) Encourage the mass media to have particular regard to the linguistic needs of the child who belongs to a minority group or who is indigenous;
(e) Encourage the development of appropriate guidelines for the protection of the child from information and material injurious to his or her well-being, bearing in mind the provisions of articles 13 and 18.

Article 18

1. States Parties shall use their best efforts to ensure recognition of the principle that both parents have common responsibilities for the upbringing and development of the child. Parents or, as the case may be, legal guardians, have the primary responsibility for the upbringing and development of the child. The best interests of the child will be their basic concern.
2. For the purpose of guaranteeing and promoting the rights set forth in the present Convention, States Parties shall render appropriate assistance to parents and legal guardians in the performance of their child-rearing responsibilities and shall ensure the development of institutions, facilities and services for the care of children.
3. States Parties shall take all appropriate measures to ensure that children of working parents have the right to benefit from child-care services and facilities for which they are eligible.

Article 19

1. States Parties shall take all appropriate legislative, administrative, social and educational measures to protect the child from all forms of physical or mental violence, injury or abuse, neglect or negligent treatment, maltreatment or exploitation, including sexual abuse, while in the care of parent(s), legal guardian(s) or any other person who has the care of the child.
2. Such protective measures should, as appropriate, include effective procedures for the establishment of social programmes to provide necessary support for the child and for those who have the care of the child, as well as for other forms of prevention and for identification, reporting, referral, investigation, treatment and follow-up of instances of child maltreatment described heretofore, and, as appropriate, for judicial involvement.

Article 20

1. A child temporarily or permanently deprived of his or her family environment, or in whose own best interests cannot be allowed to remain in that environment, shall be entitled to special protection and assistance provided by the State.
2. States Parties shall in accordance with their national laws ensure alternative care for such a child.
3. Such care could include, inter alia, foster placement, kafalah of Islamic law, adoption or if necessary placement in suitable institutions for the care of children. When considering solutions, due regard shall be paid to the desirability of continuity in a child's upbringing and to the child's ethnic, religious, cultural and linguistic background.

Article 21

States Parties that recognize and/or permit the system of adoption shall ensure that the best interests of the child shall be the paramount consideration and they shall:

(a) Ensure that the adoption of a child is authorized only by competent authorities who determine, in accordance with applicable law and procedures and on the basis of all pertinent and reliable information, that the adoption is permissible in view of the child's status concerning parents, relatives and legal guardians and that, if required, the persons concerned have given their informed consent to the adoption on the basis of such counselling as may be necessary;
(b) Recognize that inter-country adoption may be considered as an alternative means of child's care, if the child cannot be placed in a foster or an adoptive family or cannot in any suitable manner be cared for in the child's country of origin;
(c) Ensure that the child concerned by inter-country adoption enjoys safeguards and standards equivalent to those existing in the case of national adoption;
(d) Take all appropriate measures to ensure that, in inter-country adoption, the placement does not result in improper financial gain for those involved in it;
(e) Promote, where appropriate, the objectives of the present article by concluding bilateral or multilateral arrangements or agreements, and endeavour, within this framework, to ensure that the placement of the child in another country is carried out by competent authorities or organs.

Article 22

1. States Parties shall take appropriate measures to ensure that a child who is seeking refugee status or who is considered a refugee in accordance with applicable international or domestic law and procedures shall, whether unaccompanied or accompanied by his or her parents or by any other person, receive appropriate protection and humanitarian assistance in the enjoyment of applicable rights set forth in the present Convention and in other international human rights or humanitarian instruments to which the said States are Parties.
2. For this purpose, States Parties shall provide, as they consider appropriate, co-operation in any efforts by the United Nations and other competent intergovernmental organizations or non-governmental organizations co-operating with the United Nations to protect and assist such a child and to trace the parents or other members of the family of any refugee child in order to obtain information necessary for reunification with his or her family. In cases where no parents or other members of the family can be found, the child shall be accorded the same protection as any other child permanently or temporarily deprived of his or her family environment for any reason, as set forth in the present Convention.

Article 23

1. States Parties recognize that a mentally or physically disabled child should enjoy a full and decent life, in conditions which ensure dignity, promote self-reliance and facilitate the child's active participation in the community.
2. States Parties recognize the right of the disabled child to special care and shall encourage and ensure the extension, subject to available resources, to the eligible child and those responsible for his or her care, of assistance for which application

is made and which is appropriate to the child's condition and to the circumstances of the parents or others caring for the child.

3. Recognizing the special needs of a disabled child, assistance extended in accordance with paragraph 2 of the present article shall be provided free of charge, whenever possible, taking into account the financial resources of the parents or others caring for the child, and shall be designed to ensure that the disabled child has effective access to and receives education, training, health care services, rehabilitation services, preparation for employment and recreation opportunities in a manner conducive to the child's achieving the fullest possible social integration and individual development, including his or her cultural and spiritual development.
4. States Parties shall promote, in the spirit of international cooperation, the exchange of appropriate information in the field of preventive health care and of medical, psychological and functional treatment of disabled children, including dissemination of and access to information concerning methods of rehabilitation, education and vocational services, with the aim of enabling States Parties to improve their capabilities and skills and to widen their experience in these areas. In this regard, particular account shall be taken of the needs of developing countries.

Article 24

1. States Parties recognize the right of the child to the enjoyment of the highest attainable standard of health and to facilities for the treatment of illness and rehabilitation of health. States Parties shall strive to ensure that no child is deprived of his or her right of access to such health care services.
2. States Parties shall pursue full implementation of this right and, in particular, shall take appropriate measures:
   (a) To diminish infant and child mortality;
   (b) To ensure the provision of necessary medical assistance and health care to all children with emphasis on the development of primary health care;
   (c) To combat disease and malnutrition, including within the framework of primary health care, through, inter alia, the application of readily available technology and through the provision of adequate nutritious foods and clean drinking-water, taking into consideration the dangers and risks of environmental pollution;
   (d) To ensure appropriate pre-natal and post-natal health care for mothers;
   (e) To ensure that all segments of society, in particular parents and children, are informed, have access to education and are supported in the use of basic knowledge of child health and nutrition, the advantages of breastfeeding, hygiene and environmental sanitation and the prevention of accidents;
   (f) To develop preventive health care, guidance for parents and family planning education and services.
3. States Parties shall take all effective and appropriate measures with a view to abolishing traditional practices prejudicial to the health of children.

4. States Parties undertake to promote and encourage international co-operation with a view to achieving progressively the full realization of the right recognized in the present article. In this regard, particular account shall be taken of the needs of developing countries.

Article 25

States Parties recognize the right of a child who has been placed by the competent authorities for the purposes of care, protection or treatment of his or her physical or mental health, to a periodic review of the treatment provided to the child and all other circumstances relevant to his or her placement.

Article 26

1. States Parties shall recognize for every child the right to benefit from social security, including social insurance, and shall take the necessary measures to achieve the full realization of this right in accordance with their national law.
2. The benefits should, where appropriate, be granted, taking into account the resources and the circumstances of the child and persons having responsibility for the maintenance of the child, as well as any other consideration relevant to an application for benefits made by or on behalf of the child.

Article 27

1. States Parties recognize the right of every child to a standard of living adequate for the child's physical, mental, spiritual, moral and social development.
2. The parent(s) or others responsible for the child have the primary responsibility to secure, within their abilities and financial capacities, the conditions of living necessary for the child's development.
3. States Parties, in accordance with national conditions and within their means, shall take appropriate measures to assist parents and others responsible for the child to implement this right and shall in case of need provide material assistance and support programmes, particularly with regard to nutrition, clothing and housing.
4. States Parties shall take all appropriate measures to secure the recovery of maintenance for the child from the parents or other persons having financial responsibility for the child, both within the State Party and from abroad. In particular, where the person having financial responsibility for the child lives in a State different from that of the child, States Parties shall promote the accession to international agreements or the conclusion of such agreements, as well as the making of other appropriate arrangements.

Article 28

1. States Parties recognize the right of the child to education, and with a view to achieving this right progressively and on the basis of equal opportunity, they shall, in particular:
   (a) Make primary education compulsory and available free to all;

(b) Encourage the development of different forms of secondary education, including general and vocational education, make them available and accessible to every child, and take appropriate measures such as the introduction of free education and offering financial assistance in case of need;
(c) Make higher education accessible to all on the basis of capacity by every appropriate means;
(d) Make educational and vocational information and guidance available and accessible to all children;
(e) Take measures to encourage regular attendance at schools and the reduction of drop-out rates.

2. States Parties shall take all appropriate measures to ensure that school discipline is administered in a manner consistent with the child's human dignity and in conformity with the present Convention.
3. States Parties shall promote and encourage international cooperation in matters relating to education, in particular with a view to contributing to the elimination of ignorance and illiteracy throughout the world and facilitating access to scientific and technical knowledge and modern teaching methods. In this regard, particular account shall be taken of the needs of developing countries.

Article 29

1. States Parties agree that the education of the child shall be directed to:
   (a) The development of the child's personality, talents and mental and physical abilities to their fullest potential;
   (b) The development of respect for human rights and fundamental freedoms, and for the principles enshrined in the Charter of the United Nations;
   (c) The development of respect for the child's parents, his or her own cultural identity, language and values, for the national values of the country in which the child is living, the country from which he or she may originate, and for civilizations different from his or her own;
   (d) The preparation of the child for responsible life in a free society, in the spirit of understanding, peace, tolerance, equality of sexes, and friendship among all peoples, ethnic, national and religious groups and persons of indigenous origin;
   (e) The development of respect for the natural environment.
2. No part of the present article or article 28 shall be construed so as to interfere with the liberty of individuals and bodies to establish and direct educational institutions, subject always to the observance of the principle set forth in paragraph 1 of the present article and to the requirements that the education given in such institutions shall conform to such minimum standards as may be laid down by the State.

Article 30

In those States in which ethnic, religious or linguistic minorities or persons of indigenous origin exist, a child belonging to such a minority or who is indigenous shall not be denied the right, in community with other members of his or her group, to enjoy his or her own culture, to profess and practise his or her own religion, or to use his or her own language.

Article 31

1. States Parties recognize the right of the child to rest and leisure, to engage in play and recreational activities appropriate to the age of the child and to participate freely in cultural life and the arts.
2. States Parties shall respect and promote the right of the child to participate fully in cultural and artistic life and shall encourage the provision of appropriate and equal opportunities for cultural, artistic, recreational and leisure activity.

Article 32

1. States Parties recognize the right of the child to be protected from economic exploitation and from performing any work that is likely to be hazardous or to interfere with the child's education, or to be harmful to the child's health or physical, mental, spiritual, moral or social development.
2. States Parties shall take legislative, administrative, social and educational measures to ensure the implementation of the present article. To this end, and having regard to the relevant provisions of other international instruments, States Parties shall in particular:
   (a) Provide for a minimum age or minimum ages for admission to employment;
   (b) Provide for appropriate regulation of the hours and conditions of employment;
   (c) Provide for appropriate penalties or other sanctions to ensure the effective enforcement of the present article.

Article 33

States Parties shall take all appropriate measures, including legislative, administrative, social and educational measures, to protect children from the illicit use of narcotic drugs and psychotropic substances as defined in the relevant international treaties, and to prevent the use of children in the illicit production and trafficking of such substances.

Article 34

States Parties undertake to protect the child from all forms of sexual exploitation and sexual abuse. For these purposes, States Parties shall in particular take all appropriate national, bilateral and multilateral measures to prevent:

(a) The inducement or coercion of a child to engage in any unlawful sexual activity;
(b) The exploitative use of children in prostitution or other unlawful sexual practices;
(c) The exploitative use of children in pornographic performances and materials.

Article 35

States Parties shall take all appropriate national, bilateral and multilateral measures to prevent the abduction of, the sale of or traffic in children for any purpose or in any form.

Article 36

States Parties shall protect the child against all other forms of exploitation prejudicial to any aspects of the child's welfare.

Article 37

States Parties shall ensure that:

(a) No child shall be subjected to torture or other cruel, inhuman or degrading treatment or punishment. Neither capital punishment nor life imprisonment without possibility of release shall be imposed for offences committed by persons below 18 years of age;
(b) No child shall be deprived of his or her liberty unlawfully or arbitrarily. The arrest, detention or imprisonment of a child shall be in conformity with the law and shall be used only as a measure of last resort and for the shortest appropriate period of time;
(c) Every child deprived of liberty shall be treated with humanity and respect for the inherent dignity of the human person, and in a manner which takes into account the needs of persons of his or her age. In particular, every child deprived of liberty shall be separated from adults unless it is considered in the child's best interest not to do so and shall have the right to maintain contact with his or her family through correspondence and visits, save in exceptional circumstances;
(d) Every child deprived of his or her liberty shall have the right to prompt access to legal and other appropriate assistance, as well as the right to challenge the legality of the deprivation of his or her liberty before a court or other competent, independent and impartial authority, and to a prompt decision on any such action.

Article 38

1. States Parties undertake to respect and to ensure respect for rules of international humanitarian law applicable to them in armed conflicts which are relevant to the child.
2. States Parties shall take all feasible measures to ensure that persons who have not attained the age of 15 years do not take a direct part in hostilities.
3. States Parties shall refrain from recruiting any person who has not attained the age of 15 years into their armed forces. In recruiting among those persons who have attained the age of 15 years but who have not attained the age of 18 years, States Parties shall endeavour to give priority to those who are oldest.
4. In accordance with their obligations under international humanitarian law to protect the civilian population in armed conflicts, States Parties shall take all feasible measures to ensure protection and care of children who are affected by an armed conflict.

Article 39

States Parties shall take all appropriate measures to promote physical and psychological recovery and social reintegration of a child victim of: any form of neglect, exploitation, or abuse; torture or any other form of cruel, inhuman or degrading treatment or punishment; or armed conflicts. Such recovery and reintegration shall take place in an environment which fosters the health, self-respect and dignity of the child.

Article 40

1. States Parties recognize the right of every child alleged as, accused of, or recognized as having infringed the penal law to be treated in a manner consistent with the promotion of the child's sense of dignity and worth, which reinforces the child's respect for the human rights and fundamental freedoms of others and which takes into account the child's age and the desirability of promoting the child's reintegration and the child's assuming a constructive role in society.
2. To this end, and having regard to the relevant provisions of international instruments, States Parties shall, in particular, ensure that:
   (a) No child shall be alleged as, be accused of, or recognized as having infringed the penal law by reason of acts or omissions that were not prohibited by national or international law at the time they were committed;
   (b) Every child alleged as or accused of having infringed the penal law has at least the following guarantees:
      (i) To be presumed innocent until proven guilty according to law;
      (ii) To be informed promptly and directly of the charges against him or her, and, if appropriate, through his or her parents or legal guardians, and to have legal or other appropriate assistance in the preparation and presentation of his or her defence;
      (iii) To have the matter determined without delay by a competent, independent and impartial authority or judicial body in a fair hearing according to law, in the presence of legal or other appropriate assistance and, unless it is considered not to be in the best interest of the child, in particular, taking into account his or her age or situation, his or her parents or legal guardians;
      (iv) Not to be compelled to give testimony or to confess guilt; to examine or have examined adverse witnesses and to obtain the participation and examination of witnesses on his or her behalf under conditions of equality;
      (v) If considered to have infringed the penal law, to have this decision and any measures imposed in consequence thereof reviewed by a higher competent, independent and impartial authority or judicial body according to law;
      (vi) To have the free assistance of an interpreter if the child cannot understand or speak the language used;
      (vii) To have his or her privacy fully respected at all stages of the proceedings.

3. States Parties shall seek to promote the establishment of laws, procedures, authorities and institutions specifically applicable to children alleged as, accused of, or recognized as having infringed the penal law, and, in particular:
   (a) The establishment of a minimum age below which children shall be presumed not to have the capacity to infringe the penal law;
   (b) Whenever appropriate and desirable, measures for dealing with such children without resorting to judicial proceedings, providing that human rights and legal safeguards are fully respected. 4. A variety of dispositions, such as care, guidance and supervision orders; counselling; probation; foster care; education and vocational training programmes and other alternatives to institutional care shall be available to ensure that children are dealt with in a manner appropriate to their well-being and proportionate both to their circumstances and the offence.

Article 41

Nothing in the present Convention shall affect any provisions which are more conducive to the realization of the rights of the child and which may be contained in:

(a) The law of a State party; or
(b) International law in force for that State.

PART II

Article 42

States Parties undertake to make the principles and provisions of the Convention widely known, by appropriate and active means, to adults and children alike.

Article 43

1. For the purpose of examining the progress made by States Parties in achieving the realization of the obligations undertaken in the present Convention, there shall be established a Committee on the Rights of the Child, which shall carry out the functions hereinafter provided.
2. The Committee shall consist of 18 experts of high moral standing and recognized competence in the field covered by this Convention*. The members of the Committee shall be elected by States Parties from among their nationals and shall serve in their personal capacity, consideration being given to equitable geographical distribution, as well as to the principal legal systems.
3. The members of the Committee shall be elected by secret ballot from a list of persons nominated by States Parties. Each State Party may nominate one person from among its own nationals.
4. The initial election to the Committee shall be held no later than 6 months after the date of the entry into force of the present Convention and thereafter every second year. At least 4 months before the date of each election, the Secretary-General of the United Nations shall address a letter to States Parties inviting

them to submit their nominations within 2 months. The Secretary-General shall subsequently prepare a list in alphabetical order of all persons thus nominated, indicating States Parties which have nominated them, and shall submit it to the States Parties to the present Convention.

5. The elections shall be held at meetings of States Parties convened by the Secretary-General at United Nations Headquarters. At those meetings, for which two thirds of States Parties shall constitute a quorum, the persons elected to the Committee shall be those who obtain the largest number of votes and an absolute majority of the votes of the representatives of States Parties present and voting.
6. The members of the Committee shall be elected for a term of 4 years. They shall be eligible for re-election if renominated. The term of five of the members elected at the first election shall expire at the end of 2 years; immediately after the first election, the names of these five members shall be chosen by lot by the Chairman of the meeting.
7. If a member of the Committee dies or resigns or declares that for any other cause he or she can no longer perform the duties of the Committee, the State Party which nominated the member shall appoint another expert from among its nationals to serve for the remainder of the term, subject to the approval of the Committee.
8. The Committee shall establish its own rules of procedure.
9. The Committee shall elect its officers for a period of 2 years.
10. The meetings of the Committee shall normally be held at United Nations Headquarters or at any other convenient place as determined by the Committee. The Committee shall normally meet annually. The duration of the meetings of the Committee shall be determined, and reviewed, if necessary, by a meeting of the States Parties to the present Convention, subject to the approval of the General Assembly.
11. The Secretary-General of the United Nations shall provide the necessary staff and facilities for the effective performance of the functions of the Committee under the present Convention.
12. With the approval of the General Assembly, the members of the Committee established under the present Convention shall receive emoluments from United Nations resources on such terms and conditions as the Assembly may decide.

Article 44

1. States Parties undertake to submit to the Committee, through the Secretary-General of the United Nations, reports on the measures they have adopted which give effect to the rights recognized herein and on the progress made on the enjoyment of those rights
   (a) Within 2 years of the entry into force of the Convention for the State Party concerned;
   (b) Thereafter every 5 years.
2. Reports made under the present article shall indicate factors and difficulties, if any, affecting the degree of fulfilment of the obligations under the present

Convention. Reports shall also contain sufficient information to provide the Committee with a comprehensive understanding of the implementation of the Convention in the country concerned.

3. A State Party which has submitted a comprehensive initial report to the Committee need not, in its subsequent reports submitted in accordance with paragraph 1 (b) of the present article, repeat basic information previously provided.
4. The Committee may request from States Parties further information relevant to the implementation of the Convention.
5. The Committee shall submit to the General Assembly, through the Economic and Social Council, every 2 years, reports on its activities.
6. States Parties shall make their reports widely available to the public in their own countries.

Article 45

In order to foster the effective implementation of the Convention and to encourage international co-operation in the field covered by the Convention:

(a) The specialized agencies, the United Nations Children's Fund, and other United Nations organs shall be entitled to be represented at the consideration of the implementation of such provisions of the present Convention as fall within the scope of their mandate. The Committee may invite the specialized agencies, the United Nations Children's Fund and other competent bodies as it may consider appropriate to provide expert advice on the implementation of the Convention in areas falling within the scope of their respective mandates. The Committee may invite the specialized agencies, the United Nations Children's Fund, and other United Nations organs to submit reports on the implementation of the Convention in areas falling within the scope of their activities;

(b) The Committee shall transmit, as it may consider appropriate, to the specialized agencies, the United Nations Children's Fund and other competent bodies, any reports from States Parties that contain a request, or indicate a need, for technical advice or assistance, along with the Committee's observations and suggestions, if any, on these requests or indications;

(c) The Committee may recommend to the General Assembly to request the Secretary-General to undertake on its behalf studies on specific issues relating to the rights of the child;

(d) The Committee may make suggestions and general recommendations based on information received pursuant to articles 44 and 45 of the present Convention. Such suggestions and general recommendations shall be transmitted to any State Party concerned and reported to the General Assembly, together with comments, if any, from States Parties.

PART III

Article 46

The present Convention shall be open for signature by all States.

Article 47
The present Convention is subject to ratification. Instruments of ratification shall be deposited with the Secretary-General of the United Nations.

Article 48
The present Convention shall remain open for accession by any State. The instruments of accession shall be deposited with the Secretary-General of the United Nations.

Article 49
1. The present Convention shall enter into force on the thirtieth day following the date of deposit with the Secretary-General of the United Nations of the twentieth instrument of ratification or accession.
2. For each State ratifying or acceding to the Convention after the deposit of the twentieth instrument of ratification or accession, the Convention shall enter into force on the thirtieth day after the deposit by such State of its instrument of ratification or accession.

Article 50
1. Any State Party may propose an amendment and file it with the Secretary-General of the United Nations. The Secretary-General shall thereupon communicate the proposed amendment to States Parties, with a request that they indicate whether they favour a conference of States Parties for the purpose of considering and voting upon the proposals. In the event that, within 4 months from the date of such communication, at least one third of the States Parties favour such a conference, the Secretary-General shall convene the conference under the auspices of the United Nations. Any amendment adopted by a majority of States Parties present and voting at the conference shall be submitted to the General Assembly for approval.
2. An amendment adopted in accordance with paragraph 1 of the present article shall enter into force when it has been approved by the General Assembly of the United Nations and accepted by a two-thirds majority of States Parties.
3. When an amendment enters into force, it shall be binding on those States Parties which have accepted it, other States Parties still being bound by the provisions of the present Convention and any earlier amendments which they have accepted.

Article 51
1. The Secretary-General of the United Nations shall receive and circulate to all States the text of reservations made by States at the time of ratification or accession.
2. A reservation incompatible with the object and purpose of the present Convention shall not be permitted.
3. Reservations may be withdrawn at any time by notification to that effect addressed to the Secretary-General of the United Nations, who shall then inform all States. Such notification shall take effect on the date on which it is received by the Secretary-General.

Article 52

A State Party may denounce the present Convention by written notification to the Secretary-General of the United Nations. Denunciation becomes effective 1 year after the date of receipt of the notification by the Secretary-General.

Article 53

The Secretary-General of the United Nations is designated as the depositary of the present Convention.

Article 54

The original of the present Convention, of which the Arabic, Chinese, English, French, Russian and Spanish texts are equally authentic, shall be deposited with the Secretary-General of the United Nations. In witness thereof the undersigned plenipotentiaries, being duly authorized thereto by their respective Governments, have signed the present Convention.

1/ The General Assembly, in its resolution 50/155 of 21 December 1995, approved the amendment to article 43, paragraph 2, of the Convention on the Rights of the Child, replacing the word "ten" with the word "eighteen". The amendment entered into force on 18 November 2002 when it had been accepted by a two-thirds majority of the States parties (128 out of 191).

Appendix 5

The protocols to the CRC

Appendix 5a: Optional Protocol to the Convention on the Rights of the Child on the involvement of children in armed conflict

Adopted and opened for signature, ratification and accession by General Assembly resolution 54/263 of 25 May 2000

entry into force 12 February 2002

The States Parties to the present Protocol,

Encouraged by the overwhelming support for the Convention on the Rights of the Child, demonstrating the widespread commitment that exists to strive for the promotion and protection of the rights of the child,

Reaffirming that the rights of children require special protection, and calling for continuous improvement of the situation of children without distinction, as well as for their development and education in conditions of peace and security,

Disturbed by the harmful and widespread impact of armed conflict on children and the long-term consequences it has for durable peace, security and development,

Condemning the targeting of children in situations of armed conflict and direct attacks on objects protected under international law, including places that generally have a significant presence of children, such as schools and hospitals,

Noting the adoption of the Rome Statute of the International Criminal Court, in particular, the inclusion therein as a war crime, of conscripting or enlisting children under the age of 15 years or using them to participate actively in hostilities in both international and non-international armed conflicts,

Considering therefore that to strengthen further the implementation of rights recognized in the Convention on the Rights of the Child there is a need to increase the protection of children from involvement in armed conflict,

Noting that article 1 of the Convention on the Rights of the Child specifies that, for the purposes of that Convention, a child means every human being below the age of 18 years unless, under the law applicable to the child, majority is attained earlier,

Convinced that an optional protocol to the Convention that raises the age of possible recruitment of persons into armed forces and their participation in hostilities will contribute effectively to the implementation of the principle that the best interests of the child are to be a primary consideration in all actions concerning children,

Noting that the twenty-sixth International Conference of the Red Cross and Red Crescent in December 1995 recommended, inter alia, that parties to conflict take every feasible step to ensure that children below the age of 18 years do not take part in hostilities,

Welcoming the unanimous adoption, in June 1999, of International Labour Organization Convention No. 182 on the Prohibition and Immediate Action for the Elimination of the Worst Forms of Child Labour, which prohibits, inter alia, forced or compulsory recruitment of children for use in armed conflict,

Condemning with the gravest concern the recruitment, training and use within and across national borders of children in hostilities by armed groups distinct from the armed forces of a State, and recognizing the responsibility of those who recruit, train and use children in this regard,

Recalling the obligation of each party to an armed conflict to abide by the provisions of international humanitarian law,

Stressing that the present Protocol is without prejudice to the purposes and principles contained in the Charter of the United Nations, including Article 51, and relevant norms of humanitarian law,

Bearing in mind that conditions of peace and security based on full respect of the purposes and principles contained in the Charter and observance of applicable human rights instruments are indispensable for the full protection of children, in particular during armed conflicts and foreign occupation,

Recognizing the special needs of those children who are particularly vulnerable to recruitment or use in hostilities contrary to the present Protocol owing to their economic or social status or gender,

Mindful of the necessity of taking into consideration the economic, social and political root causes of the involvement of children in armed conflicts,

Convinced of the need to strengthen international cooperation in the implementation of the present Protocol, as well as the physical and psychosocial rehabilitation and social reintegration of children who are victims of armed conflict,

Encouraging the participation of the community and, in particular, children and child victims in the dissemination of informational and educational programmes concerning the implementation of the Protocol,

Have agreed as follows:

Article 1

States Parties shall take all feasible measures to ensure that members of their armed forces who have not attained the age of 18 years do not take a direct part in hostilities.

Article 2

States Parties shall ensure that persons who have not attained the age of 18 years are not compulsorily recruited into their armed forces.

Article 3

1. States Parties shall raise the minimum age for the voluntary recruitment of persons into their national armed forces from that set out in article 38, paragraph 3, of the Convention on the Rights of the Child, taking account of the principles contained in that article and recognizing that under the Convention persons under the age of 18 years are entitled to special protection.
2. Each State Party shall deposit a binding declaration upon ratification of or accession to the present Protocol that sets forth the minimum age at which it will permit voluntary recruitment into its national armed forces and a description of the safeguards it has adopted to ensure that such recruitment is not forced or coerced.
3. States Parties that permit voluntary recruitment into their national armed forces under the age of 18 years shall maintain safeguards to ensure, as a minimum, that:
   (a) Such recruitment is genuinely voluntary;
   (b) Such recruitment is carried out with the informed consent of the person's parents or legal guardians;
   (c) Such persons are fully informed of the duties involved in such military service;
   (d) Such persons provide reliable proof of age prior to acceptance into national military service.
4. Each State Party may strengthen its declaration at any time by notification to that effect addressed to the Secretary-General of the United Nations, who shall inform all States Parties. Such notification shall take effect on the date on which it is received by the Secretary-General.
5. The requirement to raise the age in paragraph 1 of the present article does not apply to schools operated by or under the control of the armed forces of the States Parties, in keeping with articles 28 and 29 of the Convention on the Rights of the Child.

Article 4

1. Armed groups that are distinct from the armed forces of a State should not, under any circumstances, recruit or use in hostilities persons under the age of 18 years.

2. States Parties shall take all feasible measures to prevent such recruitment and use, including the adoption of legal measures necessary to prohibit and criminalize such practices.
3. The application of the present article shall not affect the legal status of any party to an armed conflict.

Article 5

Nothing in the present Protocol shall be construed as precluding provisions in the law of a State Party or in international instruments and international humanitarian law that are more conducive to the realization of the rights of the child.

Article 6

1. Each State Party shall take all necessary legal, administrative and other measures to ensure the effective implementation and enforcement of the provisions of the present Protocol within its jurisdiction.
2. States Parties undertake to make the principles and provisions of the present Protocol widely known and promoted by appropriate means, to adults and children alike.
3. States Parties shall take all feasible measures to ensure that persons within their jurisdiction recruited or used in hostilities contrary to the present Protocol are demobilized or otherwise released from service. States Parties shall, when necessary, accord to such persons all appropriate assistance for their physical and psychological recovery and their social reintegration.

Article 7

1. States Parties shall cooperate in the implementation of the present Protocol, including in the prevention of any activity contrary thereto and in the rehabilitation and social reintegration of persons who are victims of acts contrary thereto, including through technical cooperation and financial assistance. Such assistance and cooperation will be undertaken in consultation with the States Parties concerned and the relevant international organizations.
2. States Parties in a position to do so shall provide such assistance through existing multilateral, bilateral or other programmes or, inter alia, through a voluntary fund established in accordance with the rules of the General Assembly.

Article 8

1. Each State Party shall, within 2 years following the entry into force of the present Protocol for that State Party, submit a report to the Committee on the Rights of the Child providing comprehensive information on the measures it has taken to implement the provisions of the Protocol, including the measures taken to implement the provisions on participation and recruitment.
2. Following the submission of the comprehensive report, each State Party shall include in the reports it submits to the Committee on the Rights of the Child, in accordance with article 44 of the Convention, any further information with respect to the implementation of the Protocol. Other States Parties to the Protocol shall submit a report every 5 years.

3. The Committee on the Rights of the Child may request from States Parties further information relevant to the implementation of the present Protocol.

Article 9

1. The present Protocol is open for signature by any State that is a party to the Convention or has signed it.
2. The present Protocol is subject to ratification and is open to accession by any State. Instruments of ratification or accession shall be deposited with the Secretary-General of the United Nations.
3. The Secretary-General, in his capacity as depositary of the Convention and the Protocol, shall inform all States Parties to the Convention and all States that have signed the Convention of each instrument of declaration pursuant to article 3.

Article 10

1. The present Protocol shall enter into force 3 months after the deposit of the tenth instrument of ratification or accession.
2. For each State ratifying the present Protocol or acceding to it after its entry into force, the Protocol shall enter into force 1 month after the date of the deposit of its own instrument of ratification or accession.

Article 11

1. Any State Party may denounce the present Protocol at any time by written notification to the Secretary- General of the United Nations, who shall thereafter inform the other States Parties to the Convention and all States that have signed the Convention. The denunciation shall take effect 1 year after the date of receipt of the notification by the Secretary-General. If, however, on the expiry of that year the denouncing State Party is engaged in armed conflict, the denunciation shall not take effect before the end of the armed conflict.
2. Such a denunciation shall not have the effect of releasing the State Party from its obligations under the present Protocol in regard to any act that occurs prior to the date on which the denunciation becomes effective. Nor shall such a denunciation prejudice in any way the continued consideration of any matter that is already under consideration by the Committee on the Rights of the Child prior to the date on which the denunciation becomes effective.

Article 12

1. Any State Party may propose an amendment and file it with the Secretary-General of the United Nations. The Secretary-General shall thereupon communicate the proposed amendment to States Parties with a request that they indicate whether they favour a conference of States Parties for the purpose of considering and voting upon the proposals. In the event that, within 4 months from the date of such communication, at least one third of the States Parties favour such a conference, the Secretary-General shall convene the conference under the auspices of the United Nations. Any amendment adopted by a majority of States Parties present and voting at the conference shall be submitted to the General Assembly of the United Nations for approval.

2. An amendment adopted in accordance with paragraph 1 of the present article shall enter into force when it has been approved by the General Assembly and accepted by a two-thirds majority of States Parties.
3. When an amendment enters into force, it shall be binding on those States Parties that have accepted it, other States Parties still being bound by the provisions of the present Protocol and any earlier amendments they have accepted.

Article 13

1. The present Protocol, of which the Arabic, Chinese, English, French, Russian and Spanish texts are equally authentic, shall be deposited in the archives of the United Nations.
2. The Secretary-General of the United Nations shall transmit certified copies of the present Protocol to all States Parties to the Convention and all States that have signed the Convention.

Appendix 5b: Optional Protocol to the Convention on the Rights of the Child on the sale of children, child prostitution and child pornography

Adopted and opened for signature, ratification and accession by General Assembly resolution 54/263 of 25 May 2000
entry into force 18 January 2002

The States Parties to the present Protocol,

Considering that, in order further to achieve the purposes of the Convention on the Rights of the Child and the implementation of its provisions, especially articles 1, 11, 21, 32, 33, 34, 35 and 36, it would be appropriate to extend the measures that States Parties should undertake in order to guarantee the protection of the child from the sale of children, child prostitution and child pornography,

Considering also that the Convention on the Rights of the Child recognizes the right of the child to be protected from economic exploitation and from performing any work that is likely to be hazardous or to interfere with the child's education, or to be harmful to the child's health or physical, mental, spiritual, moral or social development,

Gravely concerned at the significant and increasing international traffic in children for the purpose of the sale of children, child prostitution and child pornography,

Deeply concerned at the widespread and continuing practice of sex tourism, to which children are especially vulnerable, as it directly promotes the sale of children, child prostitution and child pornography,

Recognizing that a number of particularly vulnerable groups, including girl children, are at greater risk of sexual exploitation and that girl children are disproportionately represented among the sexually exploited,

Concerned about the growing availability of child pornography on the Internet and other evolving technologies, and recalling the International Conference on Combating Child Pornography on the Internet, held in Vienna in 1999, in particular its conclusion calling for the worldwide criminalization of the production, distribution, exportation, transmission, importation, intentional possession and advertising of child pornography, and stressing the importance of closer cooperation and partnership between Governments and the Internet industry,

Believing that the elimination of the sale of children, child prostitution and child pornography will be facilitated by adopting a holistic approach, addressing the contributing factors, including underdevelopment, poverty, economic disparities, inequitable socio-economic structure, dysfunctioning families, lack of education, urban–rural migration, gender discrimination, irresponsible adult sexual behaviour, harmful traditional practices, armed conflicts and trafficking in children,

Believing also that efforts to raise public awareness are needed to reduce consumer demand for the sale of children, child prostitution and child pornography, and believing further in the importance of strengthening global partnership among all actors and of improving law enforcement at the national level,

Noting the provisions of international legal instruments relevant to the protection of children, including the Hague Convention on Protection of Children and Cooperation in Respect of Intercountry Adoption, the Hague Convention on the Civil Aspects of International Child Abduction, the Hague Convention on Jurisdiction, Applicable Law, Recognition, Enforcement and Cooperation in Respect of Parental Responsibility and Measures for the Protection of Children, and International Labour Organization Convention No. 182 on the Prohibition and Immediate Action for the Elimination of the Worst Forms of Child Labour,

Encouraged by the overwhelming support for the Convention on the Rights of the Child, demonstrating the widespread commitment that exists for the promotion and protection of the rights of the child,

Recognizing the importance of the implementation of the provisions of the Programme of Action for the Prevention of the Sale of Children, Child Prostitution and Child Pornography and the Declaration and Agenda for Action adopted at the World Congress against Commercial Sexual Exploitation of Children, held in Stockholm from 27 to 31 August 1996, and the other relevant decisions and recommendations of pertinent international bodies,

Taking due account of the importance of the traditions and cultural values of each people for the protection and harmonious development of the child,

Have agreed as follows:

Article 1

States Parties shall prohibit the sale of children, child prostitution and child pornography as provided for by the present Protocol.

Article 2

For the purposes of the present Protocol:

(a) Sale of children means any act or transaction whereby a child is transferred by any person or group of persons to another for remuneration or any other consideration;

(b) Child prostitution means the use of a child in sexual activities for remuneration or any other form of consideration;
(c) Child pornography means any representation, by whatever means, of a child engaged in real or simulated explicit sexual activities or any representation of the sexual parts of a child for primarily sexual purposes.

Article 3

1. Each State Party shall ensure that, as a minimum, the following acts and activities are fully covered under its criminal or penal law, whether such offences are committed domestically or transnationally or on an individual or organized basis:
   (a) In the context of sale of children as defined in article 2:
      (i) Offering, delivering or accepting, by whatever means, a child for the purpose of:
         1. Sexual exploitation of the child;
         2. Transfer of organs of the child for profit;
         3. Engagement of the child in forced labour;
      (ii) Improperly inducing consent, as an intermediary, for the adoption of a child in violation of applicable international legal instruments on adoption;
   (b) Offering, obtaining, procuring or providing a child for child prostitution, as defined in article 2;
   (c) Producing, distributing, disseminating, importing, exporting, offering, selling or possessing for the above purposes child pornography as defined in article 2.
2. Subject to the provisions of the national law of a State Party, the same shall apply to an attempt to commit any of the said acts and to complicity or participation in any of the said acts.
3. Each State Party shall make such offences punishable by appropriate penalties that take into account their grave nature.
4. Subject to the provisions of its national law, each State Party shall take measures, where appropriate, to establish the liability of legal persons for offences established in paragraph 1 of the present article. Subject to the legal principles of the State Party, such liability of legal persons may be criminal, civil or administrative.
5. States Parties shall take all appropriate legal and administrative measures to ensure that all persons involved in the adoption of a child act in conformity with applicable international legal instruments.

Article 4

1. Each State Party shall take such measures as may be necessary to establish its jurisdiction over the offences referred to in article 3, paragraph 1, when the offences are committed in its territory or on board a ship or aircraft registered in that State.
2. Each State Party may take such measures as may be necessary to establish its jurisdiction over the offences referred to in article 3, paragraph 1, in the following cases:

(a) When the alleged offender is a national of that State or a person who has his habitual residence in its territory;
(b) When the victim is a national of that State.

3. Each State Party shall also take such measures as may be necessary to establish its jurisdiction over the aforementioned offences when the alleged offender is present in its territory and it does not extradite him or her to another State Party on the ground that the offence has been committed by one of its nationals.
4. The present Protocol does not exclude any criminal jurisdiction exercised in accordance with internal law.

Article 5

1. The offences referred to in article 3, paragraph 1, shall be deemed to be included as extraditable offences in any extradition treaty existing between States Parties and shall be included as extraditable offences in every extradition treaty subsequently concluded between them, in accordance with the conditions set forth in such treaties.
2. If a State Party that makes extradition conditional on the existence of a treaty receives a request for extradition from another State Party with which it has no extradition treaty, it may consider the present Protocol to be a legal basis for extradition in respect of such offences. Extradition shall be subject to the conditions provided by the law of the requested State.
3. States Parties that do not make extradition conditional on the existence of a treaty shall recognize such offences as extraditable offences between themselves subject to the conditions provided by the law of the requested State.
4. Such offences shall be treated, for the purpose of extradition between States Parties, as if they had been committed not only in the place in which they occurred but also in the territories of the States required to establish their jurisdiction in accordance with article 4.
5. If an extradition request is made with respect to an offence described in article 3, paragraph 1, and the requested State Party does not or will not extradite on the basis of the nationality of the offender, that State shall take suitable measures to submit the case to its competent authorities for the purpose of prosecution.

Article 6

1. States Parties shall afford one another the greatest measure of assistance in connection with investigations or criminal or extradition proceedings brought in respect of the offences set forth in article 3, paragraph 1, including assistance in obtaining evidence at their disposal necessary for the proceedings.
2. States Parties shall carry out their obligations under paragraph 1 of the present article in conformity with any treaties or other arrangements on mutual legal assistance that may exist between them. In the absence of such treaties or arrangements, States Parties shall afford one another assistance in accordance with their domestic law.

Article 7

States Parties shall, subject to the provisions of their national law:

(a) Take measures to provide for the seizure and confiscation, as appropriate, of:
   i. Goods, such as materials, assets and other instrumentalities used to commit or facilitate offences under the present protocol;
   ii. Proceeds derived from such offences;
(b) Execute requests from another State Party for seizure or confiscation of goods or proceeds referred to in subparagraph (a) (i) and (ii);
(c) Take measures aimed at closing, on a temporary or definitive basis, premises used to commit such offences.

Article 8

1. States Parties shall adopt appropriate measures to protect the rights and interests of child victims of the practices prohibited under the present Protocol at all stages of the criminal justice process, in particular by:
   (a) Recognizing the vulnerability of child victims and adapting procedures to recognize their special needs, including their special needs as witnesses;
   (b) Informing child victims of their rights, their role and the scope, timing and progress of the proceedings and of the disposition of their cases;
   (c) Allowing the views, needs and concerns of child victims to be presented and considered in proceedings where their personal interests are affected, in a manner consistent with the procedural rules of national law;
   (d) Providing appropriate support services to child victims throughout the legal process;
   (e) Protecting, as appropriate, the privacy and identity of child victims and taking measures in accordance with national law to avoid the inappropriate dissemination of information that could lead to the identification of child victims;
   (f) Providing, in appropriate cases, for the safety of child victims, as well as that of their families and witnesses on their behalf, from intimidation and retaliation;
   (g) Avoiding unnecessary delay in the disposition of cases and the execution of orders or decrees granting compensation to child victims.
2. States Parties shall ensure that uncertainty as to the actual age of the victim shall not prevent the initiation of criminal investigations, including investigations aimed at establishing the age of the victim.
3. States Parties shall ensure that, in the treatment by the criminal justice system of children who are victims of the offences described in the present Protocol, the best interest of the child shall be a primary consideration.
4. States Parties shall take measures to ensure appropriate training, in particular legal and psychological training, for the persons who work with victims of the offences prohibited under the present Protocol.
5. States Parties shall, in appropriate cases, adopt measures in order to protect the safety and integrity of those persons and/or organizations involved in the prevention and/or protection and rehabilitation of victims of such offences.
6. Nothing in the present article shall be construed to be prejudicial to or inconsistent with the rights of the accused to a fair and impartial trial.

Article 9

1. States Parties shall adopt or strengthen, implement and disseminate laws, administrative measures, social policies and programmes to prevent the offences referred to in the present Protocol. Particular attention shall be given to protect children who are especially vulnerable to such practices.
2. States Parties shall promote awareness in the public at large, including children, through information by all appropriate means, education and training, about the preventive measures and harmful effects of the offences referred to in the present Protocol. In fulfilling their obligations under this article, States Parties shall encourage the participation of the community and, in particular, children and child victims, in such information and education and training programmes, including at the international level.
3. States Parties shall take all feasible measures with the aim of ensuring all appropriate assistance to victims of such offences, including their full social reintegration and their full physical and psychological recovery.
4. States Parties shall ensure that all child victims of the offences described in the present Protocol have access to adequate procedures to seek, without discrimination, compensation for damages from those legally responsible.
5. States Parties shall take appropriate measures aimed at effectively prohibiting the production and dissemination of material advertising the offences described in the present Protocol.

Article 10

1. States Parties shall take all necessary steps to strengthen international cooperation by multilateral, regional and bilateral arrangements for the prevention, detection, investigation, prosecution and punishment of those responsible for acts involving the sale of children, child prostitution, child pornography and child sex tourism. States Parties shall also promote international cooperation and coordination between their authorities, national and international non-governmental organizations and international organizations.
2. States Parties shall promote international cooperation to assist child victims in their physical and psychological recovery, social reintegration and repatriation.
3. States Parties shall promote the strengthening of international cooperation in order to address the root causes, such as poverty and underdevelopment, contributing to the vulnerability of children to the sale of children, child prostitution, child pornography and child sex tourism.
4. States Parties in a position to do so shall provide financial, technical or other assistance through existing multilateral, regional, bilateral or other programmes.

Article 11

Nothing in the present Protocol shall affect any provisions that are more conducive to the realization of the rights of the child and that may be contained in:

(a) The law of a State Party;
(b) International law in force for that State.

Article 12

1. Each State Party shall, within 2 years following the entry into force of the present Protocol for that State Party, submit a report to the Committee on the Rights of the Child providing comprehensive information on the measures it has taken to implement the provisions of the Protocol.
2. Following the submission of the comprehensive report, each State Party shall include in the reports they submit to the Committee on the Rights of the Child, in accordance with article 44 of the Convention, any further information with respect to the implementation of the present Protocol. Other States Parties to the Protocol shall submit a report every 5 years.
3. The Committee on the Rights of the Child may request from States Parties further information relevant to the implementation of the present Protocol.

Article 13

1. The present Protocol is open for signature by any State that is a party to the Convention or has signed it.
2. The present Protocol is subject to ratification and is open to accession by any State that is a party to the Convention or has signed it. Instruments of ratification or accession shall be deposited with the Secretary- General of the United Nations.

Article 14

1. The present Protocol shall enter into force 3 months after the deposit of the tenth instrument of ratification or accession.
2. For each State ratifying the present Protocol or acceding to it after its entry into force, the Protocol shall enter into force 1 month after the date of the deposit of its own instrument of ratification or accession.

Article 15

1. Any State Party may denounce the present Protocol at any time by written notification to the Secretary- General of the United Nations, who shall thereafter inform the other States Parties to the Convention and all States that have signed the Convention. The denunciation shall take effect 1 year after the date of receipt of the notification by the Secretary-General.
2. Such a denunciation shall not have the effect of releasing the State Party from its obligations under the present Protocol in regard to any offence that occurs prior to the date on which the denunciation becomes effective. Nor shall such a denunciation prejudice in any way the continued consideration of any matter that is already under consideration by the Committee on the Rights of the Child prior to the date on which the denunciation becomes effective.

Article 16

1. Any State Party may propose an amendment and file it with the Secretary-General of the United Nations. The Secretary-General shall thereupon communicate the proposed amendment to States Parties with a request that they indicate whether they favour a conference of States Parties for the purpose of

considering and voting upon the proposals. In the event that, within 4 months from the date of such communication, at least one third of the States Parties favour such a conference, the Secretary-General shall convene the conference under the auspices of the United Nations. Any amendment adopted by a majority of States Parties present and voting at the conference shall be submitted to the General Assembly of the United Nations for approval.

2. An amendment adopted in accordance with paragraph 1 of the present article shall enter into force when it has been approved by the General Assembly and accepted by a two-thirds majority of States Parties.
3. When an amendment enters into force, it shall be binding on those States Parties that have accepted it, other States Parties still being bound by the provisions of the present Protocol and any earlier amendments they have accepted.

Article 17

1. The present Protocol, of which the Arabic, Chinese, English, French, Russian and Spanish texts are equally authentic, shall be deposited in the archives of the United Nations.
2. The Secretary-General of the United Nations shall transmit certified copies of the present Protocol to all States Parties to the Convention and all States that have signed the Convention.

Appendix 5c: Optional Protocol to the Convention on the Rights of the Child on a Communications Procedure

Adopted and opened for signature and ratification by General Assembly resolution 66/138 of 19 December 2011
Entry into Force: 14 April 2014

The States parties to the present Protocol,

Considering that, in accordance with the principles proclaimed in the Charter of the United Nations, the recognition of the inherent dignity and the equal and inalienable rights of all members of the human family is the foundation of freedom, justice and peace in the world,

Noting that the States parties to the Convention on the Rights of the Child (hereinafter referred to as "the Convention") recognize the rights set forth in it to each child within their jurisdiction without discrimination of any kind, irrespective of the child's or his or her parent's or legal guardian's race, colour, sex, language, religion, political or other opinion, national, ethnic or social origin, property, disability, birth or other status,

Reaffirming the universality, indivisibility, interdependence and interrelatedness of all human rights and fundamental freedoms,

Reaffirming also the status of the child as a subject of rights and as a human being with dignity and with evolving capacities,

Recognizing that children's special and dependent status may create real difficulties for them in pursuing remedies for violations of their rights,

Considering that the present Protocol will reinforce and complement national and regional mechanisms allowing children to submit complaints for violations of their rights,

Recognizing that the best interests of the child should be a primary consideration to be respected in pursuing remedies for violations of the rights of the child, and that such remedies should take into account the need for child-sensitive procedures at all levels,

Encouraging States parties to develop appropriate national mechanisms to enable a child whose rights have been violated to have access to effective remedies at the domestic level,

Recalling the important role that national human rights institutions and other relevant specialized institutions, mandated to promote and protect the rights of the child, can play in this regard,

Considering that, in order to reinforce and complement such national mechanisms and to further enhance the implementation of the Convention and, where applicable, the Optional Protocols thereto on the sale of children, child prostitution and child pornography and on the involvement of children in armed conflict, it would be appropriate to enable the Committee on the Rights of the Child (hereinafter referred to as "the Committee") to carry out the functions provided for in the present Protocol,

Have agreed as follows:

Part I
General provisions

Article 1
Competence of the Committee on the Rights of the Child

1. A State party to the present Protocol recognizes the competence of the Committee as provided for by the present Protocol.
2. The Committee shall not exercise its competence regarding a State party to the present Protocol on matters concerning violations of rights set forth in an instrument to which that State is not a party.
3. No communication shall be received by the Committee if it concerns a State that is not a party to the present Protocol.

Article 2
General principles guiding the functions of the Committee

In fulfilling the functions conferred on it by the present Protocol, the Committee shall be guided by the principle of the best interests of the child. It shall also have regard for the rights and views of the child, the views of the child being given due weight in accordance with the age and maturity of the child.

Article 3
Rules of procedure

1. The Committee shall adopt rules of procedure to be followed when exercising the functions conferred on it by the present Protocol. In doing so, it shall have regard, in particular, for article 2 of the present Protocol in order to guarantee child-sensitive procedures.
2. The Committee shall include in its rules of procedure safeguards to prevent the manipulation of the child by those acting on his or her behalf and may decline to examine any communication that it considers not to be in the child's best interests.

Article 4
Protection measures

1. A State party shall take all appropriate steps to ensure that individuals under its jurisdiction are not subjected to any human rights violation, ill-treatment or intimidation as a consequence of communications or cooperation with the Committee pursuant to the present Protocol.
2. The identity of any individual or group of individuals concerned shall not be revealed publicly without their express consent.

Part II
Communications procedure

Article 5
Individual communications

1. Communications may be submitted by or on behalf of an individual or group of individuals, within the jurisdiction of a State party, claiming to be victims of a violation by that State party of any of the rights set forth in any of the following instruments to which that State is a party:
   (a) The Convention;
   (b) The Optional Protocol to the Convention on the sale of children, child prostitution and child pornography;
   (c) The Optional Protocol to the Convention on the involvement of children in armed conflict.
2. Where a communication is submitted on behalf of an individual or group of individuals, this shall be with their consent unless the author can justify acting on their behalf without such consent.

Article 6
Interim measures

1. At any time after the receipt of a communication and before a determination on the merits has been reached, the Committee may transmit to the State party concerned for its urgent consideration a request that the State party take such interim measures as may be necessary in exceptional circumstances to avoid possible irreparable damage to the victim or victims of the alleged violations.
2. Where the Committee exercises its discretion under paragraph 1 of the present article, this does not imply a determination on admissibility or on the merits of the communication.

Article 7
Admissibility
The Committee shall consider a communication inadmissible when:

(a) The communication is anonymous;
(b) The communication is not in writing;
(c) The communication constitutes an abuse of the right of submission of such communications or is incompatible with the provisions of the Convention and/or the Optional Protocols thereto;
(d) The same matter has already been examined by the Committee or has been or is being examined under another procedure of international investigation or settlement;
(e) All available domestic remedies have not been exhausted. This shall not be the rule where the application of the remedies is unreasonably prolonged or unlikely to bring effective relief;
(f) The communication is manifestly ill-founded or not sufficiently substantiated;
(g) The facts that are the subject of the communication occurred prior to the entry into force of the present Protocol for the State party concerned, unless those facts continued after that date;
(h) The communication is not submitted within 1 year after the exhaustion of domestic remedies, except in cases where the author can demonstrate that it had not been possible to submit the communication within that time limit.

Article 8
Transmission of the communication

1. Unless the Committee considers a communication inadmissible without reference to the State party concerned, the Committee shall bring any communication submitted to it under the present Protocol confidentially to the attention of the State party concerned as soon as possible.
2. The State party shall submit to the Committee written explanations or statements clarifying the matter and the remedy, if any, that it may have provided. The State party shall submit its response as soon as possible and within 6 months.

Article 9
Friendly settlement

1. The Committee shall make available its good offices to the parties concerned with a view to reaching a friendly settlement of the matter on the basis of respect for the obligations set forth in the Convention and/or the Optional Protocols thereto.
2. An agreement on a friendly settlement reached under the auspices of the Committee closes consideration of the communication under the present Protocol.

Article 10
Consideration of communications

1. The Committee shall consider communications received under the present Protocol as quickly as possible, in the light of all documentation submitted to it, provided that this documentation is transmitted to the parties concerned.
2. The Committee shall hold closed meetings when examining communications received under the present Protocol.
3. Where the Committee has requested interim measures, it shall expedite the consideration of the communication.
4. When examining communications alleging violations of economic, social or cultural rights, the Committee shall consider the reasonableness of the steps taken by the State party in accordance with article 4 of the Convention. In doing so, the Committee shall bear in mind that the State party may adopt a range of possible policy measures for the implementation of the economic, social and cultural rights in the Convention.
5. After examining a communication, the Committee shall, without delay, transmit its views on the communication, together with its recommendations, if any, to the parties concerned.

Article 11
Follow-up

1. The State party shall give due consideration to the views of the Committee, together with its recommendations, if any, and shall submit to the Committee a written response, including information on any action taken and envisaged in the light of the views and recommendations of the Committee. The State party shall submit its response as soon as possible and within 6 months.
2. The Committee may invite the State party to submit further information about any measures the State party has taken in response to its views or recommendations or implementation of a friendly settlement agreement, if any, including as deemed appropriate by the Committee, in the State party's subsequent reports under article 44 of the Convention, article 12 of the Optional Protocol on the sale of children, child prostitution and child pornography or article 8 of the Optional Protocol on the involvement of children in armed conflict, where applicable.

Article 12
Inter-State communications

1. A State party to the present Protocol may, at any time, declare that it recognizes the competence of the Committee to receive and consider communications in which a State party claims that another State party is not fulfilling its obligations under any of the following instruments to which the State is a party:
   (a) The Convention;
   (b) The Optional Protocol to the Convention on the sale of children, child prostitution and child pornography;
   (c) The Optional Protocol to the Convention on the involvement of children in armed conflict.
2. The Committee shall not receive communications concerning a State party that has not made such a declaration or communications from a State party that has not made such a declaration.
3. The Committee shall make available its good offices to the States parties concerned with a view to a friendly solution of the matter on the basis of the respect for the obligations set forth in the Convention and the Optional Protocols thereto.
4. A declaration under paragraph 1 of the present article shall be deposited by the States parties with the Secretary-General of the United Nations, who shall transmit copies thereof to the other States parties. A declaration may be withdrawn at any time by notification to the Secretary-General. Such a withdrawal shall not prejudice the consideration of any matter that is the subject of a communication already transmitted under the present article; no further communications by any State party shall be received under the present article after the notification of withdrawal of the declaration has been received by the Secretary-General, unless the State party concerned has made a new declaration.

Part III
Inquiry procedure

Article 13
Inquiry procedure for grave or systematic violations

1. If the Committee receives reliable information indicating grave or systematic violations by a State party of rights set forth in the Convention or in the Optional Protocols thereto on the sale of children, child prostitution and child pornography or on the involvement of children in armed conflict, the Committee shall invite the State party to cooperate in the examination of the information and, to this end, to submit observations without delay with regard to the information concerned.
2. Taking into account any observations that may have been submitted by the State party concerned, as well as any other reliable information available to it, the Committee may designate one or more of its members to conduct an inquiry and to report urgently to the Committee. Where warranted and with the consent of the State party, the inquiry may include a visit to its territory.

3. Such an inquiry shall be conducted confidentially, and the cooperation of the State party shall be sought at all stages of the proceedings.
4. After examining the findings of such an inquiry, the Committee shall transmit without delay these findings to the State party concerned, together with any comments and recommendations.
5. The State party concerned shall, as soon as possible and within 6 months of receiving the findings, comments and recommendations transmitted by the Committee, submit its observations to the Committee.
6. After such proceedings have been completed with regard to an inquiry made in accordance with paragraph 2 of the present article, the Committee may, after consultation with the State party concerned, decide to include a summary account of the results of the proceedings in its report provided for in article 16 of the present Protocol.
7. Each State party may, at the time of signature or ratification of the present Protocol or accession thereto, declare that it does not recognize the competence of the Committee provided for in the present article in respect of the rights set forth in some or all of the instruments listed in paragraph 1.
8. Any State party having made a declaration in accordance with paragraph 7 of the present article may, at any time, withdraw this declaration by notification to the Secretary-General of the United Nations.

Article 14
Follow-up to the inquiry procedure

1. The Committee may, if necessary, after the end of the period of 6 months referred to in article 13 (5), invite the State party concerned to inform it of the measures taken and envisaged in response to an inquiry conducted under article 13 of the present Protocol.
2. The Committee may invite the State party to submit further information about any measures that the State party has taken in response to an inquiry conducted under article 13, including as deemed appropriate by the Committee, in the State party's subsequent reports under article 44 of the Convention, article 12 of the Optional Protocol to the Convention on the sale of children, child prostitution and child pornography or article 8 of the Optional Protocol to the Convention on the involvement of children in armed conflict, where applicable.

Part IV
Final provisions

Article 15
International assistance and cooperation

1. The Committee may transmit, with the consent of the State party concerned, to United Nations specialized agencies, funds and programmes and other competent bodies its views or recommendations concerning communications and inquiries

that indicate a need for technical advice or assistance, together with the State party's observations and suggestions, if any, on these views or recommendations.

2. The Committee may also bring to the attention of such bodies, with the consent of the State party concerned, any matter arising out of communications considered under the present Protocol that may assist them in deciding, each within its field of competence, on the advisability of international measures likely to contribute to assisting States parties in achieving progress in the implementation of the rights recognized in the Convention and/or the Optional Protocols thereto.

Article 16
Report to the General Assembly

The Committee shall include in its report submitted every 2 years to the General Assembly in accordance with article 44 (5) of the Convention a summary of its activities under the present Protocol.

Article 17
Dissemination of and information on the Optional Protocol

Each State party undertakes to make widely known and to disseminate the present Protocol and to facilitate access to information about the views and recommendations of the Committee, in particular with regard to matters involving the State party, by appropriate and active means and in accessible formats to adults and children alike, including those with disabilities.

Article 18
Signature, ratification and accession

1. The present Protocol is open for signature to any State that has signed, ratified or acceded to the Convention or either of the first two Optional Protocols thereto.
2. The present Protocol is subject to ratification by any State that has ratified or acceded to the Convention or either of the first two Optional Protocols thereto. Instruments of ratification shall be deposited with the Secretary-General of the United Nations.
3. The present Protocol shall be open to accession by any State that has ratified or acceded to the Convention or either of the first two Optional Protocols thereto.
4. Accession shall be effected by the deposit of an instrument of accession with the Secretary-General.

Article 19
Entry into force

1. The present Protocol shall enter into force 3 months after the deposit of the tenth instrument of ratification or accession.
2. For each State ratifying the present Protocol or acceding to it after the deposit of the tenth instrument of ratification or instrument of accession, the present Protocol shall enter into force 3 months after the date of the deposit of its own instrument of ratification or accession.

Article 20
Violations occurring after the entry into force

1. The Committee shall have competence solely in respect of violations by the State party of any of the rights set forth in the Convention and/or the first two Optional Protocols thereto occurring after the entry into force of the present Protocol.
2. If a State becomes a party to the present Protocol after its entry into force, the obligations of that State vis-à-vis the Committee shall relate only to violations of the rights set forth in the Convention and/or the first two Optional Protocols thereto occurring after the entry into force of the present Protocol for the State concerned.

Article 21
Amendments

1. Any State party may propose an amendment to the present Protocol and submit it to the Secretary-General of the United Nations. The Secretary-General shall communicate any proposed amendments to States parties with a request to be notified whether they favour a meeting of States parties for the purpose of considering and deciding upon the proposals. In the event that, within 4 months of the date of such communication, at least one third of the States parties favour such a meeting, the Secretary-General shall convene the meeting under the auspices of the United Nations. Any amendment adopted by a majority of two thirds of the States parties present and voting shall be submitted by the Secretary-General to the General Assembly for approval and, thereafter, to all States parties for acceptance.
2. An amendment adopted and approved in accordance with paragraph 1 of the present article shall enter into force on the thirtieth day after the number of instruments of acceptance deposited reaches two thirds of the number of States parties at the date of adoption of the amendment. Thereafter, the amendment shall enter into force for any State party on the thirtieth day following the deposit of its own instrument of acceptance. An amendment shall be binding only on those States parties that have accepted it.

Article 22
Denunciation

1. Any State party may denounce the present Protocol at any time by written notification to the Secretary-General of the United Nations. The denunciation shall take effect 1 year after the date of receipt of the notification by the Secretary-General.
2. Denunciation shall be without prejudice to the continued application of the provisions of the present Protocol to any communication submitted under articles 5 or 12 or any inquiry initiated under article 13 before the effective date of denunciation.

Article 23
Depositary and notification by the Secretary-General

1. The Secretary-General of the United Nations shall be the depositary of the present Protocol.
2. The Secretary-General shall inform all States of:
   (a) Signatures, ratifications and accessions under the present Protocol;
   (b) The date of entry into force of the present Protocol and of any amendment thereto under article 21;
   (c) Any denunciation under article 22.

Article 24
Languages

1. The present Protocol, of which the Arabic, Chinese, English, French, Russian and Spanish texts are equally authentic, shall be deposited in the archives of the United Nations.
2. The Secretary-General of the United Nations shall transmit certified copies of the present Protocol to all States.

Appendix 6

African Charter on the Rights and Welfare of the Child

OAU Doc. CAB/LEG/24.9/49 (1990), *entered into force* Nov. 29, 1999.

PREAMBLE

The African Member States of the Organization of African Unity, Parties to the present Charter entitled ‘African Charter on the Rights and Welfare of the Child’,

CONSIDERING that the Charter of the Organization of African Unity recognizes the paramountcy of Human Rights and the African Charter on Human and People’s Rights proclaimed and agreed that everyone is entitled to all the rights and freedoms recognized and guaranteed therein, without distinction of any kind such as race, ethnic group, colour, sex, language, religion, political or any other opinion, national and social origin, fortune, birth or other status,

RECALLING the Declaration on the Rights and Welfare of the African Child (AHG/ST.4 Rev.l) adopted by the Assembly of Heads of State and Government of the Organization of African Unity, at its Sixteenth Ordinary Session in Monrovia, Liberia. from 17 to 20 July 1979, recognized the need to take appropriate measures to promote and protect the rights and welfare of the African Child,

NOTING WITH CONCERN that the situation of most African children, remains critical due to the unique factors of their socio-economic, cultural, traditional and developmental circumstances, natural disasters, armed conflicts, exploitation and hunger, and on account of the child’s physical and mental immaturity he/she needs special safeguards and care,

RECOGNIZING that the child occupies a unique and privileged position in the African society and that for the full and harmonious development of his personality. the child should grow up in a family environment in an atmosphere of happiness, love and understanding,

RECOGNIZING that the child, due to the needs of his physical and mental development requires particular care with regard to health, physical, mental, moral and social development, and requires legal protection in conditions of freedom, dignity and security,

TAKING INTO CONSIDERATION the virtues of their cultural heritage, historical background and the values of the African civilization which should inspire and characterize their reflection on the concept of the rights and welfare of the child,

CONSIDERING that the promotion and protection of the rights and welfare of the child also implies the performance of duties on the part of everyone,

REAFFIRMING ADHERENCE to the principles of the rights and welfare of the child contained in the declaration, conventions and other instruments of the Organization of African Unity and in the United Nations and in particular the United Nations Convention on the Rights of the Child; and the OAU Heads of State and Government's Declaration on the Rights and Welfare of the African Child.

HAVE AGREED AS FOLLOWS:

PART 1: RIGHTS AND DUTIES

Chapter One: Rights and Welfare of the Child

Article 1: Obligation of States Parties

1. Member States of the Organization of African Unity Parties to the present Charter shall recognize the rights, freedoms and duties enshrined in this Charter and shall undertake to the necessary steps, in accordance with their Constitutional processes and with the provisions of the present Charter, to adopt such legislative or other measures as may be necessary to give effect to the provisions of this Charter.
2. Nothing in this Charter shall affect any provisions that are more conductive to the realization of the rights and welfare of the child contained in the law of a State Party or in any other international Convention or agreement in force in that State.
3. Any custom, tradition, cultural or religious practice that is inconsistent with the rights, duties and obligations contained in the present Charter shall to the extent of such inconsistency be discouraged.

Article 2: Definition of a Child

For tile purposes of this Charter, a child means every human being below the age of 18 years.

Article 3: Non-Discrimination

Every child shall be entitled to the enjoyment of the rights and freedoms recognized and guaranteed in this Charter irrespective of the child's or his/her parents' or legal guardians' race, ethnic group, colour, sex, language, religion, political or other opinion, national and social origin, fortune, birth or other status.

Article 4: Best Interests of the Child

1. In all actions concerning the child undertaken by any person or authority the best interests of the child shall be the primary consideration.
2. In all judicial or administrative proceedings affecting a child who is capable of communicating his/her own views, and opportunity shall be provided for the views of the child to be heard either directly or through an impartial representative as a party to the proceedings, and those views shall be taken into consideration by the relevant authority in accordance with the provisions of appropriate law.

Article 5: Survival and Development

1. Every child has an inherent right to life. This right shall be protected by law.
2. States Parties to the present Charter shall ensure, to the maximum extent possible, the survival, protection and development of the child.
3. Death sentence shall not be pronounced for crimes committed by children.

Article 6: Name and Nationality

1. Every child shall have the right from his birth no a name.
2. Every child shall be registered immediately after birth.
3. Every child has the right to acquire a nationality.
4. States Parties to the present Charter shall undertake to ensure that their Constitutional legislation recognize the principles according to which a child shall acquire the nationality of the State in the territory of which he has been born if, at the time of the child's birth, he is not granted nationality by any other State in accordance with its laws.

Article 7: Freedom of Expression

Every child who is capable of communicating his or her own views shall be assured the rights to express his opinions freely in all matters and to disseminate his opinions subject to such restrictions as are prescribed by laws.

Article 8: Freedom of Association

Every child shall have the right to free association and freedom of peaceful assembly in conformity with the law.

Article 9: Freedom of Thought, Conscience and Religion

1. Every child shall have the right to freedom of thought conscience and religion.
2. Parents and, where applicable, legal guardians shall have a duty to provide guidance and direction in the exercise of these rights having regard to the evolving capacities, and best interests of the child.
3. States Parties shall respect the duty of parents and where applicable, legal guardians to provide guidance and direction in the enjoyment of these rights subject to the national laws and policies.

Article 10: Protection of Privacy

No child shall be subject to arbitrary or unlawful interference with his privacy, family home or correspondence, or to the attacks upon his honour or reputation, provided that parents or legal guardians shall have the right to exercise reasonable supervision over the conduct of their children. The child has the right to the protection of the law against such interference or attacks.

Article 11: Education

1. Every child shall have the right to an education.
2. The education of the child shall be directed to:
   (a) the promotion and development of the child's personality, talents and mental and physical abilities to their fullest potential;
   (b) fostering respect for human rights and fundamental freedoms with particular reference to those set out in the provisions of various African instruments on human and peoples' rights and international human rights declarations and conventions;
   (c) the preservation and strengthening of positive African morals, traditional values and cultures;
   (d) the preparation of the child for responsible life in a free society, in the spirit of understanding tolerance, dialogue, mutual respect and friendship among all peoples ethnic, tribal and religious groups;
   (e) the preservation of national independence and territorial integrity;
   (f) the promotion and achievements of African Unity and Solidarity;
   (g) the development of respect for the environment and natural resources;
   (h) the promotion of the child's understanding of primary health care.
3. States Parties to the present Charter shall take all appropriate measures with a view to achieving the full realization of this right and shall in particular:
   (a) provide free and compulsory basic education;
   (b) encourage the development of secondary education in its different forms and to progressively make it free and accessible to all;
   (c) make the higher education accessible to all on the basis of capacity and ability by every appropriate means;

(d) take measures to encourage regular attendance at schools and the reduction of drop-out rates;
(e) take special measures in respect of female, gifted and disadvantaged children, to ensure equal access to education for all sections of the community.

4. States Parties to the present Charter shall respect the rights and duties of parents, and where applicable, of legal guardians to choose for their children's schools, other than those established by public authorities, which conform to such minimum standards may be approved by the State, to ensure the religious and moral education of the child in a manner with the evolving capacities of the child.
5. States Parties to the present Charter shall take all appropriate measures to ensure that a child who is subjected to schools or parental discipline shall be treated with humanity and with respect for the inherent dignity of the child and in conformity with the present Charter.
6. States Parties to the present Charter shall have all appropriate measures to ensure that children who become pregnant before completing their education shall have an opportunity to continue with their education on the basis of their individual ability.
7. No part of this Article shall be construed as to interfere with the liberty of individuals and bodies to establish and direct educational institutions subject to the observance of the principles set out in paragraph I of this Article and the requirement teal the education given in such institutions shall conform to such minimum standards as may be laid down by the States.

Article 12: Leisure, Recreation and Cultural Activities

1. States Parties recognize the right of the child to rest and leisure, to engage in play and recreational activities appropriate to the age of the child and to participate freely in cultural life and the arts.
2. States Parties shall respect and promote the right of the child to fully participate in cultural and artistic life and shall encourage the provision of appropriate and equal opportunities for cultural, artistic, recreational and leisure activity.

Article 13: Handicapped Children

1. Every child who is mentally or physically disabled shall have the right to special measures of protection in keeping with his physical and moral needs and under conditions which ensure his dignity, promote his self-reliance and active participation in the community.
2. States Parties to the present Charter shall ensure, subject to available resources, to a disabled child and to those responsible for his care, of assistance for which application is made and which is appropriate to the child's condition and in particular shall ensure that the disabled child has effective access to training, preparation for employment and recreation opportunities in a manner

conducive to the child achieving the fullest possible social integration, individual development and his cultural and moral development.

3. The States Parties to the present Charter shall use their available resources with a view to achieving progressively the full convenience of the mentally and physically disabled person to movement and access to public highway buildings and other places to which the disabled may legitimately want to have access to.

Article 14: Health and Health Services

1. Every child shall have the right to enjoy the best attainable state of physical, mental and spiritual health.
2. States Parties to the present Charter shall undertake to pursue the full implementation of this right and in particular shall take measures:
   (a) to reduce infant and child morality rate;
   (b) to ensure the provision of necessary medical assistance and health care to all children with emphasis on the development of primary health care;
   (c) to ensure the provision of adequate nutrition and safe drinking water;
   (d) to combat disease and malnutrition within the framework of primary health care through the application of appropriate technology;
   (e) to ensure appropriate health care for expectant and nursing mothers;
   (f) to develop preventive health care and family life education and provision of service;
   (g) to integrate basic health service programmes in national development plans;
   (h) to ensure that all sectors of the society, in particular, parents, children, community leaders and community workers are informed and supported in the use of basic knowledge of child health and nutrition, the advantages of breastfeeding, hygiene and environmental sanitation and the prevention of domestic and other accidents;
   (i) to ensure the meaningful participation of non-governmental organizations, local communities and the beneficiary population in the planning and management of a basic service programme for children;
   (j) to support through technical and financial means, the mobilization of local community resources in the development of primary health care for children.

Article 15: Child Labour

1. Every child shall be protected from all forms of economic exploitation and from performing any work that is likely to be hazardous or to interfere with the child's physical, mental, spiritual, moral, or social development.
2. States Parties to the present Charter take all appropriate legislative and administrative measures to ensure the full implementation of this Article which covers both the formal and informal sectors of employment and having regard to the relevant provisions of the International Labour Organization's instruments relating to children, States Parties shall in particular:

(a) provide through legislation, minimum wages for admission to every employment;
(b) provide for appropriate regulation of hours and conditions of employment;
(c) provide for appropriate penalties or other sanctions to ensure the effective enforcement of this Article;
(d) promote the dissemination of information on the hazards of child labour to all sectors of the community.

Article 16: Protection Against Child Abuse and Torture

1. States Parties to the present Charter shall take specific legislative, administrative, social and educational measures to protect the child from all forms of torture, inhuman or degrading treatment and especially physical or mental injury or abuse, neglect or maltreatment including sexual abuse, while in the care of the child.
2. Protective measures under this Article shall include effective procedures for the establishment of special monitoring units to provide necessary support for the child and for those who have the care of the child, as well as other forms of prevention and for identification, reporting referral investigation, treatment, and follow-up of instances of child abuse and neglect.

Article 17: Administration of Juvenile Justice

1. Every child accused or found guilty of having infringed penal law shall have the right to special treatment in a manner consistent with the child's sense of dignity and worth and which reinforces the child's respect for human rights and fundamental freedoms of others.
2. States Parties to the present Charter shall in particular:
   (a) ensure that no child who is detained or imprisoned or otherwise deprived of his/her liberty is subjected to torture, inhuman or degrading treatment or punishment;
   (b) ensure that children are separated from adults in their place of detention or imprisonment;
   (c) ensure that every child accused in infringing the penal law:
      (i) shall be presumed innocent until duly recognized guilty;
      (ii) shall be informed promptly in a language that he understands and in detail of the charge against him, and shall be entitled to the assistance of an interpreter if he or she cannot understand the language used;
      (iii) shall be afforded legal and other appropriate assistance in the preparation and presentation of his defence;
      (iv) shall have the matter determined as speedily as possible by an impartial tribunal and if found guilty, be entitled to an appeal by a higher tribunal;
   (d) prohibit the press and the public from trial.

3. The essential aim of treatment of every child during the trial and also if found guilty of infringing the penal law shall be his or her reformation, re-integration into his or her family and social rehabilitation.
4. There shall be a minimum age below which children shall be presumed not to have the capacity to infringe the penal law.

Article 18: Protection of the Family

1. The family shall be the natural unit and basis of society. it shall enjoy the protection and support of the State for its establishment and development.
2. States Parties to the present Charter shall take appropriate steps to ensure equality of rights and responsibilities of spouses with regard to children during marriage and in the even of its dissolution. In case of the dissolution, provision shall be made for the necessary protection of the child.
3. No child shall be deprived of maintenance by reference to the parents' marital status.

Article 19: Parent Care and Protection

1. Every child shall be entitled to the enjoyment of parental care and protection and shall, whenever possible, have the right to reside with his or her parents. No child shall be separated from his parents against his will, except when a judicial authority determines in accordance with the appropriate law, that such separation is in the best interest of the child.
2. Every child who is separated from one or both parents shall have the right to maintain personal relations and direct contact with both parents on a regular basis.
3. Where separation results from the action of a State Party, the State Party shall provide the child, or if appropriate, another member of the family with essential information concerning the whereabouts of the absent member or members of the family. States Parties shall also ensure that the submission of such a request shall not entail any adverse consequences for the person or persons in whose respect it is made.
4. Where a child is apprehended by a State Party, his parents or guardians shall, as soon as possible, be notified of such apprehension by that State Party.

Article 20: Parental Responsibilities

1. Parents or other persons responsible for the child shall have the primary responsibility of the upbringing and development the child and shall have the duty:
   (a) to ensure that the best interests of the child are their basic concern at all times-
   (b) to secure, within their abilities and financial capacities, conditions of living necessary to the child's development; and

(c) to ensure that domestic discipline is administered with humanity and in a manner consistent with the inherent dignity of the child.

2. States Parties to the present Charter shall in accordance with their means and national conditions the all appropriate measures;
   (a) to assist parents and other persons responsible for the child and in case of need provide material assistance and support programmes particularly with regard to nutrition, health, education, clothing and housing;
   (b) to assist parents and others responsible for the child in the performance of child-rearing and ensure the development of institutions responsible for providing care of children; and
   (c) to ensure that the children of working parents are provided with care services and facilities.

Article 21: Protection against Harmful Social and Cultural Practices

1. States Parties to the present Charter shall take all appropriate measures to eliminate harmful social and cultural practices affecting the welfare, dignity, normal growth and development of the child and in particular:
   (a) those customs and practices prejudicial to the health or life of the child; and
   (b) those customs and practices discriminatory to the child on the grounds of sex or other status.
2. Child marriage and the betrothal of girls and boys shall be prohibited and effective action, including legislation, shall be taken to specify the minimum age of marriage to be 18 years and make registration of all marriages in an official registry compulsory.

Article 22: Armed Conflicts

1. States Parties to this Charter shall undertake to respect and ensure respect for rules of international humanitarian law applicable in armed conflicts which affect the child.
2. States Parties to the present Charter shall take all necessary measures to ensure that no child shall take a direct part in hostilities and refrain in particular, from recruiting any child.
3. States Parties to the present Charter shall, in accordance with their obligations under international humanitarian law, protect the civilian population in armed conflicts and shall take all feasible measures to ensure the protection and care of children who are affected by armed conflicts. Such rules shall also apply to children in situations of internal armed conflicts, tension and strife.

Article 23: Refugee Children

1. States Parties to the present Charter shall take all appropriate measures to ensure that a child who is seeking refugee status or who is considered a refugee in accordance with applicable international or domestic law shall, whether

unaccompanied or accompanied by parents, legal guardians or close relatives, receive appropriate protection and humanitarian assistance in the enjoyment of the rights set out in this Charter and other international human rights and humanitarian instruments to which the States are Parties.

2. States Parties shall undertake to cooperate with existing international organizations which protect and assist refugees in their efforts to protect and assist such a child and to trace the parents or other close relatives or an unaccompanied refugee child in order to obtain information necessary for reunification with the family.
3. Where no parents, legal guardians or close relatives can be found, the child shall be accorded the same protection as any other child permanently or temporarily deprived of his family environment for any reason.
4. The provisions of this Article apply mutatis mutandis to internally displaced children whether through natural disaster, internal armed conflicts, civil strife, breakdown of economic and social order or howsoever caused.

Article 24: Adoption

States Parties which recognize the system of adoption shall ensure that the best interest of the child shall be the paramount consideration and they shall:

(a) establish competent authorities to determine matters of adoption and ensure that the adoption is carried out in conformity with applicable laws and procedures and on the basis of all relevant and reliable information, that the adoption is permissible in view of the child's status concerning parents, relatives and guardians and that, if necessary, the appropriate persons concerned have given their informed consent to the adoption on the basis of appropriate counselling;

(b) recognize that inter-country adoption in those States who have ratified or adhered to the International Convention on the Rights of the Child or this Charter, may, as the last resort, be considered as an alternative means of a child's care, if the child cannot be placed in a foster or an adoptive family or cannot in any suitable manner be cared for in the child's country of origin;

(c) ensure that the child affected by inter-country adoption enjoys safeguards and standards equivalent to those existing in the case of national adoption;

(d) take all appropriate measures to ensure that in inter-country adoption, the placement does not result in trafficking or improper financial gain for those who try to adopt a child;

(e) promote, where appropriate, the objectives of this Article by concluding bilateral or multilateral arrangements or agreements, and endeavour, within this framework to ensure that the placement of the child in another country is carried out by competent authorities or organs;

(f) establish a machinery to monitor the well-being of the adopted child.

Article 25: Separation from Parents

1. Any child who is permanently or temporarily deprived of his family environment for any reason shall be entitled to special protection and assistance;
2. States Parties to the present Charter:
   (a) shall ensure that a child who is parentless, or who is temporarily or permanently deprived of his or her family environment, or who in his or her best interest cannot be brought up or allowed to remain in that environment shall be provided with alternative family care, which could include, among others, foster placement, or placement in suitable institutions for the care of children;
   (b) shall take all necessary measures to trace and re-unite children with parents or relatives where separation is caused by internal and external displacement arising from armed conflicts or natural disasters.
3. When considering alternative family care of the child and the best interests of the child, due regard shall be paid to the desirability of continuity in a child's upbringing and to the child's ethnic, religious or linguistic background.

Article 26: Protection Against Apartheid and Discrimination

1. States Parties to the present Charter shall individually and collectively undertake to accord the highest priority to the special needs of children living under Apartheid and in States subject to military destabilization by the Apartheid regime.
2. States Parties to the present Charter shall individually and collectively undertake to accord the highest priority to the special needs of children living under regimes practising racial, ethnic. religious or other forms of discrimination as well as in States subject to military destabilization.
3. States Parties shall undertake to provide whenever possible, material assistance to such children and to direct their efforts towards the elimination of all forms of discrimination and Apartheid on the African Continent.

Article 27: Sexual Exploitation

1. States Parties to the present Charter shall undertake to protect the child from all forms of sexual exploitation and sexual abuse and shall in particular take measures to prevent:
   (a) the inducement, coercion or encouragement of a child to engage in any sexual activity;
   (b) the use of children in prostitution or other sexual practices;
   (c) the use of children in pornographic activities, performances and materials.

Article 28: Drug Abuse

States Parties to the present Charter shall take all appropriate measures to protect the child from the use of narcotics and illicit use of psychotropic substances as defined in the relevant international treaties, and to prevent the use of children in the production and trafficking of such substances.

Article 29: Sale, Trafficking and Abduction

States Parties to the present Charter shall take appropriate measures to prevent:

(a) the abduction, the sale of, or traffic of children for any purpose or in any form, by any person including parents or legal guardians of the child;
(b) the use of children in all forms of begging.

Article 30: Children of Imprisoned Mothers

1. States Parties to the present Charter shall undertake to provide special treatment to expectant mothers and to mothers of infants and young children who have been accused or found guilty of infringing the penal law and shall in particular:
   (a) ensure that a non-custodial sentence will always be first considered when sentencing such mothers;
   (b) establish and promote measures alternative to institutional confinement for the treatment of such mothers;
   (c) establish special alternative institutions for holding such mothers;
   (d) ensure that a mother shall not be imprisoned with her child;
   (e) ensure that a death sentence shall not be imposed on such mothers;
   (f) the essential aim of the penitentiary system will be the reformation, the integration of the mother to the family and social rehabilitation.

Article 31: Responsibility of the Child

Every child shall have responsibilities towards his family and society, the State and other legally recognized communities and the international community. The child, subject to his age and ability, and such limitations as may be contained in the present Charter, shall have the duty;

(a) to work for the cohesion of the family, to respect his parents, superiors and elders at all times and to assist them in case of need;
(b) to serve his national community by placing his physical and intellectual abilities at its service;
(c) to preserve and strengthen social and national solidarity;
(d) to preserve and strengthen African cultural values in his relations with other members of the society, in the spirit of tolerance, dialogue and consultation and to contribute to the moral well-being of society;

(e) to preserve and strengthen the independence and the integrity of his country;
(f) to contribute to the best of his abilities, at all times and at all levels, to the promotion and achievement of African Unity.

Part 2

Chapter Two: Establishment and Organization of the Committee on the Rights and Welfare of the Child

Article 32: The Committee

An African Committee of Experts on the Rights and Welfare of the Child hereinafter called 'the Committee' shall be established within the Organization of African Unity to promote and protect the rights and welfare of the child.

Article 33: Composition

1. The Committee shall consist of 11 members of high moral standing, integrity, impartiality and competence in matters of the rights and welfare of the child.
2. The members of the Committee shall serve in their personal capacity.
3. The Committee shall not include more than one national of the same State.

Article 34: Election

As soon as this Charter shall enter into force the members of the Committee shall be elected by secret ballot by the Assembly of Heads of State and Government from a list of persons nominated by the States Parties to the present Charter.

Article 35: Candidates

Each State Party to the present Charter may nominate not more than two candidates. The candidates must have one of the nationalities of the States Parties to the present Charter. When two candidates are nominated by a State, one of them shall not be a national of that State.

Article 36

1. The Secretary-General of the Organization of African Unity shall invite States Parties to the present Charter to nominate candidates at least 6 months before the elections.
2. The Secretary-General of the Organization of African Unity shall draw up in alphabetical order, a list of persons nominated and communicate it to the Heads of State and Government at least 2 months before the elections.

Article 37: Term of Office

1. The members of the Committee shall be elected for a tenn of 5 years and may not be re-elected, however. the term of four of the members elected at the first election shall expire after 2 years and the term of six others, after 4 years.
2. Immediately after the first election, the Chairman of the Assembly of Heads of State and Government of the Organization of African Unity shall draw lots to determine the names of those members referred to in sub-paragraph 1 of this Article.
3. The Secretary-General of the Organization of African Unity shall convene the first meeting of Committee at the Headquarters of the Organization within 6 months of the election of the members of the Committee, and thereafter the Committee shall be convened by its Chairman whenever necessary, at least once a year.

Article 38: Bureau

1. The Committee shall establish its own Rules of Procedure.
2. The Committee shall elect its officers for a period of 2 years.
3. Seven Committee members shall form the quorum.
4. In case of an equality of votes, the Chairman shall have a casting vote.
5. The working languages of the Committee shall be the official languages of the OAU.

Article 39: Vacancy

If a member of the Committee vacates his office for any reason other than the normal expiration of a term, the State which nominated that member shall appoint another member from among its nationals to serve for the remainder of the term – subject to the approval of the Assembly.

Article 40: Secretariat

The Secretary-General of the Organization of African Unity shall appoint a Secretary for the Committee.

Article 41: Privileges and Immunities

In discharging their duties, members of the Committee shall enjoy the privileges and immunities provided for in the General Convention on the Privileges and Immunities of the Organization of African Unity.

Chapter Three: Mandate and Procedure of the Committee
Article 42: Mandate

The functions of the Committee shall be:

(a) To promote and protect the rights enshrined in this Charter and in particular to:
   i. collect and document information, commission inter-disciplinary assessment of situations on African problems in the fields of the rights and welfare of the child, organize meetings, encourage national and local institutions concerned with the rights and welfare of the child, and where necessary give its views and make recommendations to Governments;
   ii. formulate and lay down principles and rules aimed at protecting the rights and welfare of children in Africa;
   iii. cooperate with other African, international and regional Institutions and organizations concerned with the promotion and protection of the rights and welfare of the child.

(b) To monitor the implementation and ensure protection of the rights enshrined in this Charter.

(c) To interpret the provisions of the present Charter at the request of a State Party, an Institution of the Organization of African Unity or any other person or Institution recognized by the Organization of African Unity, or any State Party.

(d) Perform such other task as may be entrusted to it by the Assembly of Heads of State and Government, Secretary-General of the OAU and any other organs of the OAU or the United Nations.

Article 43: Reporting Procedure

1. Every State Party to the present Charter shall undertake to submit to the Committee through the Secretary-General of the Organization of African Unity, reports on the measures they have adopted which give effect to the provisions of this Charter and on the progress made in the enjoyment of these rights:
   (a) within 2 years of the entry into force of the Charter for the State Party concerned: and
   (b) and thereafter, *every 3 years.*
2. Every report made under this Article shall:
   (a) contain sufficient information on the implementation of the present Charter to provide the Committee with comprehensive understanding of the implementation of the Charter in the relevant country; and
   (b) shall indicate factors and difficulties, if any, affecting the fullfilment of the obligations contained in the Charter.
3. A State Party which has submitted a comprehensive first report to the Committee need not, in its subsequent reports submitted in accordance with paragraph I (a) of this Article, repeat the basic information previously provided.

Article 44: Communications

1. The Committee may receive communication, from any person, group or non-governmental organization recognized by the Organization of African Unity, by a Member State, or the United Nations relating to any matter covered by this Charter.
2. Every communication to the Committee shall contain the name and address of the author and shall be treated in confidence.

Article 45: Investigations by the Committee

1. The Committee may, resort to any appropriate method of investigating any matter falling within the ambit of the present Charter, request from the States Parties any information relevant to the implementation of the Charter and may also resort to any appropriate method of investigating the measures the State Party has adopted to implement the Charter.
2. The Committee shall submit to each Ordinary Session of the Assembly of Heads of State and Government every 2 years, a report on its activities and on any communication made under Article [44] of this Charter.
3. The Committee shall publish its report after it has been considered by the Assembly of Heads of State and Government.
4. States Parties shall make the Committee's reports widely available to the public in their own countries.

Chapter Four: Miscellaneous Provisions

Article 46: Sources of Inspiration

The Committee shall draw inspiration from International Law on Human Rights, particularly from the provisions of the African Charter on Human and Peoples' Rights, the Charter of the Organization of African Unity, the Universal Declaration on Human Rights, the International Convention on the Rights of the Child, and other instruments adopted by the United Nations and by African countries in the field of human rights, and from African values and traditions.

Article 47: Signature, Ratification or Adherence

1. The present Charter shall be open to signature by all the Member States of the Organization of African Unity.
2. The present Charter shall be subject to ratification or adherence by Member States of the Organization of African Unity. The instruments of ratification or adherence to the present Charter shall be deposited with the Secretary-General of the Organization of African Unity.
3. The present Charter shall come into force 30 days after the reception by the Secretary-General of the Organization of African Unity of the instruments of ratification or adherence of 15 Member States of the Organization of African Unity.

Article 48: Amendment and Revision of the Charter

1. The present Charter may be amended or revised if any State Party makes a written request to that effect to the Secretary-General of the Organization of African Unity, provided that the proposed amendment is not submitted to the Assembly of Heads of State and Government for consideration until all the States Parties have been duly notified of it and the Committee has given its opinion on the amendment.
2. An amendment shall be approved by a simple majority of the States Parties.

Index

B. Milne, *Rights of the Child*, Children's Well-Being: Indicators and Research 11,
DOI 10.1007/978-3-319-18784-6